TIGERS
IN
COMBAT II

TIGERS
IN
COMBAT II

✚ WOLFGANG SCHNEIDER ✚

STACKPOLE
BOOKS

Published in 2005 by
STACKPOLE BOOKS
5067 Ritter Road
Mechanicsburg, PA 17055
www.stackpolebooks.com

www.jjfpub.mb.ca

Printed in the United States of America

10 9 8 7 6 5 4 3 2 1

FIRST EDITION

Library of Congress Cataloging-in-Publication Data

Schneider, Wolfgang, Oberleutnant.
  Tigers in combat II / Wolfgang Schneider.— 1st ed.
    p. cm.
  Includes bibliographical references.
  ISBN 0-8117-3203-7
  1. Tiger (Tank) 2. World War, 1939–1945—Tank warfare. 3. Germany—Armed Forces—Armored troops. I. Title.

UG446.5.S32835 2004
940.54'1343—dc22
                                        2004018902

TABLE OF CONTENTS

WAFFEN-SS

SCHWERE SS-PANZER-ABTEILUNG

PREFACE

This volume marks the completion of my treatment of the combat history of the units and formations equipped with the Tiger tank. The first volume, originally published by J. J. Fedorowicz Publishing, Inc., was soon sold out, and the response was really overwhelming. There were a large number of letters and telephone calls—back then e-mails were still somewhat of a novelty—and all of them were positive and encouraging with regard to both the content and the format of the book.

Some of these contacts provided me with more information, others invited further inquiries. Hitherto unknown details concerning aspects of the combat operations roused special interest as well as the marking and coloring of the vehicles. As each edition is reprinted, I hope to be able to update the information contained in each one.

✚

This second volume presents the remaining Wehrmacht and Waffen-SS formations and units equipped with the Tiger tank. The most famous of these were the Tiger companies in the German Army's Panzer-Grenadier-Division "Großdeutschland" and the first three divisions of the Waffen-SS that were formed: SS-Panzer-Grenadier-Division "Leibstandarte SS Adolf Hitler," SS-Panzer-Grenadier-Division "Das Reich" and SS-Panzer-Grenadier-Division "Totenkopf." In all four instances of the aforementioned divisions, the companies were later expanded to battalions, with several of them ultimately being detached to form separate battalions with habitual relationships to a corps.

In addition, several other units are mentioned—and certainly not all of them—that were equipped with a few Tigers for a short time. That generally happened in the final weeks of the war, and thus information is rather scarce. From the ad hoc formations where information exists, there are virtually no photographs available, which is understandable with regard to the circumstances prevailing at the time.

✚

There are quite a few books concerning the Waffen-SS that also mention the Tiger units and formations it had. Almost without exception, these narratives concentrate on the fighting at Kursk in July 1943 and in Normandy in 1944, or they restrict themselves to the operations of the "most successful tank commander of WW II," SS-Hauptsturmführer Michael Wittmann. Wittmann continues to fascinate many readers abroad, resulting in several dozen books and contributions to periodicals having been published.

It is striking that among these publications, all greatly differing in value, that there is none which documents the events sufficiently completely and, therefore, completely accurately. To the professional or otherwise knowledgeable reader, such products are often greeted with skepticism, because they usually focus on such factors as how many armored vehicles were knocked out or how many decorations were awarded. Other factors are far more important when it comes to analyzing the outcome of a highly successful engagement or the career of a successful tank commander: What weapon systems were involved; what was the over-all situation; what was the tactical situation; etc. It is perhaps worthwhile mentioning that there were a number of tank commanders—and not only in Tiger units—who achieved more "kills" than Wittmann.

✜

The facts mentioned above also point to the gap between serious history writing and publications pursuing other agendas. A typical example of the arbitrary handling of facts is the description of the so-called "Tank Battle of Prokhorovka," which took place on 12 July 1943 during Operation "Citadel." The 5th Guards Tank Army suffered a shocking number of casualties—more than 400 tanks on one day. In order to screen the poor operational leadership resulting in such losses, Rotmistrov, the commander-in-chief, did not hesitate to declare the engagement to have been won for the Soviets.

He stated the heaviest losses had been suffered by the Germans and claimed that more than seventy Tigers had been destroyed. This claim has been accepted uncritically in most of the available literature. The fact is that the German formations in this sector of the front had a total of only forty-three Tigers at their disposal, namely, the heavy tank companies of the three aforementioned SS armored divisions. On 12 July 1943, the heavy tank company of SS-Panzer-Regiment 1 reported a total of one complete loss. In the course of the Operation "Citadel," the three SS Tiger companies lost four tanks. Up until this point in time, the "destruction of the German tank force at Kursk" has been reported with monotonous mantra-like regularity in military literature and on television.

✜

I feel obliged here to renew my thanks to the numerous former tankers who actively supported me by lending out their personal documents and by patiently answering my countless inquiries. Thanks to their cooperation, it was possible for the first time to shed some light on the combat history of the more-or-less unknown SS units and formations. Numerous bits of fascinating information are now known. For instance, it was discovered that the 3. SS-Panzer-Division "Totenkopf" retained its heavy tank company until the end of the war (in contrast to its sister formations, the 1. SS-Panzer-Division "Leibstandarte SS Adolf Hitler" and the 2. SS-Panzer-Division "Das Reich").

It also needs to be mentioned that the chapters on the 13./SS-Panzer-Regiment 1 and schwere SS-Panzer-Abteilung 101 (501) were written primarily by the former SS-Oberscharführer Horst Wendt, whose aim was to document the combat history of his own battalion. I should like to express my special gratitude to this fellow tanker.

✛

One final note: The search for photographs of SS formations proved to be extremely difficult—quite different from the Army formations. There were several reasons, but the most common was that the end of the war was approaching, and the SS soldiers frequently destroyed all their personal documents and most of their photos. When they were captured, they normally found themselves exposed to rather harsh treatment, the more harmless aspect of which was that they were stripped of all their personal belongings and photos. As a result, the collection of photographs for this book had to be based on a greatly restricted fund.

Wolfgang Schneider
Germany
January 1998

PUBLISHERS' ACKNOWLEDGEMENTS

We wish to thank Jean Restayn for his superb color artwork. We also wish to thank George Bradford for the preparation of the wonderful organizational tables.

We also wish to thank you the reader for purchasing this book and all those of you who have purchased our other books. Your kind words of praise and encouragement have led us to redouble our efforts in providing our readership with the finest military-history titles on World War II subjects available today.

For a complete list of titles published by J.J. Fedorowicz Publishing, visit our website at www.jjfpub.mb.ca.

John Fedorowicz,
Michael Olive,
Robert J. Edwards,
and Ian Clunie

EDITORS' NOTES

Modern American Army terminology is generally used wherever an equivalent term is applicable. In cases where there may be nuances where we think the reader might enjoy learning the German term, we have included it with an explanation

In cases where the German term is commonly understood or there is no good, direct English equivalent, we have tended to retain the original German term, e.g., Schwerpunkt (point of main effort), Auftragstaktik (mission-type orders) etc.

In an attempt to highlight the specific German terminology, we have italicized German-language terms and expressions. Since most of the terms are repeated several times, we have not included a glossary. There is a rank-comparison table at the back of the book listing German Army, Waffen-SS, Commonwealth and US Army equivalents.

Unit designations follow standard German practice, i.e., an Arabic numeral before the slash (e.g., 1./schwere SS-Panzer-Abteilung 501) indicates a company or battery formation. A Roman numeral indicates the battalion within the regiment (e.g., III./ Panzer-Regiment "Großdeutschland"). Since this book deals primarily with battalion formations, the reader will encounter company designations most frequently.

J. J. Fedorowicz

J. J. Fedorowicz Publishing have a well earned reputation for publishing exceptionally high-quality books on German World War II subjects, and *Tigers in Combat II* is a prime example. I've been a huge fan of their books for years, and so I jumped at the chance to introduce this book to a whole new audience of readers in an attractive and very affordable edition. Those familiar with the original will note that some changes have been made due to the exigencies of publishing in a new format, but always with a mind to maintaining the same high standards to create a comprehensive photographic survey and detailed historical record of the Tiger tank in combat.

Chris Evans
History Editor
Stackpole Books

Tigers in Detail

TIGERS OF PANZER-GRENADIER-DIVISION "GROßDEUTSCHLAND"

Equipment

As with the three early SS Mechanized Infantry Divisions—SS-Panzer-Grenadier-Division "Leibstandarte SS Adolf Hitler," SS-Panzer-Grenadier-Division "Das Reich" and SS-Panzer-Grenadier-Division "Totenkopf"—Panzer-Grenadier-Division "Großdeutschland" was the only German Army division to have an organic unit with Tiger tanks. Although it was otherwise organized like a Panzer-Grenadier-Division, it had an entire tank regiment as opposed to the normal battalion. In early 1943, it received a heavy tank company with Tiger Is, which was assigned to the II./Panzer-Regiment "Großdeutschland." In February 1943, the company only had two platoons due to its only having nine Tiger I tanks. The tanks were of the second model version and did not have submachine-gun firing ports at the right turret rear. The six remaining tanks delivered in May 1943 already had the loader's vision block.

This company—with a strength of nine Tigers after suffering six losses—merged into the new III./Panzer-Regiment "Großdeutschland," which consisted of two other Tiger companies that were consolidated with this battalion after having originally been earmarked for the two "African" battalions, schwere Panzer-Abteilung 501 and schwere Panzer-Abteilung 504. The twenty-eight Tigers delivered in June 1943 were already fitted with the new HL230P45 engine. This was also true for the three command tanks issued to the battalion headquarters section.

The battalion received Tiger I tanks of virtually all known variants during the rest of the war, but it was never issued any Tiger II tanks. As a result, the battalion always had a mix of equipment of various variants—with or without Zimmerit, the anti-magnetic paste applied to the tanks to keep explosive charges from sticking—and different arrangements for spare track links.

Organization

In the beginning, the heavy tank company had only nine tanks. The company commander and one and the remaining eight tanks were divided into two platoons of four tanks each. The turret identification alphanumerics consisted of a capital S (for *schwere*, or "heavy") and two digits, the first one indicating the platoon number and the second one the tank within the platoon. Only a single numeral was painted on the rear turret stowage box; it indicated the platoon number. The company command tank was marked S01. When six more tanks were delivered, two more platoons of three tanks each were formed. The platoon leader tanks had the final digit 0, so that the four platoon leaders had the tactical markings S10, S20, S30, and S40.

The III./Panzer-Regiment "Großdeutschland" had the standard organization of forty-five tanks in three tank companies (fourteen each) and three Tigers in the battalion headquarters. The battalion used a unique tactical marking system. Each company had a different letter: A for the 9./Panzer-Regiment "Großdeutschland," B for the 10./Panzer-Regiment "Großdeutschland" and C for the 11./Panzer-Regiment "Großdeutschland." The letters were followed by two digits, which indicated the platoon and the tank within the platoon. The battalion headquarters tanks were marked S01, S02, and S03.

Camouflage and Markings

The first tanks issued had the *panzergrau* ("armor gray") color. The tactical markings were painted on the middle of the turret side, but they varied in size. Initially, the alphanumeric was very small; over time, it grew in size. During the initial fielding phase, either the S or the two-digit number was sometimes bigger than the rest. The Balkenkreuz—German national insignia—was in the middle of the hull side.

Prior to Operation "Citadel," the tanks were covered with large yellow-olive and small green spots. This camouflage was applied in random patterns by the individual crews with considerable variations in the final product. The tactical marking remained the same as before with a Balkenkreuz also painted on the left hull rear.

In the initial phase of the battalion's activation, the majority of the tanks received no camouflage beside the factory-applied yellow-olive coating. In the autumn of 1944, newly delivered tanks received the same coloring as the rest of the regiment: Irregular broad brown bands across the tank's superstructure.

Due to the constant new tank deliveries, the camouflage patterns within the battalion varied considerably, especially in the last few months of the war.

SCHWERE PANZER-KOMPANIE "HUMMEL"
Equipment and Organization

Because the company received most of its tanks and other equipment from the Panzer-Ersatz- und-Ausbildungs-Abteilung 500 (500th Armor replacement and Training Battalion), it had a mixture of several Tiger I variants, including some with steel-rimmed roadwheels. Some Tigers also came from depot-level maintenance facilities and had differing turret and hull arrangements (e.g., early hull with a late-model turret, etc.). The company had a standard table of organization and equipment with three four-tank platoons and two company headquarters tanks.

Camouflage and Markings

Due to its hodgepodge of equipment, there was no standardized camouflage scheme within the company. Before the company was consolidated with schwere Panzer-Abteilung 506, it had no tactical markings at all. After the consolidation, the company had three-digit numerals that started with a 4 for vehicle identification. The numerals were painted in dark green and outlined in white. This system followed the standard German military coloring sequence of white, red, yellow, green, brown, etc. The tank companies of the heavy tank battalions had colors assigned to them in accordance with that sequence.

SCHWERE PANZER-KOMPANIE "MEYER"
Equipment and Organization

This unit was formed in July 1943 and rushed to Italy in response to the Allied invasion of Sicily. It did not reach full company strength and was only equipped with eight new Tiger

I tanks. These tanks were among the last ones of the mid-production series and were still equipped with rubbed-rimmed roadwheels.

The company was never organized by platoon. As a result, the tanks were simply numbered from 1 to 8.

Camouflage and Markings
The tanks were painted dark yellow with small dark-green and larger dark-brown splotches. The single digit turret numerals were painted on the forward third of the turret side in solid black. The tanks did not feature Balkenkreuze. Instead, they had a Baltenkreuz (Baltic Cross) in black on a small white crest right in the upper center of the hull bow. The reason for this was that Leutnant Meyer was born in the Baltics. Every tank crew christened its tank: *Mausi* ("Mousie"), *Strolch* ("Tramp"), and *(Tiger) von Eschnapur* (after the movie of the same name) were some of the names chosen. All these markings and the camouflage were applied in Northern Italy. After the company was consolidated with schwere Panzer-Abteilung 508, these markings gradually vanished.

TIGER-GRUPPE "FEHRMANN"
This "unit"—like all the other ones hastily activated at the end of the war—had a mixture of different variants or even accidentally integrated subsystems due to the fact that the depot-level maintenance facilities had to use anything available to get tanks operational again. Photographs document that Tiger-Gruppe "Fehrmann" had at least one Tiger with steel-rimmed roadwheels and an older turret with the drum-shaped commander's cupola.

Consequently, the camouflage and markings varied considerably. The tanks had very distinct markings, however, with an alphanumeric consisting of an F (standing for Fehrmann) and a two-digit numeral painted in red and outlined in white.

The other German Army units and formations equipped with Tigers or supported temporarily by them were not organized in accordance with standard German tables of organization and equipment. Because there is so much variance, their equipment and organization will be discussed in the respective sections.

13./SS-PANZER-REGIMENT 1
Equipment
The ten Tiger I tanks issued to this unit in December 1942 belonged to the second variant, which did not have the second pistol port on the right rear turret side. The tanks had spare track sections on the hull bow. Like all the other early Tiger units, the company was also equipped with the Panzerkampfwagen III (fifteen of the J Model). The five replacement Tigers delivered in May 1943 still had the old drum-shaped commander's cupola, but they featured a loader's vision block. Several tanks had track links attached vertically on the turrets' rear sides. By that time, the remaining Panzer IIIs were handed over to other units in the division's tank regiment.

The five Tigers issued in July 1943 came too late for Operation "Citadel"; these tanks had the new HL230P45 engine. When the division was transferred to Italy, the company kept only its light vehicles and turned the Tigers over to SS-Panzer-Grenadier-Division "Das Reich" (nine Tigers) and SS-Panzer-Grenadier-Division "Totenkopf" (eight Tigers).

The establishment of the new heavy tank battalion for the I. SS-Panzer-Korps started in northern Italy. Twenty-seven Tigers (including two command tanks) arrived in August 1943. They still retained the old drum-shaped commander's cupola. The tanks had vertically arranged track links on both rear sides of the turret. The battalion was rushed back to the Eastern Front while it was still being activated. The twenty-seven tanks merged into one unit and were again employed as the heavy company within SS-Panzer-Regiment 1.

In order to compensate for losses, five new Tigers with the new commander's cupola were issued to this unit in mid-February 1944.

It was shortly thereafter that the crews handed over the remaining tanks to the regiment or turned them in for depot-level maintenance and repair. The personnel then started the journey back to the rest of the battalion, which had been designated as schwere SS-Panzer-Abteilung 101 by then.

It was during this phase that another six brand-new tanks arrived at the Eastern Front. These vehicles were the very last ones with the old suspension. The crews of these tanks had to stay with the division longer and did not made their way back to the battalion until April 1944.

Organization

With its twenty-five tanks, the company formed four tank platoons. One light platoon had five Panzer IIIs. The other three consisted of two sections, of which the 1st Section had three Tigers and the 2nd Section had three Panzer IIIs. The company headquarters section had one Tiger and one Panzer III. Since the unit was designated as the 4./SS-Panzer-Regiment 1, the three-digit identification markings started with a 4. The Tigers were numbered 405, 411, 412, 414, 421, 422, 423, 431, 432 and 433; the Panzer IIIs were numbered 404, 414, 415, 416, 424, 425, 426, 434, 435 and 436. The tanks of the light platoon were numbered from 4L1 to 4L5.

Prior to Operation "Citadel," the company turned in its Panzer IIIs and shifted to the standard organization of three platoons of four Tigers each. The company headquarters section had one Tiger for the company commander. The company was redesignated as the 13./SS-Panzer-Regiment 1 and renumbered its vehicles accordingly. The tanks adopted a unique four-digit marking system: 1311 to 1314 for the 1st Platoon, 1321 to 1324 for the 2nd Platoon and 1331 to 1334 for the 3rd Platoon. The company commander's tanks was marked 1305. Later on, when a second tank was issued for the company headquarters section, it was numbered 1304.

At the time of its redeployment in autumn 1943, the company was overstrength and had twenty-seven Tigers on its property books. Five tank platoons of five tanks each were formed. Being the regiment's *schwere* (heavy) company, it used a large S along with a two-digit number for the individual vehicle identifiers. The 1st Platoon consisted of S11, S12, S13, S14 and S15 and the remaining platoons were numbered analogously. The headquarters tanks were marked S05 and S04.

After the departure of the majority of the company back to schwere Panzer-Abteilung 101, the small *Kampfgruppe* (company team or task force) of the six remaining Tigers had single digit numbering from 1 to 6.

Camouflage and Markings

The early Tigers still had the overall *panzergrau* color. In an attempt to put some camouflage paint on the vehicles, large yellow-olive spots were applied. The turret numerals were about half the height of the turret sides and were painted in the center. They were also applied to the turret rear stowage box. They were black outlines with open ends. The Balkenkreuz was in the middle of the hull side. A distinguishing feature was the divisional insignia, a crest with a skeleton key, which is variously interpreted to represent the key to the Reich chancellery or a play on the family name of the commander, Sepp Dietrich). The Panzer IIIs also were painted in *panzergrau*. The divisional insignia was painted on the right hull front.

Prior to the operation to retake Kharkov, the tanks received a winter camouflage of whitewash. The area around the turret numerals, the Balkenkreuze and the divisional insignia were left free of paint.

In the spring of 1943, the new-production tanks were delivered with the new yellow-olive base paint. The old ones were also repainted in that color. The camouflage pattern was made of curved brown lines on the yellow-olive base coat.

The new four-digit identification system had two differing-sized digits. The second pair of numerals was 30% smaller in height than the first one. They were positioned on the turret sides, moved some distance to the rear and the large pair of digits was about 40% of the turret height. They were outlined with a double line—a small black one inside and a small white outside—and all the numerals had open ends. (The numeral 3 also had a cornered upper end.) The numerals were also painted on the rear turret stowage boxes. The Balkenkreuz was on its center hull position. The divisional insignia was applied in white on the left front hull (by the driver's station). No Zimmerit was applied.

In the autumn of 1943, the overstrength company of twenty-seven tanks applied its camouflage and markings prior to entrainment in Italy. The camouflage pattern was rather unusual; it consisted of curved green, brown and dark-olive lines of different thicknesses. The alphanumeric combination was positioned on the bottom of the forward turret sides and was about 50% of its height. These markings also had a black and white double outline. The tanks did not have Zimmerit.

The six tanks delivered in early 1944 received a coat of whitewash and had small black single digit numerals painted on the forward portion of the turret sides and also on the rear turret stowage box. Spare track links were attached on both sides of the hull front and on the rear turret sides.

8./SS-PANZER-REGIMENT 2

Equipment

In December 1942, the company received ten Tiger I tanks and twelve Panzer IIIs. The Tigers lacked the submachine-gun firing port on the right-hand side of the turret of the very early models. The next six Tigers, which were delivered in May 1943, had the loader's vision block but still the old engine. Most of the tanks carried track links on the front hull bow. After Operation "Citadel," nine former Tigers of the 13./SS-Panzer-Regiment 1 were received resulting in an overstrength company of twenty-two tanks. The six last Tigers produced in December 1943 did not arrive until February 1944. They featured the new commander's cupola, but they still had the old rubber-rimmed roadwheels.

Organization

Like the other mixed units that were outfitted with both the Tiger and the Panzer III, the company was organized in a unique way. The 8./SS-Panzer-Regiment 2 had four mixed platoons and two platoons without any Tigers. The mixed platoons each had three Tigers and one Panzer III, the remaining two platoons had four Panzer IIIs each. The company commander had one Tiger.

Prior to the Kursk Offensive, the company had a standard fourteen-tank organization. During its overstrength phase after Operation "Citadel," the company was organized in three overstrength platoons of five tanks each. There was also a headquarters platoon with five tanks.

The *Kampfgruppe* of six Tigers formed in February and March 1944 had no special form of organization. The tanks were simply numbered from 01 to 06.

Camouflage and Markings

All tanks initially issued to the company had the *panzergrau* base color. The characteristic divisional insignia—the *Wolfsangel*—was painted either in yellow or black (whitewash) on the left hull front and to the left of the rear hull Balkenkreuz.

Prior to the fighting at Kharkov, the tanks were whitewashed. The turret numerals were painted in solid black, with the same height as previously. The areas around the divisional insignia and the Balkenkreuze were left free of whitewash.

The new tanks delivered in the spring already had the new yellow-olive base paint. The old tanks were repainted in the same way. The camouflage paint consisted of red-brown and olive-green spots. All tanks were without an application of Zimmerit. The numerals were applied slightly larger than 50% of the turret height and were white outlines that appeared to have been applied with stencils. Identification markings were also painted on the rear turret stowage boxes. The Balkenkreuz was about twice the normal width and was painted slightly forward on the hull side.

The alphanumerics—an S followed by two digits—applied prior to Operation "Citadel" were white outlines with closed ends. They were about 40% of the turret height. The markings also appeared on the turret rear stowage box. The company insignia—a devil—was painted in solid white in the most forward turret side section just in front of the lifting bolts. These symbols were of Russian origin and quite common during the time. Their function was to scare away bad spirits.

The tactical division identification sign for Operation "Citadel"—a double-bar rune—was painted in white on the radio-operator's side of the hull front and also on the left rear track fender or on the rear hull. The Balkenkreuze were positioned in the middle of the hull side and also a single one on the left rear hull section. The camouflage pattern remained unchanged.

The new tanks delivered in early 1944 had an application of Zimmerit and received whitewash at once. The turret numbers were painted in black on the front turret sides; their size was about 60% of the turret height.

9. SS-PANZER-REGIMENT 3

Equipment

The first nine Tiger I tanks were of the second model without the submachine-gun firing port in the right turret rear. The company was also issued ten Panzer IIIs (Model J). The six Tigers delivered in May 1943 still had the old engine, but they already featured the loader's vision block. The five replacement tanks issued in September 1943 had the new commander's cupola.

Having lost the rest of its equipment in Northern Romania in the spring of 1944, the company was reequipped in May 1944 with new tanks featuring the steel-rimmed road-wheels. In July 1944, it received five more tanks; these had the three lifting eyes on the turret roof. The five Tigers picked up in Warsaw came from depot-level maintenance facilities and included models with the older rubber-rimmed roadwheels.

Organization

Like its sister units in the other two SS tank regiments, this company started with a mix of nine Tiger I tanks and ten Panzer IIIs. They were organized into four tank platoons, with each consisting of two sections of one Tiger and one Panzer III each. The company headquarters was formed by one Tiger and two Panzer IIIs. Analogous to the 13./SS-Panzer-Regiment 1, the 9./SS-Panzer-Regiment 3 was also initially designated the 4./SS-Panzer-Regiment 3. This resulted in the following numbering system: 401, 411, 413, 421, 423, 431, 433, 441 and 443 for the Tigers and 402, 403, 412, 414, 422, 424, 432, 434, 442 and 444 for the medium tanks.

In May 1943, the company turned in its remaining Panzer IIIs and converted to the standard Tiger company organization with three platoons of four tanks each. The company headquarters had three Tigers instead of the standard two, however. Being the last company in the new II./SS-Panzer-Regiment 3, the tank markings changed to have a 9 starting the three-digit vehicle identification number.

This numbering system was kept until the end of the company's existence in May 1945, but the company was overstrength with up to twenty-three tanks in the second half of 1943. This resulted in establishing a fourth tank platoon (with five tanks) that then had the turret numbers 941 to 945. During several phases of high losses and subsequent deliveries of replacement vehicles, the newly arrived tanks did not even get a turret number.

Camouflage and Markings

The tanks originally had the *panzergrau* base coat. The Panzer IIIs bore the divisional insignia—a Totenkopf ("Death's Head")—painted in white on the right hull front. This insignia was not applied to the Tigers. In preparation for the Kharkov operation, the tanks received whitewash. The turret numbers were located on the central side section and painted in black. They were about 50% of the turret height. The Balkenkreuz had the regular hull side center position. The tanks lacked an application of Zimmerit.

In the transition phase prior to the springtime, the tanks received large yellow-olive spots and smaller brown ones after the removal of the whitewash, which almost completely covered the former *panzergrau* base paint. The numerals had the same arrangement and size, but they were painted in white and outlined with a small black line. The vehicle identification numerals were also painted on the rear turret stowage box.

In the weeks before Operation "Citadel," the tanks received a uniform camouflage pattern with large brown-olive and small green-olive spots and the yellow-olive base paint. The newly delivered tanks already had the yellow-olive base coat, to which the camouflage pattern described above was applied.

The turret numbers were about 35% of the turret height and were painted not quite in the center of the turret sides in a slightly raised position. They were outlined in black and also painted on the rear turret stowage box. The Balkenkreuz was positioned as usual in the middle of the hull side. The divisional tactical insignia for the operation—triple parallel vertical bars—was painted in black on the right hull front on the driver's glacis.

In the winter of 1943–44, the whitewashed tanks had very unusual vehicle identification numerals. Each crew had a rectangular white wooden signboard and the number painted on it in black.

After refitting in the late spring of 1944, the Zimmerit-coated tanks featured large brown-olive and dark green cloud-like spots on the obligatory yellow-olive base paint. The numerals were white outlines and positioned in the forward third of the turret side; they were about half the turret height. They also appeared on the rear turret stowage box. The Balkenkreuz on the hull side was moved slightly to the rear.

SCHWERE SS-PANZER-ABTEILUNG 101
(SCHWERE SS-PANZER-ABTEILUNG 501)

Equipment

The first ten Tiger I tanks arrived in November 1943 and featured the new commander's cupola. Another one produced during the same month had originally been purchased by Japan, but it was later issued to the battalion, because there was no way to get it shipped there. The other nine Tigers—still with the old rubber-rimmed roadwheels—featured the rear gun-tube lock. After arrival in Normandy, schwere SS-Panzer-Abteilung 101 was the only battalion using tanks with the old-style roadwheels. The twenty-five tanks issued in April 1944 were of a later variant and featured steel-rimmed roadwheels, the four-centimeter turret roof, the new loader's hatch and the monocular gun sight aperture. All tanks were coated with Zimmerit. With a few exceptions, the tanks had tracks links on the rear turret sides and the front hull bow.

The fourteen Tiger II tanks received by the 1./schwere SS-Panzer-Abteilung 101 in July and August 1944 were models with production turrets. All but one were lost and the battalion was reequipped with thirty-four Tiger IIs in October and November 1944. Prior to transport to the Ardennes offensive, eleven Tiger II tanks from schwere Panzer-Abteilung 509 were received in order to ensure the battalion was at full strength. To compensate the losses in the Ardennes operation (fifteen tanks), six more Tiger IIs were issued end of January 1945.

Organization

The twenty-seven tanks of the "Italian" delivery in August 1943, which had been earmarked for the 1. and 2./schwere SS-Panzer-Abteilung 101 and the battalion headquarters, were diverted to the Eastern Front to deal with a crisis. While these vehicles and crews were gone, subsequent tanks issued went to form the 3./schwere SS-Panzer-Abteilung 101. As a result, this company was also overstrength and had four tank platoons of four tanks each. Two tanks belonged to the company headquarters section. This resulted in a standard three-digit numbering system with 341, 342, 343 and 344 for the fourth platoon. The company command tanks had the tactical markings of 305 and 304. The remaining two tanks were the battalion command vehicles, Tigers 007 and 008.

After the battalion was reconstituted in April 1944, it had a mixture of variants. The 2./schwere SS-Panzer-Abteilung 101 had Tigers featuring the old-style suspension, while the 2./schwere SS-Panzer-Abteilung 101 had Tigers with the new, steel-rimmed roadwheel suspension. The 1./schwere SS-Panzer-Abteilung 101 had Tigers with steel-rimmed roadwheels except for the 3rd Platoon, which was previously the 4th Platoon in the "old" 3./schwere SS-Panzer-Abteilung 101. The third battalion command tank to be received—Tiger 009—also had the new suspension featuring steel-rimmed roadwheels.

After the first engagements in Normandy, the 1./schwere SS-Panzer-Abteilung 101 was pulled out of the line and sent back to Germany for reconstitution after it had suffered the most losses. The three remaining tanks of the company, including one command tank, beefed up the 3./schwere SS-Panzer-Abteilung 101 so it had a reporting strength of eleven Tigers. The 2./schwere SS-Panzer-Abteilung 101 had ten tanks on its property books at the time. The 1./schwere SS-Panzer-Abteilung 101 received a full complement of fourteen new Tiger II tanks, but it did not rejoin the battalion in France.

Prior to the Ardennes Offensive, the battalion, which had been redesignated as schwere SS-Panzer-Abteilung 501 in September, was equipped with forty-five Tiger IIs. It had the standard battalion organization of three tank companies of fourteen tanks each. There were 3 tanks in the battalion headquarters section. One important divergence from the battalion's table of organization and equipment needs to be mentioned. The combat elements of the headquarters Company—the reconnaissance, combat-engineer and Flak platoons—were concentrated into a fourth "light" company. The peculiarity was maintained until the end of the war.

Camouflage and Markings

The twenty old-suspension Tigers delivered in late 1943 were camouflaged with curved vertical green-olive and brown-olive stripes on the yellow-olive base paint. The turret numerals were quite large—about 60% of the turret height—and painted in white on the forward turret sides and also on the turret rear stowage boxes.

The insignia of the I. SS-Panzer-Korps—with two keys instead of the usual one in the 1. SS-Panzer-Division "Leibstandarte SS Adolf Hitler"—was painted in white on the left hull front. The tanks had an application of Zimmerit. The tanks of the battalion command section received turret markings in the same way.

After arrival of the other twenty-five Tigers, the white turret numbers of the 3./schwere SS-Panzer-Abteilung 101, which had proven to be too conspicuous, were repainted. They were changed to blue with a yellow outline. This was a combination that no other Tiger formation used. The headquarters tanks retained the solid white numbers. The new tanks—all covered with an application of Zimmerit—received differently painted turret numbers for each company. The 1./schwere SS-Panzer-Abteilung 101 had green-olive numerals with a white outline, and the 2./schwere SS-Panzer-Abteilung 101 had red numerals with a white outline. All vehicle identification numerals also appeared on the rear turret stowage boxes.

A peculiarity of the 1./schwere SS-Panzer-Abteilung 101 was the tactical insignia for a tank company—a rhombus—was painted in white on the right front hull plate and also on the right hull rear. Inside the rhombus was a small white Latin s; to its right was a small 1, which was also painted in white.

In contrast to the rest of the battalion, the 2./schwere SS-Panzer-Abteilung 101 painted the corps insignia on the right hull front. The 1./schwere SS-Panzer-Abteilung 101 also had the corps insignia on the left hull rear. On the tanks of the 1. and 3./schwere SS-Panzer-Abteilung 101, the Zimmerit was removed in a square underneath the insignia. The Balkenkreuz on the hull side was moved slightly rearward. The camouflage consisted of broad brown and green-olive spots on the yellow-olive base paint.

The reequipped 1./schwere SS-Panzer-Abteilung 101 received fourteen of the very first Tiger II tanks with the Henschel production turret. They were camouflaged with large brown-olive and irregularly shaped green-olive spots of different size on a yellow-olive base. The yellow turret numerals were painted in the middle of the turret side beneath the Balkenkreuz. The numerals did not appear on the turret rear. All tanks had an application of Zimmerit and spare track links on the front and rear turret sides.

The thirty-four Tiger IIs delivered in late autumn 1944 were painted in the new ambush scheme and did not have Zimmerit any more. The 1./schwere SS-Panzer-Abteilung 501 employed black numerals with a white outline, which were painted right in the middle of the turret side; they were about 40% of the turret height. There were no Balkenkreuze. The 2./schwere SS-Panzer-Abteilung 501 maintained its white-outlined red identification numerals and the 3./schwere SS-Panzer-Abteilung 501 also kept its yellow-outlined blue numerals. The battalion command tanks had large red numerals with a white outline.

Some of the eleven tanks received from schwere Panzer-Abteilung 509 still had the old camouflage. They received hurriedly applied yellow turret numerals. The numerals were not painted on the turret rear.

SCHWERE SS-PANZER-ABTEILUNG 102
(SCHWERE SS-PANZER-ABTEILUNG 502)
Equipment

Despite the fact that only three Tigers (with the old rubber-rimmed roadwheels) were available, the battalion was sent to the Eastern Front, where it was sporadically used in combat. It was attached to the parent division of most of the cadre, the SS-Panzer-Grenadier-Division "Das Reich."

After redeployment to the Netherlands, the battalion received its entire complement of forty-five Tiger I tanks. All vehicles were of the same version and featured steel-rimmed roadwheels and the monocular gun sight. They still lacked the three lifting mounts on the turret roof, however. In contrast to the other two Normandy Tiger formations, the battalion did not attach track links on the hull front.

In February and March 1945, the battalion, which had been redesignated as schwere SS-Panzer-Abteilung 502 in September, was reequipped with Tiger IIs.

Organization

The Normandy campaign saw the battalion with the standard forty-five-tank organization and semi-standard vehicle marking system. The exception in the markings occurred within the company headquarters sections of each company, where the two Tigers had a 4 in their identification numbers: 141, 142, 241, 242, 341 and 342. The battalion command tanks were numbered 001, 002 and 003.

As a result of the ubiquitous shortage of tanks, the battalion was reorganized in accordance with the downscaled battalion strength model of thirty-one tanks (only three tanks per platoon and only one command tank at all levels of command). The battalion kept the old numbering system with the exception of the battalion command Tiger, which received the unusual marking of 555.

Camouflage and Markings

The "Normandy" tanks had camouflage painting with large brown and green-olive segments that almost completely covered the yellow-olive base coating. The turret numerals were white outlines and were about half the height of the turret. The numerals painted on the rear turret stowage boxes were in black and outlined in white. The battalion insignia was a Blitzrune (lightning-bolt rune) painted in pink on the left hull front and the left hull rear as well. All tanks had an application of Zimmerit.

The Tiger II tanks deployed to the Oder Front all had the ambush scheme. Not all tanks had turret numerals; some were in solid white, others merely white outlines. Some tanks had a Balkenkreuz in the middle of the turret side; some had none at all.

SCHWERE SS-PANZER-ABTEILUNG 103
(SCHWERE SS-PANZER-ABTEILUNG 503)
Equipment

Born under a bad sign, the battalion had to give away every single Tiger I tank it was ever issued. It was not until autumn 1944 that it started to receive Tiger IIs. Even then, only four arrived. The battalion reached nearly full strength in January 1945 with thirty-nine tanks.

Organization

The battalion had no chance to get properly organized, because the last thirteen tanks arrived the day before departure to the front. The lack of cohesion was compounded by the fact that battalion assets were divided up right from the beginning, and it fought in several locations without contact with each other. As a result, the battalion's operations were at the company level from the very beginning, but the tanks were employed individually or in sections more often than not. The companies had twelve or thirteen tanks each, and the platoons consisted of either three or four tanks. The only exception to unit's fighting with unit integrity was the 3rd Platoon of the 2./schwere SS-Panzer-Abteilung 503, which was employed as an integral platoon of four tanks.

Camouflage and Markings

The Tiger II tanks had the ambush camouflage scheme and most of them had a Balkenkreuz in the middle of the turret side. Several tanks of the 1./schwere SS-Panzer-Abteilung 503 were seen with very large turret numbers outlined in black in the middle of the turret sides. Most of the tanks had no numerals at all.

After arrival of the six new tanks, the numerals were painted bigger to make them more visible. In addition, they were also then painted on the rear turret stowage box.
HARMS

Besides the appearance of the Balkenkreuz on the hull sides, an additional one was painted on the left rear of the hull. The Balkenkreuz is a form the national markings, commonly referred to as an "Iron Cross." A Balkenkreuz has right angles on the cross.

The markings were also occasionally applied by the crewmembers, which resulted in some variance in the size of the markings, as can be seen on this command tank from the 9./Panzer-Regiment "Großdeutschland."

Prior to Operation "Citadel," the Tiger company—by then, the 13./SS-Panzer-Regiment 1—received its characteristic four-digit markings. These were placed on the turret sides, painted in black and had a white outline. WENDT

The numerals were also applied to the rear turret stowage box.

When the company was overstrength, it employed the S (for "schwere," or "heavy") system for its excess tanks (as was employed within the 13./Panzer-Regiment "Großdeutschland" and the 8./SS-Panzer-Regiment 2).

The 8./SS-Panzer-Regiment 2 started its numbering with an 8. The three-digit markings were painted in black on the turret sides and on the rear turret stowage box. FINK

This Tiger had yet another type of numeral applied. TiKi has its numerals in a solid white. The name was applied when the vehicles were repainted yellow-olive in the spring as part of their efforts to renew their camouflage schemes.

Shortly before Operation "Citadel," the tanks received the new markings which had an S prefix. The identification markings consisted of white outlines. FINK

These markings also appeared on the rear turret stowage box. The Doppelrune (double runic symbol) that served as a divisional insignia can be seen on the right front hull. FINK

This nice image shows a grouping of tanks from SS-Panzer-Grenadier-Division "Totenkopf" in February 1943. The initial tanks were assigned to the 4./SS-Panzer-Regiment "Totenkopf" before the regiment received its second battalion. HOFMANN

After reaching full strength as a Tiger company, the tanks were remarked with a three-digit series starting with 9. This was prior to Operation "Citadel." The numerals were painted as black outlines on the turret sides and on the rear turret stowage box. BENEKE

After removal of the winter whitewash, the numerals were repainted in white with a thin black outline. VAN KERKOHM

The number 3 has a sharp upper part. These numbers were not visible under battle conditions, and this was the reason for the change to numbers with white outlines. VAN KERKOHM

For Operation "Citadel," the divisional insignia was the triple bar runic symbol that was painted in black on the right hull front. BENEKE

In the winter of 1943–1944, the white-washed Tigers did not receive markings that were painted directly on the vehicles. Instead, the vehicle's identification numeral was painted in black on a piece of wood that was tied on the turret sides.

The lonely 3./schwere SS-Panzer-Abteilung 101 used large white numerals on the tanks in early 1944. In addition to being painted on the turret sides, they also appeared on the rear turret stowage box.
WENDT

The 1./schwere SS-Panzer-Abteilung 101 was reconstituted with Tiger IIs. When employed in northern France, the company used yellow three-digit numerals for vehicle identification. They appeared below a centrally painted Balkenkreuz.

During the Ardennes Offensive and the period following it, the 2./schwere SS-Panzer-Abteilung 501 had red numerals on its turrets that were outlined in white. It did not paint Balkenkreuze on the turrets. IWM

Some of the Tigers that were hurriedly reissued to schwere SS-Panzer-Abteilung 501 received simple yellow numerals, such as Tiger 222.

The captured Tiger 332 sports blue numerals with yellow outlines. It is seen here in front of the railway station at Spa prior to its shipment back to the United States for evaluation.

Schwere SS-Panzer-Abteilung 102 (later: schwere SS-Panzer-Abteilung 502) used a three-digit identification scheme with the white-outlined numerals. A command tank—Tiger 142—can be seen here. KLÖCKNER

Most of the Tiger IIs of schwere SS-Panzer-Abteilung 502 and schwere SS-Panzer-Abteilung 503 had no numerals painted on them at all. As an exception, a tank of the 1./schwere SS-Panzer-Abteilung 503 can be seen with large black-outlined digits.

13./Panzer-Regiment "Großdeutschland"

A heavy tank company was formed for the II./Panzer-Regiment "Großdeutschland" by an order of Military District III dated 5 January 1943. It was organized in accordance with Kriegsstärkenachweis 1176b (table of organization and equipment) dated 15 December 1942. The activation orders also provided for a maintenance platoon in accordance with Kriegsstärkenachweis 1185d, which was also dated 15 December 1942. The new unit's designation: 13./Panzer-Regiment. It was to be ready for deployment no later than 3 February 1943.

Cadre came from the 3./Panzer-Abteilung 203 and the battalion's maintenance platoon. The activation took place at the Neuhammer Training Area, starting on 13 January 1943. The designated replacement formation was Grenadier-Ersatz-Brigade "Großdeutschland" at Cottbus (Military District III). The first company commander was Hauptmann Wallroth.

Initially, only nine Tiger I tanks available.

✚

End of February 1943: Integration into the newly formed Panzer-Regiment "Großdeutschland" (now with two battalions) and transport to Poltava.

17 February 1943: First elements arrive in Poltava.

26 February 1943: Assembly in the area around Reschetilowka for the counteroffensive to retake Kharkov.

28 February 1943: Operational tanks: 4.

3 March 1943: Operational tanks: 5.

5 March 1943: Assembly area of Kampfgruppe (Oberst Graf) Strachwitz (commander of Panzer-Regiment "Großdeutschland") in the southeast part of Tschutowo. Operational tanks: 7.

6 March 1943: Operational tanks: 6.

7 March 1943: Start of attack via Tschabanowka (0615 hours)-Mosulewka-Alexandrowka (0730 hours)-Molodezkij (0830 hours) against the western outskirts of Komtakusowo (0950 hours). After breaking weak enemy resistance, the southern part of Perekop is reached in the late afternoon. Strong enemy resistance near Gosow and Petrowskij is broken; one Tiger is damaged. The day's objective, the railway/road crossing at Schljach is not taken.

8 March 1943: Initial assault through dense snowdrifts from Kowjagi to the east up to Schljach; then advance further to the north on Staryj Mertschik. The fighting continues into the night hours; the regiment knocks out more than twenty tanks.

9 March 1943: Assault to the road Olschany-Bogoduchoff in order to contain enemy breakout to the east. The movements are hampered by the critical road conditions. Due to a lack of fuel, no further advance to the northwest. In the evening, covering positions are occupied in Popowka. Operational tanks: 7.

10 March 1943: Tanks are short of fuel; no gains. Operational tanks: 6. Assembly area in the rear area of Hill 190.7, south of Kryssino (for the attack on Bogoduchoff).

11 March 1943: Attack to the northeast via the Merla Sector near Moltschany. After two hours of fighting, Bogoduchoff is reached in a pincer movement from the east via Ssennjanka at 1130 hours. Pursuit of the enemy as far as Leskowka and Schtscherbaki. In the evening, fighting positions in Ssennjanka are occupied. Operational tanks: 6.

12 March 1943: Panzer-Regiment "Großdeutschland" initially advances towards Graiworon. At noon, the jump-off position of Kampfgruppe Strachwitz is at Schewtschenko. Attack via Maximowka to the east and then via Graiworonka on Graiworon, which is seized at 1410 hours. Operational tanks: 4.

13 March 1943: Attack ordered for 0500 hours is not possible because a blown-up bridge near Maximowka forces the supply trucks to a time consuming detour. They finally reach the tanks at 1200 hours. The attack continues, passing Antonowka and moving via Sosuli up to the edges of Borissowka, which is reached at 1700 hours. All-round defensive positions established covering Striguny-Dubino-Belenko-Lokinskij. Operational tanks: 6.

14 March 1943: Enemy attacks east of Borissowka are contained by the I./Panzer-Regiment "Großdeutschland" and the Tiger company; forty-six out of sixty enemy tanks are knocked out. Operational tanks: 4.

15 March 1943: Starting at 2430 hours, several enemy attacks against the eastern and northeastern part of Borissowka are pushed back; twenty-seven tanks are knocked out. Operational tanks: 3.

16 March 1943: Several enemy tank attacks are repelled again; forty tanks are knocked out. The pursuit stalls at Striguny due to strong resistance. Only one Tiger operational.

17 March 1943: No engagements; two Tigers operational.

18 March 1943: Attack on Bessonowka via Stanowoje-Chwostowka (fifteen enemy tanks destroyed) and then via Point 240.5. Contact with elements of the II. SS-Panzer-Korps advancing towards Bjelgorod is established in Dolbino at 1600 hours. No Tigers operational.

19 March 1943: Attack on Tomarowka from the east via Bessonowka-Nowaja-Derewnja after fierce tank engagements near Kalinina. Following this, movement towards Borissowka in order to control the eastbound road in the enemy's rear that is being used for his advance. Thirty-one tanks and twenty-nine antitank guns destroyed; no Tigers operational.

20 March 1943: Covering positions occupied. Since 7 March 1943, the company has knocked out thirty tanks. No Tigers operational.

21 March 1943: No engagements. No Tigers operational.

22 March 1943: Light engagements during these days; the division is to be relieved in place and then transported into the area north of Poltava.

23 March 1943: Relief in place by the 167. Infanterie-Division and assembly in the area around Graiworon.

24 March 1943: Road marches of the division start in the evening. The II./Panzer-Regiment "Großdeutschland" and other elements of the division form Kampfgruppe Beuermann and stay in Borissowka as a reserve.

26 March 1943: One Tiger operational. After arrival in the new area, battlefield reconstitution and preparations for Operation "Citadel."

31 March 1943: Only one Tiger operational.

10 April 1943: Operational tanks: 3.

20 April 1943: Operational tanks: 3.

30 April 1943: All nine tanks operational.

13 May 1943: Six new Tigers arrive.

Total tanks: 9.

20 May 1943: Operational tanks: 4.

21 May 1943: Infanterie-Division (mot.) "Großdeutschland" is redesignated Panzer-Grenadier-Division "Großdeutschland."

30 May 1943: All fifteen Tigers operational.

10 June 1943: Operational tanks: 12.

30 June 1943: Operational status as 10.6. and 20.6.43.

4 July 1943: During the night, relocation out of the northern part of Moschtschenoje to the area south of Point 229.8.

5 July 1943: Attack starts at 0400 hours via the railway line. After the time-consuming breaching of several mine barriers, the Gerzowka Creek east of Bereswyji is reached at 0530 hours. By divisional order, the attached Panzer-Brigade 10 assumes command of Panzer-Regiment "Großdeutschland." (Panzer-Brigade 10 was a temporary formation designed to consolidate the newly introduced Panther medium tank into a massed strike force of two battalions.) That night, Panzer-Regiment "Großdeutschland" is diverted from the creek area north of Point 229.8 to the west in order to use a crossing gained by the 3. Panzer-Division. Failing to do that, it rests in open terrain for the night. Three Tigers operational; no casualties.

6 July 1943: In the morning, advance via Butowo into the area around Point 244.5. The attack is started at 1040 hours on the left side of the road together with the I./Panzer-Regiment "Großdeutschland" and Panzer-Regiment 39. About 1230 hours, the tank ditch southwest of Point 241.1 is seized. At 1400 hours, a further advance behind the Panthers. Point 241.1 is taken. Two Tigers are operational.

7 July 1943: Continuation of the advance at 0845 hours. Due to fierce enemy shelling, the tanks are retrieved to the reverse slope of Hill 247.2. Later on, an attack in a right pincer movement on Hill 230 to the east. A mine belt is hit in a balka—a gully formed by a washout, similar to a desert wadi—east of Hill 230; the last of the Tigers breaks down.

8 July 1943: Attack starts at 0530 hours along the road Ssyrzewo-Werchopenje. In the evening, advance on Werchopenje, which is strongly defended by antitank guns and dug-in tanks. All-round defensive positions established southeast of Werchopenje. Eight Tigers operational

9 July 1943: Advance is resumed at 0800 hours with ten Tigers; assault from the hills east of Werchopenje to the hills in the northern part of the village. Antitank guns and artillery positions engaged. Subsequent assault from the southwest on the hill near Point 260.8. Positions taken up on the left side of the hill. Covering positions established for the left pincer movement in the direction of Nowosselowka; numerous enemy tanks are knocked out. Pursuit in a right-hand bypass operation and establishment of contact northeast of Werchopenje. During the subsequent attack, an antitank-gun belt is contacted. The tanks are withdrawn at 1900 hours; new approach towards Hill 258.5. Advance commences only up to the defile southwest of Nowosselowka. Rest positions established; more than thirty enemy tanks are spotted at dawn. Three Tiger Is still operational.

10 July 1943: After defending against enemy counterattacks on the line east of Werchopenje-Beresowka-Dolaij, the road four kilometers west of Werchopenje is crossed.

11 July 1943: Operational tanks: 11. Attack starts at 0700 hours. The Panthers follow the Tigers; the enemy forces show signs of dissolution. The day's objective—Hill 342.8—is seized by 1000 hours. Combat engineer and terrain and route reconnaissance elements are accompanied by two Tigers toward the Pena Sector; a minefield is encountered, and one Tiger is immobilized. All-round defensive positions established when the infantry finally closes with the tanks.

12 July 1943: Departure at 0530 hours along the former line of attack to a small patch of woods west of Point 260.8; several hours of rest there. About 1500 hours, occupation of jump-off positions for sealing and clearing an enemy penetration. Operation changed shortly thereafter: Continuation of the attack to the north. After taking Hill 260.8, an order is received to march back because of an enemy penetration in the southwest out of the direction of Werchopenje. Enemy counterattacks are repelled by five Tiger I tanks at the woodline two kilometers west of Werchopenje. Night engagement at the hill in front of the woods north of Point 258.5. Covering positions occupied starting at 2200 hours. Five Tigers are operational.

13 July 1943: Operations around the hill 4.5 kilometers west of Werchopenje. Assembly area northeast of Beresowka.

14 July 1943: Attack from the area east of Tschopajew; enemy resistance on the hill three kilometers north of Tschopajew crushed. Further advance to the high ground 2.5 kilometers southeast of Nowenkoje.

15 July 1943: Five Tiger Is in action. Assault to the depression southeast of Nowenkoje; sixteen enemy tanks knocked out.

16 July 1943: Several enemy attacks are stopped. Operational tanks: 5.

17 July 1943: Operational tanks: 8.

18 July 1943: Order is given to withdraw the division from the line and relocate it to the area of operations of Heeresgruppe Mitte (Army Group Center) (relief in place by the 3. Panzer-Division).

19 July 1943: Attack is stopped; withdrawal to the line of departure. Railway transport to Brjansk; bivouac area in the vicinity of Karatschew. Enemy penetration threatens the main road Karatschew-Brjansk.

20 July 1943: Operational tanks: 10.

25 July 1943: Two Tigers support elements of Panzer-Aufklärungs-Abteilung "Großdeutschland" (armored reconnaissance battalion) during its attempt to make contact with the enemy.

30 July 1943: Two Tigers (Leutnant Folke) have to give up their attempt to relieve German forces at Point 211.7.

31 July 1943: Operational tanks: 6.

1 August 1943: Operational tanks: 5. No combat engagements; no engagements on 2 August 1943 either.

3 August 1943: Attack to the northwest starting from the southern part of Ismorosnj. Three Tigers break down during their support of the assault of the II./Panzer-Grenadier-Regiment "Großdeutschland" on the "Yellow Hill." Six T-34s are knocked out. The original main line of resistance is seized again.

4 August 1943: The division is ordered to redeploy. Relief in place by the 8. Panzer-Division. Railway transport from Brjansk into the area of Achtyrka, where a crisis arises from the enemy penetration near Tomarowka-Borissowka.

7 August 1943: Operational tanks 6.

8 August 1943: Detrainment in Trostjanez; several enemy attacks are repelled. In all, six Tigers lost during the most recent engagements.

Total tanks: 9.

10 August 1943: Only one Tiger operational.

14 August 1943: Consolidation with the III./Panzer-Regiment "Großdeutschland" as the 9./Panzer-Regiment "Großdeutschland."

15 August 1943: Consolidation of the company's maintenance platoon into the Maintenance Company of Panzer-Regiment "Großdeutschland."

✚

In all, the company destroyed more than 100 tanks.

COMPANY COMMANDER

Hauptmann Wallroth   13 January 1943–15 August 1943

A photograph taken during the fighting around Bogoduchoff. This Tiger has broken down and the engine is being checked out after the engine-deck access cover has been raised.

The maintenance vehicles with enclosed cabins were highly prized by the maintenance personnel and also performed a valuable function: they allowed repairs on sensitive equipment in a more controlled environment. NÄGELE

The wheeled vehicles of the division have started their road movement. A sight like this was only possible in the rear area and where there was little threat from the air.

The terrain conditions during these operations were extremely difficult, because the spring thaw had started. Traversing ice-covered bodies of water could prove hazardous. The company commander's tank—Tiger S01— got stuck in a way that facilitated its recovery. Less fortunate is Tiger S13, which has also gotten stuck in its efforts to recover a comrade. The later image was taken outside of Borissowka.

Maintenance is rarely mentioned in the after-action reports, but it is a major prerequisite for winning the battle. These photographs were taken at the end of the fighting around Bogoduchoff under cold-weather conditions. The 5-ton crane on the 18-ton prime mover can be seen to good advantage. It was used to remove engines and lesser loads from the Tigers; it was not suitable for lifting the turret. NÄGELE

After the successful offensive, Panzer-Grenadier-Division "Großdeutschland" was relieved and transported to Poltawa. HAASLER

This interesting series of photographs was taken in early May 1943 and shows maintenance work done in preparation for Operation "Citadel."

Additional views of the preparations for train movement to Poltawa.

Spring has arrived and Tiger S12 can be extricated from its unpleasant situation. It had broken through the ice during its attempt to cross the river during the March offensive.

The Tigers were still an unfamiliar sight for many soldiers, even though they had been in various stages of employment since the middle of 1942. For this reason, the division held several demonstrations and exercises for onlookers. In this picture, we see Leutnant Zierenberg hosting a group of visitors. RAISCH

Maintenance personnel search for "partisans" in their uniform items. Lice were a constant and unwelcome visitor. NÄGELE

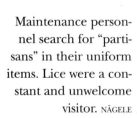

This respite was also used to train new drivers. These two photographs were taken while instructing a driver how to ford a shallow body of water.

Another small exercise was held to instruct personnel on how to negotiate a small body of water using pontoons and prefabricated bridging sections. Tiger S22 checks the quality of the engineers' efforts. HARMS

During offensive operations, the tanks constantly encountered mines, such as these two shown here. This photograph also demonstrates a unique characteristic of the 13./Panzer-Regiment "Großdeutschland": In order to make it easier for maintenance personnel and recovery teams to spot disabled tanks from a distance, the broken-down Tigers put small pennants on top of their aerials. RAISCH

In order to remove the Tiger's gearbox, the turret had to be removed from the vehicle. This also required the removal of the ammunition stowed in the hull and the mounting brackets for it.

Oberleutnant Stadler mugs for the camera in June 1943. RAISCH

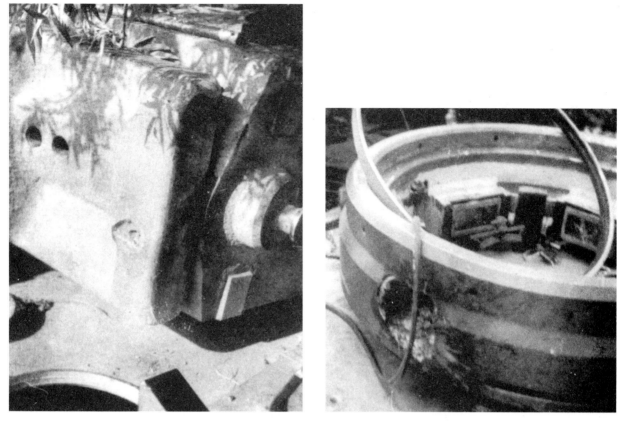

During Operation "Citadel," all of the tanks received numerous hits, but their armor proved superior on the battlefield. Only a few Tigers were lost during that operation. RAISCH

The recovery platoon in full swing. The eighteen-ton prime movers were constantly employed to recover disabled Tigers from the combat zone.

The division commander, Generalmajor Hoernlein, salutes successful Tiger crews. He is accompanied by the regimental commander, Oberst Graf Strachwitz.

In early August 1943, the division was moved to Achtyrka. RAISCH

This 7.62-centimeter hit that penetrated the barrel was quite unusual, but it could have meant big trouble for the crew if it had attempted to then fire the main gun. RAISCH

13./ Panzerregiment
"Großdeutschland" – 13 May 1943

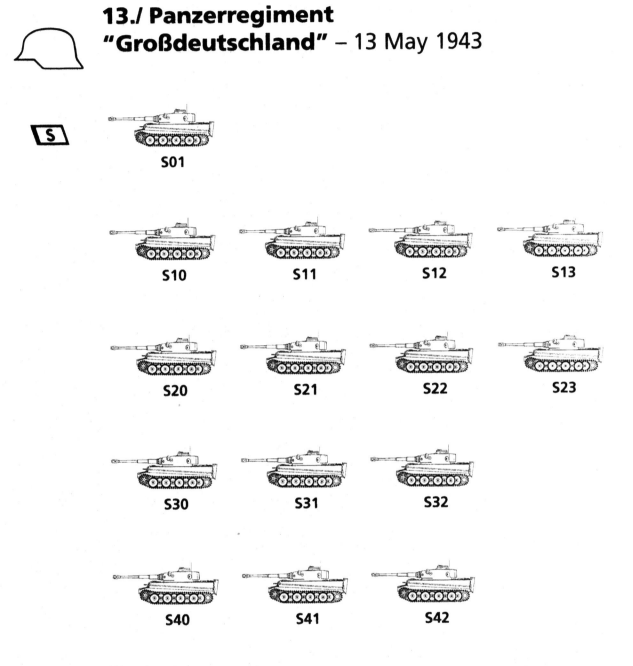

S01

S10 S11 S12 S13

S20 S21 S22 S23

S30 S31 S32

S40 S41 S42

III./Panzer-Regiment "Großdeutschland" (schwere Panzer-Abteilung "Großdeutschland")

Establishment of the III./Panzer-Regiment "Großdeutschland" at the Senne Training Area. First commander is Major Gomille.

✙

29 June 1943: Three Tiger I tanks are delivered for the battalion headquarters.

1 July 1943: The 13./Panzer-Regiment "Großdeutschland," about to go into action for Operation "Citadel," is consolidated with the battalion and redesignated as the 9./Panzer-Regiment "Großdeutschland." The 3./schwere Panzer-Abteilung 501 becomes the 10./Panzer-Regiment "Großdeutschland" and 3./schwere Panzer-Abteilung 504 becomes the 11./Panzer-Regiment "Großdeutschland." The two consolidated and redesignated companies join the battalion fully equipped.

July 1943: The battalion—minus the 9./Panzer-Regiment "Großdeutschland"—is entrained at the Neuhaus Railway Station near Paderborn and moved to Ssumy.

27 July 1943: Panzer-Kompanie (Funklenk) 311 is attached to the battalion (order: OpAbt III Nr. 7249/43). Movement to Gomel is ordered.

5–6 August 1943: Achtyrka.

14 August 1943: Detrainment at Nish. Ssirowatka. During the transport four tanks of the 11./Panzer-Regiment "Großdeutschland" burn out. The equipment of the maintenance section is lost as well.

Total tanks: 27.

Road march of 110 kilometers to Jassenowoje (ten kilometers west of Achtyrka). In the evening, sixteen Tigers are operational. The seven SPWs of the reconnaissance platoon still lack their machine guns. The Headquarters Company has not been formed; neither has the bulk of the Maintenance Company. Assembly area near Persche Trawnja. Attachment to Kampfgruppe (Oberstleutnant) Natzmer, the operations officer of the division. The Reconnaissance Platoon of Leutnant Janetzke is ordered to conduct terrain reconnaissance in the direction of Belsk. Departure after 1830 hours to Grun with the mission to defend the town. Assembly in Persche Trawnja (five kilometers northeast of Grun), because Grun is already in enemy hands.

15 August 1943: Jump-off position for the attack at the southwestern outskirts of Jassenowoje. At 0530 hours, the Tigers lead the attack on Grun. The leading Tiger is stopped after running over a mine. A left-hand pincer movement is ordered across the dominating high ground. In order to cross two ditches, the 11./Panzer-Regiment "Großdeutschland" attacks under cover of the 10./Panzer-Regiment "Großdeutschland." Dug-in antitank guns and SU 122s open fire from the right flank, the northeast edges of the town. The Tiger of the company commander of the 10./Panzer-Regiment "Großdeutschland" receives eight direct hits from a 12.2-centimeter antitank gun; Hauptmann von Villebois is severely wounded. Oberleutnant Arnold assumes acting command. After neutralizing their opponents, the town is captured. Five Tigers suffer battle damage after being hit and are non-operational; with the exception of six tanks, all the rest suffer mechanical problems. Attack on Budy, where dug-in antitank and antiaircraft guns are destroyed. After refueling and rearming, three Tigers advance on Belsk at about 1900 hours. It is taken shortly after midnight. The battalion has destroyed eight tanks and twenty-one guns. The 9./Panzer-Regiment "Großdeutschland" joins the battalion with its nine Tigers.

Total tanks: 36.

16 August 1943: March from Belsk via Grun to the forest two kilometers west of Achtyrka. Operational tanks: 5.

17 August 1943: Operational tanks: 10. Maintenance is performed.

18 August 1943: Fifteen Tigers attack Mosheni along the right side of the road Achtyrka-Michailowka. Shortly after Achtyrka is passed, eight Tigers run over mines. Five antitank guns are destroyed. In the evening, only four tanks remain operational.

19 August 1943: The operational tanks under Oberleutnant Arnold start an attack with the rest of the tank regiment on Parchomowka, where they penetrate strong antitank-gun belts. Twelve tanks and eighteen antitank guns are destroyed. One Tiger is heavily damaged by an SU 122; two more break down due to mechanical problems. In the evening, five Tigers are operational again.

20 August 1943: Attack from Parchomowka towards Kodelewka; five tanks knocked out. Three of the Tigers break down after mechanical problems. Operational tanks: 8.

21 August 1943: Attack on the southeast part of Parchomowka.

22 August 1943: One Tiger counterattacks northeast of Parchomowka; six antitank guns destroyed. Operational tanks: fifteen.

23 August 1943: Two Tigers push back several attacks together with other tanks of the regiment east and northeast of Michailowka (twelve kilometers southeast of Achtyrka); twenty-five tanks are knocked out. The main gun of one Tiger is put out of action.

24 August 1943: Gepanzerte Gruppe Gomille (two Tigers and five Panthers) push back several attacks; during the night, the division withdraws to the line Parchomowka-Bugrowatij.

25 August 1943: The battalion establishes a bivouac area near Budischtscha.

26 August 1943: Two partially damaged Tigers are sent to Kotelowa; one of them breaks down after gearbox failure. The last tank—Tiger B02—knocks out two T-34s but is destroyed after several hits.

Total tanks: 35.

Six new Tigers arrive in Poltava; after a land march of more than forty-five kilometers, only one tank is still operational.

Total tanks: 41.

During the last eight days of combat operations, the battalion has destroyed forty-two tanks and assault guns and fifty-four antitank guns. The low operational status results from the fact that the battalion still lacks a Maintenance Company.

31 August 1943: Operational tanks: 3.

1 September 1943: Counterattack near Teplyj after a road march of 220 kilometers. Operational tanks: 3.

2 September 1943: Relief in place by the 112. Infanterie-Division.

3 September 1943: Only eight tanks in the entire regiment still operational.

4 September 1943: Redeployment order to the a new sector near Oposhnaja.

5 September 1943: The division's tank regiment assembles north of Sesekli; several artillery barrages are received.

6 September 1943:   Blocking positions occupied south of Oposhnaja.

9 September 1943:   Positions in Tschupanoso occupied. Two tanks lost in early September.

Total tanks: 39.

10 September 1943: Operational tanks: 10.

11 September 1943: Several Tigers cover Makuchi-Romjany-Okari.

12 September 1943: Fighting positions occupied on Hill 184.8 and on the northwest outskirts of Oposhnaja.

13 September 1943: Positions maintained in Oposhnaja. Panzer-Grenadier-Division "Großdeutschland" is the covering force for the withdrawal across the Dnjepr River and then the withdrawal to the small Pssel River on the I Line.

20 September 1943: Operational tanks: 17.

27 September 1943: The M2 Line near Krementschug is held; local counterattacks. The regiment starts to leave the bridgehead.

29 September 1943: Operational tanks: 10. Counterattack led by the commander of the 11./Panzer-Regiment "Großdeutschland" (Oberleutnant Bayer) against the Dnjepr Bridgehead near Mischurin-Borodajewska; four Tigers are knocked out.

Total tanks: 35.

30 September 1943: Operational tanks: 9.

1 October 1943: Operational tanks: 9.

3 October 1943: Attack on Borodajewska. In the days that follow, defensive operations are conducted against several attacks, and a local counterattack by two Tigers is conducted against the high ground north of Borodajewska.

9 October 1943: A Tiger group of five tanks under the command of Oberleutnant Arnold attacks east of Point 172.2, but the accompanying infantry does not keep contact. The Tigers are trapped and all are knocked out. Oberleutnant Reinke becomes the new commander of the 10./Panzer-Regiment "Großdeutschland."

Total tanks: 30.

10 October 1943: Operational tanks: 6.

15 October 1943: Defensive operations against enemy forces attacking the bridgehead. Delaying action up to the area of Sofijewka (east of Kriwoj-Rog).

17 October 1943: Tiger C33 of Feldwebel Rampel, which is not completely operational, destroys several T-34s near Taranzoff.

18 October 1943: Tiger C33 repels a massive armor assault, knocking out seventeen out of around forty tanks. The tank then reaches the maintenance facility, heavily damaged but under its own power. Rampel is later awarded Knight's Cross. A train with ten new Tiger I tanks (coming from the Panzer-Lehr-Division) is captured near Pjatischatki by the Soviets!

20 October 1943: Operational tanks: 2. Seven Tigers have been destroyed during the last few days.

Total tanks: 23.

October 1943: Crews without tanks relieve Grenadier-Regiment "Großdeutschland" north of Sofijewka and fight as infantry, suffering substantial losses! Six tanks are lost in the last week of October.

Total tanks: 17.

1 November 1943: Operational tanks: 3.

6 November 1943: Attack on both sides of Krassnyj Orlik to the northeast in order to capture the high ground northwest of Nowo Kijewka. The attack passes between Ssofijewka and Prokowka and subsequently turns south.

8–15 November 1943: Employment of dismounted tank crews in two infantry companies. Three Tigers lost.

Total tanks: 14.

10 November 1943: All 14 Tigers in maintenance.

14 November 1943: Operations around Rantzau-Piz.

15 November 1943: Defensive positions occupied northeast of Ljubimowka; approximately twenty tanks are knocked out.

16 November 1943: Fighting positions occupied east of Ljubimowka; the battalion covers the withdrawal movements of the front. Oberleutnant Bayer destroys ten tanks. Oberfeldwebel Rampel's tank is a total loss.

Total tanks: 13.

17 November 1943: Kampfgruppe Gomille continues defensive operations.

20 November 1943: Operational tanks: 4.

26 November 1943: Kampfgruppe Gomille (with thirteen Tigers) counterattacks west of Menshinka; twenty-nine T-34s are knocked out.

27 November 1943: The front is moved back to the E Line (Jekaterinowka-defile south of Menshinka-Point 143.7-Schirokaja).

30 November 1943: Operational tanks: 2. No operations.

5 December 1943: First snowfall; redeployment to the east in reaction to reported strong enemy amour concentrations.

6 December 1943: Employment in the sector of the 13. Panzer-Division; attack on Wesely.

10 December 1943: Only one Tiger operational.

December 1943: Defensive operations near Kirowograd.

21 December 1943: Operational tanks: 7.

25 December 1943: Repeated counterattacks on Wyssockij.

31 December 1943: Operational tanks: 13.

1 January 1944: Attack on Hill 50 east of Wyssockij. Operational tanks: 9.

2 January 1944: Skirmishes near Wyssockij.

3 January 1944: Relief in place southwest of Kirowograd; counterattack to the northeast.

9 January 1944: Railway transport from Pawlozolije to the area south of Fedorowka (Panzergruppe Oberleutnant Bayer).

9–10 January 1944: Attack on Karlowka and Nasarjewka.

11 January 1944: Attack on Karlowka and local defensive operations.

27 January–8 February 1944: Several elements are employed to assist the 11. Panzer-Division in the Tscherkassy sector. The company commander of the 9./Panzer-Regiment "Großdeutschland," Hauptmann Wallroth, is killed in action; Oberleutnant Stadler assumes acting command.

1 February 1944: Operational tanks: 6.

February 1944–early March 1944: Battlefield reconstitution southwest of Kirowograd.

29 February 1944: Operational tanks: 10.

1 March 1944: Operational tanks: 10.

6 March 1944: Six Tigers delivered.

Total tanks: 19.

7 March 1944: The operational tanks of the regiment get the mission to cover the area on both sides of the main road Kirowograd-Rownoje.

8 March 1944: The Russian offensive west of Kirowograd is contained (until 13 March 1944); the division is then relieved in place. One Tiger lost.

Total tanks: 18.

10 March 1944: Three bogged-down Tigers are blown-up eight kilometers out of Perwomaisk.

Total tanks: 15.

15 March 1944: Transport to Rybniza.

21 March 1944: During the road march towards Kistimu, one Tiger and one quad light Flak vehicle are blown up after mechanical problems.

Total tanks: 14.

End of March 1944: Assembly in the area of Kischinew.

31 March 1944: Operational tanks: 10.

5 April 1944: Two Tigers in covering positions near Tochiresti; two other tanks are employed to support the attack of parts of Panzer-Grenadier-Regiment "Großdeutschland" on Hill 170.2 in the direction of Parliti Sat.

10 April 1944: Start of the counterattack from Jassy against enemy forces that have penetrated German positions at Targul. In the evening, the city is occupied.

11 April 1944: Tigers support the division's combat-engineer battalion, which is advancing via Valea Otlor to the north in the direction of Palieni.

16 April 1943: Counterattack and retaking of Bals.

20 April 1944: Operational tanks: 14. In the days that follow delivery is taken of six new Tiger I tanks.

Total tanks: 20.

25 April 1944: Attack towards Vascani under command of Oberstleutnant Baumungk. A Kampfgruppe of the division's tank regiment, including three Tigers, prepares for the attack on Ruginoasa.

26 April 1944: Attack into an enemy concentration along the main road to Vascani.

27 April 1944: Counterattack of the Tiger battalion against Dumbravita, Vascani and Hill 372.

30 April 1944: Operational tanks: 8. Assembly area in Baccau.

1 May 1944: Attack north of Dumbravita and in the area of Point 372.

2 May 1944: The Soviet offensive is pushed back on both sides of Targul Frumos, starting on the left in the sector of Panzer-Grenadier-Regiment "Großdeutschland" and then towards noon on the right in the sector of Panzer-Füsilier-Regiment "Großdeutschland." During the night, two mixed armored Kampfgruppen are in position so that they are able to cover the sectors in front of the two regiments.

3 May 1944: Repeated enemy attacks are repelled from reverse-slope positions; numerous tanks are knocked out.

4–5 May 1944: Fighting positions occupied near Point 296.

6 May 1944: Eight Tigers are delivered; two are transferred to the Tiger company of SS-Panzer-Regiment 3 "Totenkopf," the friendly force to the left. In addition, two other Tigers from on-hand stocks are also transferred to the SS tankers.

Total tanks: 24.

7 May 1944: Attack against Hill 344. Enemy artillery positions are destroyed with indirect fire.

18 May 1944: Six Tiger I tanks arrive in Roman. 2 are transferred to SS-Panzer-Regiment 3 "Totenkopf."

Total tanks: 28.

31 May 1944: Defensive positions occupied in the sector of Panzer-Grenadier-Regiment "Großdeutschland" north of the main road Jassy-Targul Framos.

1 June 1944: Six Tiger I tanks are delivered. Operational tanks: 19.

Total tanks: 34.

2 June 1944: Attack towards Orsoaei, the hill west of Point 146 and Hill 178.3 (three kilometers south of Isvoare-Epureni).

3 June 1944: Covering positions occupied north of Ursonaei; later on, attack on Hill 181. Local counterattack against the woods at Epureni.

4 June 1944:Attack on Hill 181, against Moimestti (four Tigers) and into the depression one kilometer southwest of Paprikanii Coarba. Covering positions occupied and defensive operations conducted west of Zahorna.

5 June 1944: Attack against the woods one kilometer southwest of Paprikanii Coarba.

10 June 1944–26 July 1944: Battlefield reconstitution in the area of Bacau.

June 1944: Six Tigers are manned with crews from Panzer-Ersatz- und Ausbildungs-Abteilung 500 in Paderborn. The battalion is transported by rail to East Prussia.

Total tanks: 40.

During detrainment, two Tigers are destroyed by fighter-bombers while changing their tracks.

Total tanks: 38.

1 July 1944: Operational tanks: 26.

26 July 1944: Start of railway transport to Gumbinnen.

5 August 1944: The first Tiger is immediately committed from the railhead in support of Panzer-Grenadier-Regiment "Großdeutschland," which is attacking to the northeast from Wirballen-the Kowno rail line-Gumbinnen.

6 August 1944: Attack from Wirballen to the northeast (Oberleutnant Leusing). Tigers C11, C12, C13 and C14 are knocked out by Josef Stalin heavy tanks.

Total tanks: 34.

9 August 1944: Assembly in the area of Wilkowischken. Attack within the regiment towards Wilkowischken. The battalion commander's tank is knocked out, and he is severely wounded. Hauptmann Bock assumes acting command. Two Tigers of the 10./Panzer-Regiment "Großdeutschland" (Leutnant Kurz and Oberfeldwebel Machleit) and Tiger C24 (Feldwebel Drenkhan) are knocked out. Several Tigers in action in Wilkowischken with Panzer-Füsilier-Bataillon "Großdeutschland."

Total tanks: 30.

10 August 1944: Covering positions occupied north of Wolfsburg. One Tiger (Stabsfeldwebel Will) starts burning after two hits from antitank guns; the crew manages to bail out.

Total tanks: 29.

11 August 1944: Withdrawal into the area of Skaudvile.

16 August 1944: Participation in Operation "Doppelkopf" from Tauroggen (XXXX. Panzer-Korps) and Schaulen. Operational tanks: 21.

17 August 1944: Kursenai is taken. Delivery of twelve new Tiger I tanks.

Total tanks: 41.

18 August 1944: Covering positions occupied near Guragiau (northwest of Kursenai); attack on Schaulen.

19 August 1944: Covering the area of Gytariai; Attack on Tukums starts.

20 August 1944: The Tigers support the capture of Tukums.

21 August 1944: Tigers support the 1. Infanterie-Division and parts of Panzer-Brigade 104 in the area of Schaulen.

23 August 1944: Attack at noon, which breaks through an enemy battle position five kilometers north of Autz. One Tiger fires at a Josef Stalin 1; the direct hit sets off the round in the breech of the Josef Stalin, which subsequently hits and knocks out the Tiger!

Total tanks: 40.

24 August 1944: Continuation of the attack in the area around Ile and ten kilometers northeast of Bene.

25 August 1944: Attack towards Doblen stalls at the crossing near Lemkini-Skola, eight kilometers in front of the objective. The attack force has to go over to defensive positions.

26 August 1944: Contact with the 81. Infanterie-Division is established north of Doblen.

27 August 1944: Several weak enemy attacks are repelled.

1 September 1944: Operational tanks: 19.

15 September 1944: Assembly for the offensive, Operation "Cäsar."

16 September 1944: Attack is started; advance as far as seven kilometers east of Ile.

17 September 1944: Hill 92.0, 4 kilometers west of Lake Abguldes, is reached.

18 September 1944: Sesave, two kilometers west of Lake Abguldes is passed. The attack is then called off; the forces occupy defensive fighting positions.

1 October 1944: Operational tanks: 11. During the fighting in September, the battalion lost seven tanks.

Total tanks: 33.

4 October 1944: After a road march via Autz-Laizuva-Vieksniai, arrival in Tryskiai. Assembly area around Raudenai; the Soviets have established several bridgeheads across the Venta River.

5 October 1944: Covering positions occupied around Raudenai.

7 October 1944: Several Tigers do not withdraw in time to the new position east of Telsche, but they succeed in breaking out without loss.

8 October 1944: The area between Lake Plinksin and Lake Tausalas is recaptured.

9 October 1944: Withdrawal in the direction of Memel; several Tigers have to be blown up due to a lack of fuel. Tiger C24 of Oberfeldwebel Windheuser is knocked out by T-34s. German close-air-support aircraft destroy five Tigers!

10 October 1944: Kampfgruppe Schwarzrock (with several Tigers) occupies the line Liepgiviai-southern shore of Lake Virksos and subsequently withdraws across the bridge near Salantai into the Memel via Darbenai and Polangen.

11 October 1944: Due to a lack of fuel, only stationary employment; several enemy attacks are repulsed.

14 October 1944: A single Tiger is in action with Panzer-Füsilier-Regiment "Großdeutschland."

16 October 1944: Attack against an enemy penetration east of Schweppeln is not successful.

22 October 1944: Three Tigers support the I./Panzer-Grenadier-Regiment "Großdeutschland" in the attack on Kunken Görge.

25 October 1944: The three Tigers are still in support of the battalion at Kunken Görge.

26 October 1944: The first eight Tigers arrive after sea transport in Pillau. The rest of the division relocates during the next several weeks to East Prussia. It is designated as an OKH reserve in the area of Rastenburg-Sensburg.

1 November 1944: Operational tanks: 8. The battalion lost eighteen tanks in October. *Total tanks: 15.*

November 1944: Tiger C24 is transferred to schwere Panzer-Abteilung 502.

1 December 1944: Operational tanks: 12. During battlefield reconstitution in East Prussia in November and December, the operational training status was improved. Several command-post exercises are held for the leadership.

13 December 1944: The III./Panzer-Regiment "Großdeutschland" is redesignated as schwere Panzer-Abteilung "Großdeutschland."

16 December 1944: Four Tiger I tanks delivered from depot-level maintenance; two of them are soon transferred to schwere Panzer-Abteilung 502.

Total tanks: 17.

11 January 1945: Redeployment into the area of Milau-Praschnitz; several immediate counterattacks are conducted.

13 January 1945: The 2./Panzer-Abteilung 302 (Funklenk) is attached to the battalion; assembly area southeast of Praschnitz. At midnight, covering positions are occupied east of the bridge near Podos Stary.

15 January 1945: Attack out of the Krasnosielc Bridgehead on Wola Pienicka; this is followed by engagements in the area of Dworskie. At night, two Tigers of the 11./Panzer-Regiment "Großdeutschland" (3./schwere Panzer-Abteilung "Großdeutschland") (Leutnant Oertel and Feldwebel Herwagen) and one Tiger of the 10./Panzer-Regiment "Großdeutschland" (2./schwere Panzer-Abteilung "Großdeutschland") (Feldwebel Bühler) screen at Gansewo. Operational tanks: 4.

16 January 1945: Early in the morning, withdrawal to Gansewo. Skirmishes near Dworskie.

18 January 1945: Operations at Ch.-Zalogi.

19 January 1945: Several strongpoints south of Szlachecki and Lipa and in the area to the south are held.

21 January 1945: Counterattack towards Roggen.

22 January 1945: In the evening, counterattack near Leinau.

24 January 1945: Enemy forces attacking via Mensguth are contained along the road to Wartenburg.

25 January 1945: Counterattack near Cronau.

26 January 1945: Blocking positions occupied near Schönau.

27 January 1945: Crews without tanks formed into companies and employed as infantry; empty trucks are used for transport.

29 January 1945: Liebstadt is lost.

30 January 1945: Last attack of the regiment along the Haff road in the direction of Waldburg-Maulen and Wundlacken (under command of Hauptmann Bock); sixty-eight tanks are knocked out. Hauptmann Bock is awarded the Knight's Cross.

1 February 1945: Operational tanks: 4. The battalion lost six tanks in January. A Kampfgruppe is formed out of the remaining tanks of the division (schwere Panzer-Abteilung "Großdeutschland" is dissolved). The majority of the personnel is relocated to Paderborn and trained on Tiger IIs (the tank drivers are trained in Kassel).

Total tanks: 11.

4–5 February 1945: Three Tigers are in action (Leutnant Vogelsang) near Federal Road 1 near Waldburg.

20 February 1945: Employment at the Heiligen Berg west of Zinten.

1 March 1945: Engagement near Groß Klingbeck with Fallschirm-Panzer-Division 1 "Hermann Göring." Operational tanks: 4. Three tanks lost in February.

Total tanks: 8.

The battalion consists of a heavy tank company (including one Sturmpanzer), a medium tank company (five Panthers and one Panzer IV) and a mixed assault-gun battery (two Sturmgeschütze and two Panzerjäger IVs). The ad hoc battalion headquarters consists of one Tiger and two Panzer IVs. The crews without tanks are employed as infantry and suffer heavy casualties.

6 March 1945: Several Tigers accompany an abortive counterattack of Panzer-Füsilier-Bataillon "Großdeutschland" in the forest north of Amalienwalde.

13 March 1945: Blocking positions occupied near Pokarben. The Tiger of Leutnant Doerr is knocked out.

Total tanks: 7.

14 March 1945: Fighting positions at Waldberg-Maulen occupied; one Tiger is knocked out. An infantry battalion under the command of Hauptmann Zabel is formed with three companies: 1st Company under Oberleutnant Welke; 2nd Company under Leutnant Vogelsang; and the 3rd Company under Leutnant Plästerer. It occupies defensive positions near Kobbelbude.

Total tanks: 6.

15 March 1945: All six remaining Tigers operational.

17 March 1945: One tank—Tiger C12—is knocked out near Pörschken; it cannot be recovered and is blown up by the crew. One Panzer IV of the headquarters section runs out of fuel and is destroyed by the crew using two Panzerfäuste (German handheld anti-tank rocket-propelled grenades).

Total tanks: 5.

19 March 1945: The remaining Tigers are either knocked out or abandoned by their crews (Unteroffizier Feuerpfeil, Unteroffizier Kroneis) in the Balga Pocket. Some of the crews can escape across the Frisches Haff into the German Samland province and are used as infantry again. Later on, they are transported by ferries to the Hela Peninsula. They engage in their last skirmishes, and the survivors are captured by the Soviets.

1 April 1945: The elements that had been sent to Paderborn are also employed as infantry (west of Paderborn). Later on, they withdraw through the Teutoburg Woods in the direction of Höxter and Einbeck. They are employed as Panzer-Jagd-Kommando Fröhlich (roughly, Antitank Detachment "Fröhlich"); they then withdraw to the Harz Mountains, where they ultimately surrender to US forces.

✠

The battalion's total score was more than 500 tanks.

BATTALION COMMANDERS

Major Gomille	June 1943–April 1944
Oberstleutnant Baumungk	April 1944–9 August 1944 (wounded)
Hauptmann Bock	9 August 1944–April 1945

KNIGHTS' CROSS RECIPIENTS

Oberfeldwebel Rampel	17 December 1943 (posthumously)
Hauptmann Bock	30 January 1945

The operational tanks assemble for an attack on Oarchomowka on 19 August 1943. Tiger C22 occupies center stage in this photograph. BRÖNNER

In Mid-August 1943, the 10./ and 11./Panzer-Regiment "Großdeutschland" were employed in an attack on Grun. Tiger B22 can be identified in this photograph. SCHMIDT

During the movement to the area around Achtyrka, Tiger C11 has halted beside a column from Panzer-Jäger-Abteilung 41. MÜNCH

These two photographs were taken in August 1943. The top picture shows the company commander's tank of the 10./Panzer-Regiment "Großdeutschland"—Tiger B01—passing a column of Füsilier-Regiment "Großdeutschland." Several hours later, it suffered a mechanical problem and broke down. TOP—MÜNCH; BOTTOM—ANDERSON

In September 1943, the battalion had some time for rest and used the opportunity to perform urgent repair and maintenance work. This sequence shows personnel of the maintenance company working on Tiger A12. HARMS

Sometimes, even the crane vehicle needed urgent repair work. In this photograph, the drive sprocket and the final drive have been replaced on the vehicle. HARMS

In January 1944, the regiment was transported by rail to the Fedorowka area of operations. This photograph was taken upon the battalion's arrival at Rowynaji.

The relief attack on the Tscherkassy Pocket took place under severe weather conditions. Tiger C13 refuels during a short maintenance halt.

Two other photographs from this period demonstrate repair work involving the indispensable portal crane: Tigers B14 and S02. NÄGELE

The crew of Feldwebel Stuckenbröcker's Tiger A22 pose right after detraining. RAISCH

In April 1944, the Soviet offensive against Targul Framos was about to start. General der Panzertruppen von Manteuffel and his Panzer-Grenadier-Division "Großdeutschland" had prepared their defensive plan well. In this photograph, he is being briefed by Major Wietersheim, while Major Remer looks on. RAISCH

The tanks occupied well-concealed hide positions and awaited the Soviet onslaught.

The terrain in northern Romania is quite open, thus offering the Tigers more opportunities for employing their main guns to the maximum range possible. HARMS

The battalion commander, Oberstleutnant Baumungk, scans the terrain near Targul Framos from the rear deck of Tiger S02, which was one of the original Tigers received by the formation as can be discerned from the old-style drum-shaped commander's cupola. His adjutant, Oberleutnant Welke, stands behind him. WELKE

Because many of the Tigers' opponents were beginning to be the newly introduced Josef Stalin heavy tanks and the SU-122 assault guns, any hits received from them tended to inflict severe battle damage.

New tanks on the way to the battalion in May 1944. No formation insignia is identifiable, but the crewmembers wear the telltale "Großdeutschland" cuff titles on their tunics. SPAETER

This photo depicts the arrival of Panzer-Regiment "Großdeutschland" in Gumbinnen in late July 1944.

In June 1944, six Tigers were shipped from Paderborn to Gumbinnen in East Prussia, where they awaited the rest of the battalion. They had a unique two-color camouflage scheme and lacked turret numbers. SPAETER

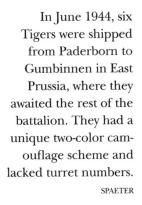

The Tigers cross a bridge during their movement to Wirballen.

On 6 August 1944, the entire 3rd Platoon of the 11./Panzer-Regiment "Großdeutschland" was knocked out near Wirballen. Several days later, the badly damaged tanks were entrained and sent to the rear for depot-level maintenance and repair at the factory. HARMS

This photograph of the divisional commander, General der Panzertruppen von Manteuffel, and the armor regiment commander, Oberst Langkeit, was taken on 10 August 1944 near Wolfsburg in East Prussia. WELKE

In September 1944, the battalion took part in the successful counteroffensive codenamed Operation Cäsar, which started in northern Lithuania.

In October, the division was pushed back towards Memel. The tanks covered the withdrawal of the infantry formations that tried to reach the harbor.

On 9 October 1944, five Tigers were erroneously attacked by German close-air-support aircraft. One of the losses was Tiger A22, which is being inspected by a Russian soldier in this photograph.

In October 1944, the remaining Tigers were transported by sea from Memel to Pillau.
RAISCH

In November and December 1944, the battalion was allowed to rest in East Prussia and prepare for the fierce fighting to come.

The struggle for East Prussia was very hard. Although the war was lost, the Tiger crews continued fighting after witnessing the cruelties of the invading Soviet forces.

The tanks continued to be employed until it was no longer possible to keep them operational. This Tiger is being towed by a Bergepanther, an armored recovery vehicle based on a Panther tank chassis. ANDERSON

III./PANZER-REGIMENT "GROßDEUTSCHLAND"

Vehicles on Hand/Deliveries

Date	Tiger I	Tiger II	On hand	Remarks
February 1943	9		9	13./Panzer-Regiment "Großdeutschland"
13 May 1943	6		15	13./Panzer-Regiment "Großdeutschland"
July 1943	28		28	3./schwere Panzer-Abteilung 501 and 3./schwere Panzer-Abteilung 504
29 June 1943	3		31	Battalion staff
14 August 1943	(9)		36	Former 13./Panzer-Regiment "Großdeutschland"'
August 1943	6		41	
18 October 1943	10			Lost
15 February 1944	10			Not arrived
6 March 1943	6		19	
20 April 1944	6		20	
6 May 1944	8		24	4 to the 9./SS-Panzer-Regiment 3
18 May 1944	6		28	2 to the 9./SS-Panzer-Regiment 3
1 June 1944	6		34	
June 1944	6		40	
17 August 1944	12		41	
16 December 1944	(4)		17	Depot-level maintenance; 2 later transferred to schwere Panzer-Abteilung 511
Grand Total	96	0		

Losses

Date	Losses	On hand	Remarks
July–August 1943	6	9	13./Panzer-Regiment "Großdeutschland"
14 August 1943	4	27	Burnt out
26 August 1943	1	35	Knocked out
9 September 1943	2	39	Knocked out
29 September 1943	4	35	Knocked out
9 October 1943	5	30	Knocked out
October 1943	13	17	?
November 1943	3	14	?
15 November 1943	1	13	Knocked out
8 March 1944	1	18	?
10 March 1944	3	15	Destroyed by own crew
21 March 1943	1	14	Destroyed by own crew
June 1944	2	38	Ground-attack aircraft
6 August 1944	4	34	Knocked out
9 August 1944	4	30	Knocked out
10 August 1944	1	29	Knocked out by an antitank gun
23 August 1944	1	40	Knocked out by a JS tank
September 1944	7	33	?
October 1944	18	15	?
January 1945	6	11	?
February 1945	3	8	?
13 March 1945	1	7	Knocked out
14 March 1945	1	6	Knocked out
17 March 1944	1	5	Destroyed by own crew
March 1945	5	0	?
Grand Total	98		

Of the losses suffered by the battalion, 33% were due to self-destruction (to prevent capture), 63% were lost in combat operations and 4% were lost due to other causes.

III./ Panzerregiment "Großdeutschland" – August 1943

S01   **S02**   **S03**

9.

???

???   **???**   **???**   **???**

???   **???**   **???**   **???**

10.

B01   **B02**

B11   **B12**   **B13**   **B14**

B21   **B22**   **B23**   **B24**

B31   **B32**   **B33**   **B34**

11.

C01   **C02**

C??   **C??**   **C??**   **C??**

C??   **C??**   **C??**   **C??**

III./ Panzerregiment "Großdeutschland" – early Sept.1943

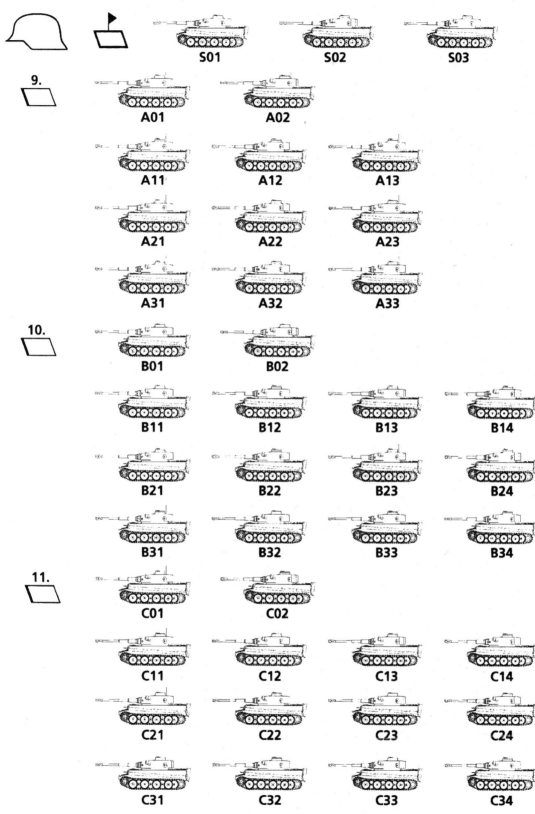

III./Panzerregiment "Großdeutschland" – 17.8.44

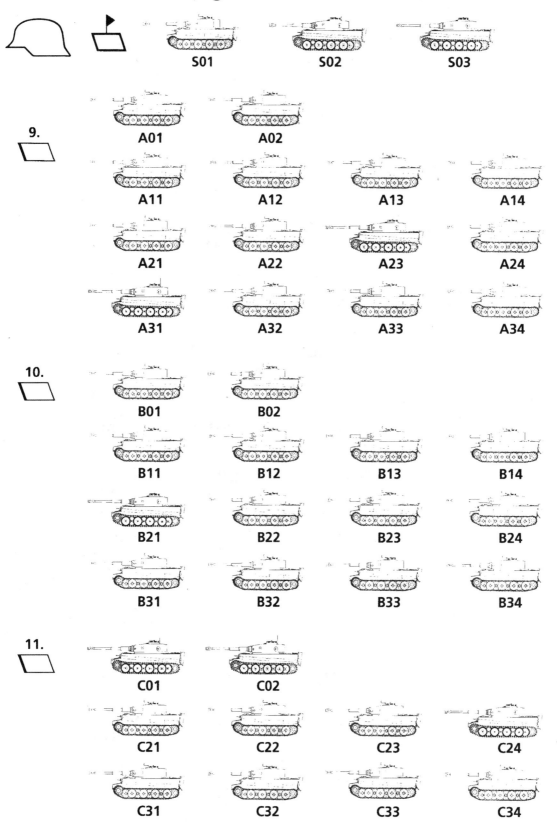

Schwere Panzer-Kompanie "Hummel"

In early July 1944, an alert unit is established by Military District VI in Paderborn, which is named after the company commander, Oberleutnant Hummel. The unit is equipped with fourteen Tiger I tanks out of the inventory of Panzer-Ersatz- und Ausbildungs-Abteilung 500. Some of the personnel come from the 2./schwere Panzer-Abteilung 504.

✠

18 September 1944: Alert at the Senne Training Area and entrainment on the following day.

19 September 1944: Detrainment in Bocholt. Eighty-kilometer road march towards Arnhem; attachment to the 10. SS-Panzer-Division "Hohenstaufen." All tanks except two break down on the way. Attack with these two Tigers (Leutnant Knaack and Feldwebel Barnecki) on the same evening; both are immobilized by PIAT fire. (The PIAT—Projectile, infantry, anti-tank—was the British version of the US bazooka.)

24 September 1944: Skirmishes as part of Kampfgruppe Spindler east of Arnhem. Several tanks crash through bridges in the Oosterbeck sector.

25 September 1944: Attack on Arnhem from the east.

Late September 1944: Delaying actions in Holland: Doetinchem, Elst, Valburg, Lienden, Ghent, Ede, Utrecht, S'Hertogenbosch and Enspijk).

Early November 1944: Engagements near Aachen.

19 November 1944: Two Tigers support elements of the 15. Panzer-Grenadier-Division near Tripsrath. One Tiger is knocked out by an antitank gun.

20 November 1944: Hauptmann Hummel is killed near Lindern; Leutnant Flöhr becomes the acting commander.

18 December 1944: Consolidated with schwere Panzer-Abteilung 506, where it becomes the 4th Company (See also, *Tigers in Combat I*). Participation in the engagements of this battalion; employment in the Eifel Mountains and in the area west of the Rhine (Heisdorf, Eselborn, Beiler, Oberpierscheid and Wallersheim).

16 February 1945: The company is relieved from assignment to schwere Panzer-Abteilung 506 and is allocated to the LXXXI. Armee-Korps in the area of Etzweiler. The company bivouacs in the forest of Elsdorfer Bürge.

24 February 1945: Two Tiger Is take part in the engagements of Panzer-Regiment 33 (9. Panzer-Division) west of the Rhine and are transported to the other bank after they break down.

25 February 1945: One Tiger I knocks out an M 26 Pershing in Elsdorf. While pulling back, it becomes entangled in the debris of a building and has to be abandoned. two Tiger Is are knocked out near Dormagen by M 24 Chaffees (4th Cavalry Group).

March 1945: Road march via Weidenbach and Brockscheid, then crossing of the Rhine near Koblenz. Further movement to the provinces of Dill and the Sauerland (Höhr-Grenzhausen, Hilgert, Odersberg, Münchhausen, Würdinghausen and Oberhunden).

5 April 1945: Allocation to the LII. Armee-Korps and attachment to Panzer-Brigade 106 (11 Tiger Is).

April 1945: Engagements in the area of Grevenbrück, Herscheid, Werdohl and Altena.

This knocked-out Tiger represents one of the first losses of the company during its employment in eastern Holland. DE MEYER

There were some casualties during the Ardennes offensive. This vehicle was knocked out on 15 January 1945 near Oberwampach (ten kilometers east of Bastogne). The internal explosion in the turret caused the gun mantlet tube jacket to be pushed forward.

The first operations of the company were conducted while attached to schwere Panzer-Abteilung 506. This was in autumn 1944 during the fighting around Aachen. This Tiger of the company was photographed on 16 October 1944 near Geilenkirchen. KEMP

One of the first newly introduced US M26 Pershings was knocked out by this Tiger at Elsdorf. During its attempt to pull back, the tank got stuck in the debris behind it and was abandoned by its crew.

In the springtime, the snow melted and allowed the turret number of this Tiger to become visible: 411. DE MEYER

This Tiger I from schwere Panzer-Kompanie "Hummel" got stuck near Brunskappel on 6 April 1945, when the company was attached to Panzer-Brigade 106. The company changed to a different numbering system soon after it was detached from schwere Panzer-Abteilung 506, since this tank features a white 111 crudely painted on the front part of the turret sides. BOTH—DE MEYER

Schwere Panzer-Kompanie "Meyer"

Established by special order of Panzer-Ersatz- und Ausbildungs-Abteilung 500 (order: Abt Ia Br.B.Nr. 851/43 (SECRET), dated 26 July 1943).

Equipped with eight Tiger I tanks; acting company commander is Oberleutnant Meyer.

+

End of July 1943: Entrainment and rail transport to Innsbruck.

31 July 1943: The Brenner Pass is crossed. Road march through Sterzing and Brixen to Bozen.

8 August 1943: Four Tigers support Kampfgruppe Furbach, the commander of Reichs-Grenadier-Regiment 132 (44. Reichs-Grenadier-Division "Hoch- und Deutschmeister"), for the disarmament of Italian formations.

10 September 1943: Operational tanks: 5.

30 September 1943: Operational tanks: 7.

Early October 1943: Relocation into the area of Borgoforte (near Mantua).

25 October 1943: Rest in Ginzano.

Early November 1943: Relocation into the Voghera-Tortona-Alessandria area. The maintenance facilities of SS-Panzer-Grenadier-Division "Leibstandarte SS Adolf Hitler" are used.

20 November 1943: Operational tanks: 7. Redeployment to Modena.

26 November 1943: Subordination to the 8. Armee; railway transport to Rome.

Early December 1943: Railway transport from Modena to Ceccignola (south of Rome). Route and terrain reconnaissance via Fiumicino and Ostia to Terracina. The approach roads—the Pontinian Swamps!—and firing positions for both land and sea targets are carefully marked on the tactical maps. The designated company commander, Hauptmann Schwebbach, arrives.

22 January 1944: At 0300 hours, the Allies start landing at the Anzio-Nettuno Beachhead. The company moves into an assembly area in the olive groves near Pavona at noon. The pre-planned employment against the landing zone at Anzio is called off without any reason given. An immediate attack of the company out of the reconnoitered positions could have been successful! The attack four days later fails.

23 January 1944: Withdrawal to Procula near Ardea.

25 January 1944: Cecina is transited during the night.

26 January 1944: Limited-objective attack under command of Kampfgruppe Haen (commander of Panzer-Abteilung 103 of the 3. Panzer-Grenadier-Division) near Aprilia has to be stopped. Hauptmann Schwebbach is killed in Tiger 2 after receiving a hit on the cupola's hatch.

30–31 January 1944: Employment at the crossing north of Campoleone.

1 February 1944: Operations near Cecina. Numerous enemy vehicles move under cover of a Red Cross flag.

3 February 1944: Assembly near Hill 95 together with tanks of the Panzer-Abteilung 190 of the 90. Panzer-Grenadier-Division.

4 February 1944: Assault on Hill 95. Company commander's tank is penetrated at 300 meters by an armor-piercing round.

10 February 1944: Air-strike on Cecina; 1 Tiger is hit on its rear.

11 February 1944: Maintenance is performed on vehicles in Ceccignola.

12 February 1944: Operational tanks: 0.

13 February 1944: Briefing of the newly arrived schwere Panzer-Abteilung 508 near Forte Tiburtina (vicinity of Rome).

15 February 1944: Training exercise at Ceccignola; issues with the umpires about the refusal to leave concrete roads right in the middle of marshy ground.

16 February 1944: Attack on the ill-fated "Finger Woods" stalls because the German infantry cannot maintain contact.

18 February-1 March 1944: Skirmishes and relief attacks in the area of Cisterna, near La Isabella and Ponte Rotto.

2 March 1944: Attack on La Isabella near Cisterna.

3 March 1944: The company is consolidated with schwere Panzer-Abteilung 508 (see also *Tigers in Combat I*). Oberleutnant Meyer becomes the battalion adjutant.

This well known but previously unidentified propaganda photograph shows schwere Panzer-Kompanie "Meyer" while encamped next to the Brenner Pass road. GRETSCHEL

Schwere Panzer-Kompanie "Meyer" approached the Brenner Pass on 30 July 1943. This is the Tiger of Feldwebel Puchegger. MEYER

On 8 August 1943, the company Tigers supported a Kampfgruppe of the 44. Reichs-Grenadier-Division "Hoch- und Deutschmeister" in the disarmament of Italian formations.

The company continued to move south. During this period, the tanks of the company lacked all markings.

Leutnant Meyer and his tank during a maintenance halt on the road march to Vipiteno Sterzing. MEYER

Leutnant Meyer . . . although he was a young officer, he was the acting commander of this unit until the designated commander, Hauptmann Schwebbach, could arrive. MEYER

Although this area belongs to Italy, most of the residents are ethnic Germans and welcome the arriving tanks with open arms. MEYER

On 25 October 1943, the company conducted an extended maintenance halt at Ginzano (near Mantova). MEYER

Preparations for a company outing near Bozen. MEYER

In Ceccignola, the tanks were prepared for the expected Allied landings. The maintenance platoon used the facilities of a road construction company to work on the vehicles, to include the cranes. MEYER

It is not difficult for a tank to find a parking space! In early December 1943, the company was transported by rail to Ceccignola via Rome. The tanks have had their tactical markings applied, including the unit symbol—the Baltic cross—on the front bow. MEYER

During the engagements near Cisterna during February 1944, Tiger 5 is seen towing another Tiger while passing a Sturmpanzer IV. JAUGITZ

Hauptmann Schwebbach was killed near Aprilia on 26 January 1944 when his tank—Tiger 2, christened Mausi ("Mousie")—received a hit on the commander's cupola. MEYER

13./SS-Panzer-Regiment 1

At the end of November 1942, the nucleus for a heavy tank company is formed from elements of SS-Panzer-Regiment "Leibstandarte SS Adolf Hitler" of SS-Panzer-Grenadier-Division "Leibstandarte SS Adolf Hitler" at Fallingbostel (KStN 1176 dated 15 August 1942). The original concept had been to form a heavy-tank battalion for the newly organized SS-Panzer-Korps, however, the divisions pleaded to have a Tiger company at their disposal for each of their tank regiments, and the request was approved.

The heavy tank company was originally designated as the 4./SS-Panzer-Regiment "Leibstandarte SS Adolf Hitler" and was to be formed at Fallingbostel. The first company commander was SS-Hauptsturmführer Kling, with an effective date of command of 24 December 1942. In fact, he arrived on 2 December 1942 at his new duty assignment.

✚

20 December 1942: Several tank commanders and drivers are detached to the production works of Henschel und Wegmann in Kassel.

21 January 1943: The company receives ten Tiger Is and fifteen Panzer IIIs. Three tank platoons are organized, each with three Tiger Is and three Panzer IIIs. In addition, the company has a maintenance platoon of its own.

28 January 1943: Orders for redeployment are issued.

31 January 1943: Beginning of entrainment at Fallingbostel.

2 February 1943: The last (third) transport is entrained.

3 February 1943: Transport passes Berlin to the north and Stargard.

4 February 1943: Wilna-Kowno.

5 February 1943: Minsk-Gomel.

7 February 1943: The first transport arrives in Kharkov.

8 February 1943: Arrival of the second transport in Kharkov.

9 February 1943: After a longer delay at Stargard (caused by a rail car burning) the last transport with three Tigers and five Panzer IIIs (under the command of SS-Untersturmführer Wittmann) arrives in Kharkov. In the evening, it is diverted to Poltava. This group stays there until it the rejoins the company in early March.

11 February 1943: Five advancing Tigers support the successful assault at Merefa.

12 February 1943: One Tiger (SS-Unterscharführer Aus der Wischen) catches fire while moving from Merefa in the direction of Poltava and has to be blown up on 16 February 1943.

Total tanks: 9.

15 February 1943: Orders to withdraw from Kharkov.

16 February 1943: The defensive blocking position at Alexejewna is reached. In the night, enemy counterattacks are repulsed.

21 February 1943: The company is ordered to move to Krassnograd. Operational tanks: 6.

25 February 1943: The company is assembled at the railway station of Poltava (nine Tigers and around ten Panzer IIIs). Beginning of the mud period. Operational tanks: 7.

2 March 1943: Operational tanks: 8.

3 March 1943: Enemy breakout attempts near Berestowaja thwarted. Operational tanks: 8.

4 March 1943: Enemy counterattacks from the direction of Staroverovka. Operational tanks: 8.

5 March 1943: Redeployment of the company to an area thirty kilometers north of Krassnograd; one Tiger (SS-Unterscharführer Brandt) catches fire along the route and burns out. Only four Tigers complete the march. The rest are not operational.

Total tanks: 8.

6 March 1943: Assault by the 1./SS-Panzer-Regiment "Leibstandarte SS Adolf Hitler" and the four operational Tigers in the direction of Walki. Outside of Blagodatnoje, an antitank-gun belt is penetrated; several T-34s and antitank guns are destroyed. Tiger 422 (SS-Hauptscharführer Pöttschlag) is immobilized by several hits. Outside of Sneschkov Kut, eight more T-34s are destroyed. SS-Untersturmführer Wendorff's tank breaks through the ice of the Msha River and is recovered some days later.

7 March 1943: Assembly at the Peski Bridgehead; attack starts in the afternoon. After an antitank-gun belt is penetrated, Walki is captured. Operational tanks: 5.

8 March 1943: The assault is continued via Bolgar to the railway and road crossing at Schljach. Operational tanks: 4.

9 March 1943: Ljubotin is captured. Operational tanks: 4.

10 March 1943: The few operational tanks of the company are attached to the 1./SS-Panzer-Grenadier-Regiment 1 and support the assault at Zirkuny (via Dergatschi). Operational tanks: 3.

11–15 March 1943: The operational tanks take part in the capture of Kharkov.

11 March 1943: After destroying six enemy tanks and eight antitank guns, the Tiger of SS-Untersturmführer Philipsen is damaged by a direct hit from close range through the optical system. (The tank receives a new mantlet in April.) The center of Kharkov is reached. No Tigers are operational by the evening.

12 March 1943: No Tigers operational.

14 March 1943: Street fighting in Kharkov continues. One Tiger operational.

15 March 1943: Same situation as the previous day.

16 March 1943: Advance on Bolschije Prochody. Operational tanks: 2.

17 March 1943: Pursuit of the fleeing enemy forces towards Bjelgorod. Operational tanks: 2.

18 March 1943: The Tiger of SS-Unterscharführer Modes returns from the Maintenance Company and road marches via Walki and Olschany to Kharkov. There it is attached to Kampfgruppe Peiper. It takes part in the assault at Bjelgorod, where five enemy tanks and one antitank gun are destroyed. With a further Tiger and three Panzer IIIs, the small Kampfgruppe covers the northern outskirts.

19 March 1943: Both of the Tigers and the 7./SS-Panzer-Regiment "Leibstandarte SS Adolf Hitler become engaged northwest of Bjelgorod near Strelezkoje while trying to establish contact with Panzer-Grenadier-Division "Großdeutschland." They knock out one KV-2 and one T-34. In the evening, they withdraw to the northern outskirts of Bjelgorod. Operational tanks: 3.

20 March 1943: In the morning, Kampfgruppe Peiper and the Tiger company advance along the road in the direction of Kursk. Fierce enemy resistance is encountered near Gonki; the front is pulled back as far as Oskotschnoje (twelve kilometers north of Bjelgorod). Operational tanks: 3.

21 March 1943: No engagements. Operational tanks: 3.

22 March 1943: Support of the assault at Strelezkoje to establish contact with Panzer-Grenadier-Division "Großdeutschland". Operational tanks: 3.

23 March 1943: Three Tigers operational. No engagements.

24 March 1943: The SS-Panzer-Korps is informed that the three divisional Tiger companies are to be consolidated into a Tiger battalion at corps level by increasing the strength of each company to fourteen tanks. Four Tigers operational. No operations.

25 March 1943: The company takes up quarters at the northern outskirts of Kharkov. Operational tanks: 4.

26 March 1943: Operational tanks: 4. The division commander refuses to dispatch six tank crews to Paderborn for planned establishment of the new Tiger battalion.

31 March 1943: Five Tigers operational.

5 April 1943: Visit of Generaloberst Model.

10 April 1943: Six Tigers operational.

Middle of April 1943: Inspection by Generaloberst Guderian.

20 April 1943: Six Tigers operational.

22 April 1943: Orders received for reorganization in accordance with KStN 1176e dated 5 March 1943.

26 April 1943: Alert and march into an assembly area for Operation "Citadel."

30 April 1943: Eight Tigers operational.

5 May 1943: Return to Kharkov.

Beginning of May 1943: Approximately forty Luftwaffe airmen are transferred into the company.

10 May 1943: Three Tigers operational.

13 May 1943: Equipment detail under SS-Hauptscharführer Hartel arrives with five Tigers; the Panzer IIIs are handed over to the regiment.

Total tanks: 13.

20 May 1943: Operational tanks: 9.

30 May 1943: Operational tanks: 7.

10 June 1943: Operational tanks: 10.

20 June 1943: Operational tanks 7.

28 June 1943: The company is alerted for movement. Road march to Olschany and assembly area in the village. One tank has damage to its carburetor and another one suffers an engine failure.

30 June–1 July 1943: Operational tanks: 11. Just prior to Operation "Citadel" one more Tiger is delivered from the II. SS Panzer-Korps.

Total tanks: 14.

2 July 1943: During the night, the company is ordered into its forward assembly area for Operation "Citadel." Eleven Tigers operational.

4 July 1943: Assembly area south of the road Tomarovka-Bykova near Point 222.3; twelve Tigers operational.

5 July 1943: Advance on Point 228.6, attack at Hill 220.5 and penetration of a defensive line (1 Tiger hit from the rear by an antitank gun). After the high ground is taken, advance on Bykovka. Two Tigers, those of Wittmann and Wendorff, are immobilized. Several antitank-gun belts are eliminated; numerous enemy tanks and antitank guns are destroyed. In the late afternoon, Bykovka is captured.

6 July 1943: Penetration of a fortified, mined enemy position with three Tigers east of Jakovlevo at Point 243.2; another assault at Pokrovka. SS-Obersturmführer Schütz is badly wounded. During the two days of fighting, the 13./SS-Panzer-Regiment "Leibstandarte SS Adolf Hitler" knocks out fifty T-34s, one KV-1, one KV-2, and forty-three antitank guns.

In the evening, SS-Obergruppenführer Dietrich visits the company; among other things, he decides that a badly battle-damaged tank—that of SS-Unterscharführer Brandt—is to be cannibalized for parts. In the night, one Tiger knocks out three T-34s that had passed through Teterewino.

Total tanks: 13.

7 July 1943: In the morning, attack at Teterewino. The company then supports the advance of SS-Panzer-Grenadier-Division "Das Reich" near Teterewino towards the east and the north. One Tiger knocks out three T-34s in Teterewino. Fierce enemy counterattacks out of Jasnaya Polyana and against the left flank northwest of Teterewino are repulsed.

8 July 1943: Assault from the area of Teterewino towards Vessely via Gresnoye (east of Hill 239.6) in conjunction with the armored group of the division. Two tanks suffer track damage. Fighting for Hill 224.5 east of Kotschetovka. Several dug-in enemy tanks are destroyed; two Tigers are immobilized.

Attacking enemy tanks swing in from the bend in the Pssel River to Teterewino.

SS-Unterscharführer Staudegger moves his battle-damaged Tiger 1322 to Teterewino and knocks out seventeen enemy tanks. After the enemy concentrates again, he knocks out a further five tanks and thus stabilizes a potentially dangerous situation. The enemy tanks take to flight, panic-stricken.

Staudegger cannot achieve further success because he runs low on armor-piercing ammunition.

The company's tally for the day: forty-two T-34s and three M-3 Lees.

9 July 1943: Advance on Rylsky, then Ssuch. Solotino.

10 July 1943: Attack of SS-Panzer-Grenadier-Regiment 2 with the division's assault-gun battalion and the Tiger company against the line railroad bend—Iwanovski Wysselok—forested area southwest of the Komssomilez collective farm. Several enemy counterattacks are repulsed. Operational tanks: 5.

SS-Unterscharführer Staudegger is awarded the Knight's Cross. The advance in the direction of Prochorovka is ordered for the next morning; as a result, the company starts about midnight for its assembly area to the southwest of Teterewino.

11 July 1943: Heavy thunderstorms soak the roads, so the scheduled beginning of the attack at 0600 hours must be postponed until 1045 hours. After getting over an tank ditch, four Tigers carry on the attack at the railway line Teterewino-Wesselyj. In the further attack on Prochorovka, twenty-eight antitank guns and six artillery pieces are destroyed. During these two days, twenty-four T-34s are knocked out. Four Tigers are operational.

The tank regiment is held back as a quick-reaction force in the area of Oserovskiy; SS-Untersturmführer Wittmann takes over acting command of the company, because SS-Hauptsturmführer Schütz is wounded.

12 July 1943: Fierce Soviet tank attacks from the direction of Jamki, Prochorovka and Petrovka (on both sides of Kalinin) are pushed back. The II./SS-Panzer-Regiment "Leibstandarte SS Adolf Hitler" and the Tiger company knock out 163 enemy tanks. One Tiger is knocked out; nine Tigers undergo repair.

Total tanks: 12.

13 July 1943: At 1030 hours, the attack is stopped, because it proves to be impossible to penetrate the enemy positions immediately south of the Oktyabrskiy collective farm. Protection of the flank along the railway line Teterewino-Prochorovka. One enemy tank is destroyed; nine Tigers undergo repair.

14 July 1943: The divisional armored group, located at Point 247.6 to the northeast of Komsomolez, is directed to report directly to the II. SS-Panzer-Korps. The assault planned at Yamki is called off.

The company has knocked out 150 enemy tanks up to this point in Operation "Citadel."

15 July 1943: The planned southward advance towards Mal. Yablonovo cannot be realized, since there are considerable delays during the approach march due to heavy rains. Operational tanks: 8.

The company is redeployed into defensive positions along the railway line. The order to evacuate the Pssel bridgehead is expected for the night of 17–18 July 1943.

16 July 1943: Nine Tigers operational. Five new tanks arrive.

Total tanks: 17.

17 July 1943: Covering positions occupied along the railroad line to Prochorovka. During the night, the company is moved to the area west of Bjelgorod.

18 July 1943: March into the new area; the division's tank regiment moves to Ssomskoye.

19 July 1943: Entrainment without changing tracks and transport to Artemovsk (north of Stalino).

20 July 1943: Operational tanks: 14.

21 July 1943: Detraining at Slaviansk; twelve Tigers operational.

22 July 1943: Operational tanks: 12.

24 July 1943: The planned attack against an enemy penetration on both sides of Bogorodischnoye is called off shortly after midnight

26 July 1943: The remaining Tigers are handed over to SS-Panzer-Grenadier-Division "Das Reich" (nine Tigers) and SS-Panzer-Grenadier-Division "Totenkopf" (eight Tigers).

Total tanks: 0.

Rest period near Slaviansk.

29 July 1943: March to Gorlowka.

31 July 1943: The company loads trains at Gorlowka.

1 August 1943: Departure of the company with the transport train. It is sent at high speed towards Italy.

2 August 1943: Fastov and Berditschev are transited.

3 August 1943: Lemberg (Lvov).

4 August 1943: Krakow-Kattowitz.

5 August 1943: Hirschberg-Görlitz-Dresden.

6 August 1943: Zwickau-Hof.

7 August 1943: Regensburg-Rosenheim. In the evening, arrival in Innsbruck. Detraining and spending the night on the vehicles.

8-12 August 1943: Accommodations in a school in Innsbruck.

12 August 1943: Start of the road march to Italy via Sterzing, Bozen, Trient, Verona, Mantova, Parma, Regio Nell Emilia.

13 August 1943: Assembly area to the northwest of the town of Reggio.

15–25 August 1943: Twenty-seven Tigers, including two command tanks, are delivered and taken over by the company. Two companies are provisionally organized.

23–28 August 1943: Replacement personnel arrive from the Sehne Training Area for organizing the new schwere SS-Panzer-Abteilung 101.

30 August 1943: The company is placed on alert status; it must be ready to move with three hours' notice. Operational tanks: 23.

31 August 1943: Operational tanks: 20.

1 September 1943: Operational tanks: 20.

8 September 1943: Highest alert status is ordered at 2000 hours.

9 September 1943: Tank crews support the detachments disarming Italian forces in Reggio. The company supplies itself with Italian motor vehicles.

10 September 1943: Operational tanks: 20.

16 September 1943: Awards presented to the participants in Operation "Citadel."

19-20 September 1943: Small-arms practice.

21 September 1943: Company party.

23 September 1943: Movement to Corregio to the northeast of Reggio-Emilia; twenty-six Tigers operational. A course for noncommissioned officers is held.

30 September 1943: Operational tanks: 20.

1 October 1943: Operational tanks: 21.

12 October 1943: Movement to Pontecurone (southeast of Voghera). Operational tanks: 25.

14 October 1943: Additional awards presented to participants in Operation "Citadel."

20 October 1943: Operational tanks: 25.

22 October 1943: The SS-Panzer-Regiment "Leibstandarte SS Adolf Hitler" is redesignated as SS-Panzer-Regiment 1 "Leibstandarte SS Adolf Hitler."

27 October 1943: Entrainment in Voghera and initiation of rail movement back to the Eastern front. SS-Untersturmführer Stich is killed when he touches the overhead electrical wires. Parma, Verona and Padua are transited. An equipment detail is sent to Burg (near Magdeburg) to pick up ten new tanks.

28 October 1943: Treviso-Udine-Gemona-Carnia.

29 October 1943: Arnoldstein-Villach-Klagenfurt.

30 October 1943: St. Veit-Neumark-Leoben-Semmering-Vienna.

1 November 1943: As the battalion is neither combat-ready nor complete, a company is task organized out of the combat-ready elements and integrated back into the division (again referred to as the 13./SS-Panzer-Regiment 1). The company commander is SS-Hauptsturmführer Kling. Lemberg is transited.

2 November 1943: Tarnopol. The ten new tanks reach Lemberg by rail and are directed back to Paderborn.

3 November 1943: Kasatin.

4 November 1943: Fastov.

5 November 1943: Detrainment in Krivoi Rog.

6 November 1943: March into the area east of Kirowograd.

10 November 1943: Due to critical developments on the northern wing of Army Group South, the company is entrained again without changing tracks. It departs without its wheeled elements.

11 November 1943: Znamenka is transited.

12 November 1943: Arrival and detraining in Berditschew.

14 November 1943: Eighteen Tigers operational. Company in positions north of Zydovce near the railroad line to Fastov.

15 November 1943: The company rejoins SS-Panzer-Regiment 1 "Leibstandarte SS Adolf Hitler." The 1st Platoon of SS-Obersturmführer Michalsky is attached to SS-Panzer-Grenadier-Regiment 1 to support a counterattack that is stopped by antitank-gun fire. One Tiger is immobilized. The platoon leader orders another Tiger (SS-Unterscharführer Kleber) to recover the damaged tank during the fighting. Then, when both tanks must be abandoned, the platoon leader precipitously orders both vehicles to be set on fire. A few days later, the platoon leader is transferred for disciplinary reasons to the 8./SS-Panzer-Regiment 1 "Leibstandarte SS Adolf Hitler."

Total tanks: 25.

On this day, the company also provided flank protection for SS-Panzer-Grenadier-Regiment 2 between Kornin-Lisovka-Solovyevka. Several night engagements.

16 November 1943: Two tanks under the command of SS-Untersturmführer Kalinovski that are coming back from the maintenance facilities relieve the encircled 11./SS-Panzer-Grenadier-Regiment 1 near Wodoty. SS-Oberscharführer Brandt annihilates an enemy rifle battalion near Brusilov with three Tigers. The company commander destroys eight anti-tank guns and another battalion near Lisovka in two assaults with five Tigers.

17 November 1943: In a counterattack, ten Tigers advance with SS-Panzer-Grenadier-Regiment 2 towards Lutschin; five T-34s are knocked out. SS-Unterscharführer Bartl is killed when his commander's cupola is shot off.

18 November 1943: During the night, an enemy assault from Fedorovka directed towards Lutschin is beaten back. Towards noon, another enemy assault, this time from Goljaki, pushes the Kampfgruppe back into the western part of Lutschin. Eight T-34s and twenty-five antitank guns are destroyed.

19 November 1943: After being relieved by parts of 25. Panzer-Division, the company assembles near Solovyevka .

20 November 1943: Enemy tank attacks from the northeast in the direction of Morosovka. Twenty-one T-34s and several antitank guns are knocked out. One Tiger is hit by an antitank gun. Operational tanks: 12.

21 November 1943: Assaults at Brusilov; thirteen T-34s are knocked out and seven anti-tank guns destroyed.

22 November 1943: Several Tigers start an attack from Ulscha towards Jastrebenka together with the 1./SS-Panzer-Grenadier-Regiment 2. Twenty guns of an antitank-gun belt front are destroyed. SS-Unterscharführer Höld is killed, when his commander's cupola is shot off.

23 November 1943: Four Tigers attack Lasarovka (via Dubrovka) with the II./SS-Panzer-Grenadier-Regiment 1 and the III./SS-Panzer-Grenadier-Regiment 2. Several T-34s are knocked out. In the evening, the tanks are refueled at Mestetschko.

24–25 November 1943: Company performs maintenance.

26 November 1943: March to Radomyschl.

28 November 1943: Advance with the III./SS-Panzer-Grenadier-Regiment 2 on very muddy roads across the Belka passage to the north of Sabelotschje as far as the road junction south of Radomyschl. Several antitank guns are destroyed; Garborov is captured. During the evening, the company moves into covered positions southeast of Garborov.

29 November–1 December 1943: The company is held as a reserve in Garborov.

1 December 1943: Operational tanks: 2. Fourteen are being repaired and nine are on their way back to the company.

2–5 December 1943: Movement into the Siljanschtschino area. Operational tanks: 5. During this time frame, Tigers coming from the Maintenance Company are often sent on missions individually, without the company commander being informed.

4 December 1943: An enemy tank column is eliminated near Styrty. Operational tanks: 4. Since the start of the fighting in the Kharkov area, the company has destroyed 205 enemy tanks and 130 antitank guns.

5 December 1943: Counterattack together with the armored group of the division from the area northwest of Tschernjachov. Pekarschtina and a fifty-ton-bridge are captured in a night attack.

6 December 1943: Advance towards Styrty (starting from Andrejew). Wittmann's platoon eliminates an antitank-gun belt. During the pursuit towards Tortschin, three T-34s are knocked out. One Tiger (SS-Untersturmführer Kalinovski) is hit in the flank and two Tigers run over mines; all three tanks are recovered in the night.

7 December 1943: Advance from Tortschin towards Tschaikovka; the advance is stopped by antitank-gun fire. After outflanking Tschaikovka, the company advances beyond Point 213 (at Ljachovaya).

8 December 1943: Kampfgruppe Peiper captures Chodory; attack continues towards Sabolot. One Tiger is knocked out; the tank commander (SS-Unterscharführer Langner) shoots himself when the Russians board his tank.

Total tanks: 24.

9 December 1943: Advance from the area southeast of Medelevka towards Meschiritschka. At 2200 hours, four Tigers attack Wel. Ratscha from the west bank of the Teterev River; the attack is halted by fierce antitank-gun fire.

10 December 1943: An antitank-gun belt is engaged outside of Krasnoborki. Operational tanks: 4.

11 December 1943: In the morning, the company assembles northwest of Meshiritschka. At noon, there is an attack towards Welikaya Ratschka (via Krasoborki-Hill 170); several antitank guns and tanks destroyed. One Tiger I operational.

12–13 December 1943: Maintenance is performed.

14 December 1943: The northward advance along the road Werpin-Fedorovka is continued. Three T-34s are knocked out. The tanks pull back, because the river cannot be crossed outside of Vyrva.

15 December 1943: Rest area at Sabolot.

17–18 December 1943: Night marches to the sector three kilometers west of Meleni.

19 December 1943: Seven operational tanks start an attack at 0900 hours on Meleni. Afterwards, they advance across the railroad line Kiev-Korosten in the direction of Baljarka. One T-34 and several antitank guns are destroyed and one Tiger is knocked out.

Total tanks: 23.

20 December 1943: The railroad station of Tschepowitschi is captured; several enemy tanks are knocked out. Three Tigers are operational, with twenty in for repairs. SS-Hauptsturmführer Kling is recommended for the Knight's Cross, but the recommendation is not approved.

21 December 1943: An enemy attack at the railroad station is beaten back; several enemy tanks are knocked out. Two Tigers are operational.

22 December 1943: In the morning, the company is relieved in place by the 1. Panzer-Division. Two Tigers are employed near Meleni; two T-34s are knocked out.

23 December 1943: Three Tigers stop enemy tank attacks in the section of the 291. Infanterie-Division. Four T-34s are destroyed.

24 December 1943: SS-Hauptsturmführer Kling supports the advance of the I./Panzer-Grenadier-Regiment 113 (1. Panzer-Division) to the north through Sevtschenko and into the area south of Schatrischtsche with twenty-five tanks of the armored group, including a number of his Tigers. Afterwards, the remaining operational tanks are sent to Sobollevka.

SS-Panzer-Grenadier-Division "Leibstandarte SS Adolf Hitler" is pulled from the line and marches south. Seven disabled Tigers have to be blown up near Tschepowitschi.

Total tanks: 16.

25 December 1943: Assembly near Ivankovo (southeast of Shitomir). 5 Tigers operational.

27 December 1943: SS-Untersturmführer Wendorff knocks out two T-34s. Wendorff's platoon advances with four Tigers along the railroad line and encounters enemy tanks near Tschubarovka; eleven T-34s are knocked out by SS-Untersturmführer Wendorff alone.

Soon afterwards, a counterattack is launched at Jusevovka; three T-34s are knocked out. During the night, company elements cover the bridge across the Guiva River in Ivankovo. Five Tigers operational.

28 December 1943: Counterattack of four Tigers (SS-Untersturmführer Wendorff) against enemy tanks near Antopol-Bojarka. Eleven T-34s knocked out; one Tiger is lost (SS-Unterscharführer Sadzio).

Total tanks: 15.

29 December 1943: An enemy tank attack at Antopol-Bojarka is beaten back; eight T-34s are destroyed. During the evening, the company withdraws as far as Solotwin. Two disabled Tigers have to be blown up.

Total tanks: 13.

30 December 1943: Two Tigers employed in a screening line. SS-Hauptsturmführer Kling is awarded the German cross in Gold.

31 December 1943: Operational tanks: 2.

1 January 1944: SS-Untersturmführer Wendorff knocks out five T-34s near Trajanov. No Tigers are operational. All the tanks are undergoing repairs at Pjatki.

2 January 1944: Withdrawal in the direction of Staro Konstantinovka continued; four Tigers are lost.

Total tanks: 9.

7 January 1944: The two operational Tigers are moved to Ssmela.

8 January 1944: An enemy tank assault in the area of Sherepki is pushed back by four Tigers; several enemy tanks are knocked out.

9 January 1944: The immediate counterattack of the 3./SS-Panzer-Aufklärungs-Abteilung 1 is supported by two Tigers after an enemy tank attack near Sherepki; twelve T-34s are knocked out.

10 January 1944: SS-Untersturmführer Wittmann is recommended for the Knight's Cross for knocking out sixty-six enemy tanks.

11 January 1944: During the night, the company withdraws south of Ssmela; four Tigers operational.

12 January 1944: Two Tigers coming from the Maintenance Company (SS-Untersturmführer Wittmann and SS-Oberscharführer Lötzsch) knock out three enemy tanks that had broken through German lines and advanced as far as Ulanoff. Six tanks operational.

13 January 1944: A large enemy tank formation advancing from Chutorysko in the direction of Tschessnovka is stopped by Armored Group Peiper and destroyed; thirty-four enemy tanks knocked out. Two Tigers support Infanterie-Regiment 188 near Bespetschena.

SS-Untersturmführer Wittmann is recommended for the award of the Oak Leaves to the Knight's Cross after achieving his 88th "kill."

14 January 1944: The armored group advances from the area west of Ssmela to the northeast of Choturysko and right into an enemy assembly area. The Soviets take flight leaving behind their heavy equipment. The company commander knocks out two enemy tanks.

In a small village, the division commander, SS-Oberführer Wisch, awards the Knight's Cross to SS-Untersturmführer Wittmann.

15 January 1944: Five operational tanks involved in fighting around Stetkovzy; the attack is called off, because the antitank-gun fire is too fierce.

17 January 1944: SS-Hauptsturmführer Kling is appointed commander of the II./SS-Panzer-Regiment "Leibstandarte SS Adolf Hitler."

Since November 1942 the company has destroyed 343 enemy tanks, 8 assault guns, and 255 antitank guns.

18 January 1944: SS-Untersturmführer Wittmann's gunner, SS-Rottenführer Woll, is awarded the Knight's Cross for eighty "kills."

19 January 1944: The company is relieved by parts of the 371. Infanterie-Division; it withdraws from the frontline and marches to Chmelnik. One Tiger operational.

19–21 January 1944: After the withdrawal, two Tigers are sent for depot-level maintenance.

Total tanks: 6.

24 January 1944: Transfer into the area northeast of Winniza. Mud creates extremely difficult terrain conditions.

25 January 1944: The company forms the spearhead of Kampfgruppe Kuhlmann west of the railroad line Kalinovka-Uman. It advances as far as Point 316.6 west of Otscheretnja. Several enemy tanks knocked out.

26 January 1944: Attack south with four Tigers across a tank ditch as far as Rossoschje (via Napadovka).

27 January 1944: Capture of the Lipowez Railroad Station and the road crossing north of it. Several enemy tanks destroyed.

28–31 January 1944: Four operational Tigers cover the Lipowez Railroad Station; several enemy tanks knocked out.

30 January 1944: SS-Untersturmführer Wittmann becomes the 380th member of the German armed forces to receive the Oak leaves to the Knight's Cross. He is simultaneously promoted to SS-Obersturmführer. In twenty-two days (since 7 January), he has knocked out sixty-one enemy tanks. His total: 117. SS-Untersturmführer Wendorff is also promoted to SS-Obersturmführer.

31 January 1944: Operational tanks: 2. Skirmishes during covering-force missions. Several enemy tanks knocked out.

1 February 1944: Withdrawal from the enemy and movement to the Monastyrischtsche Railroad Station. Six Tigers transported by rail to Krasnyi. When SS-Obersturmführer Wittmann is ordered to the Führer Headquarters for the award of the Oak leaves, SS-Obersturmführer Wendorff is given acting command of the company.

5 February 1944: Arrival at Krasnyi; three operational tanks join the attack of Kampfgruppe Kuhlmann to relieve the Tscherkassy Pocket.

6 February 1944: Two Tigers and nine Panthers advance at Tinovka. Several enemy tanks are destroyed.

7 February 1944: Four operational tanks almost without fuel are encircled between Tinovka and Woytilevka; several enemy tanks are destroyed.

8 February 1944: In the evening, some Panzer IVs arrive with a fuel truck in tow.

9 February 1944: Enemy attack north of Tatjanovka is beaten back; two enemy tanks knocked out.

10 February 1944: Five new Tigers are promised for delivery, however, they do not arrive until early March in the Tarnopol area.

12 February 1944: SS-Obersturmführer Wendorff is awarded the Knight's Cross.

14 February 1944: Attachment to elements of the 34. Infanterie-Division. Only one Tiger is operational, the others have to be towed. Two are left behind and destroyed by the crews.

Total tanks: 4.

15 February 1944: In defensive positions near Tatjanovka.

16 February 1944: Relief from attachment and movement to Frankovka. Three Tigers in tow; one operational. One later blown up.

Total tanks: 3.

17 February 1944: During the night, three operational Tigers are moved to Oktjabr; several enemy tanks and antitank guns are destroyed. The first Tscherkassy soldiers who break out of the pocket are passed through the lines.

19 February 1944: One Tiger (SS-Unterscharführer Kleber) has to be blown up near Rosskosechewka because of damage to the steering system.

Total tanks: 2.

Through 20 February 1944: Enemy tank attacks between Oktjabr and Lyssjanka are turned back.

22 February 1944: The front is pulled back to Shabinka. The company is designated as a reserve and is pulled back as far as Schubennyi Staw.

23 February 1944: SS-Hauptsturmführer Kling is awarded Knight's Cross.

24 February 1944: The division is concentrated in the area of Talnoje. The last Tigers evacuated for urgently needed maintenance.

Total tanks: 0.

29 February 1944: Entrainment and transport into the area of Proscurov-Tarnopol. The five new Tigers are integrated into the armored group of SS-Panzer-Division "Leibstandarte SS Adolf Hitler."

1 March 1944: The 13./SS-Panzer-Regiment 1 is officially deactivated. The remaining elements that do not stay with the remaining tanks are entrained at Christianovka and moved to Belgium.

5 March 1944: Six new Tigers delivered.

6 March 1944: All six Tigers operational.

7 March 1944: Two operational Tigers in the area Babijevka-Gnorovka.

8 March 1944: Operational tanks: 4.

9 March 1944: Four operational Tigers and four Tigers of schwere Panzer-Abteilung 503 support Kampfgruppe Kuhlmann in its attack to open the highway to Manatschin; at about 1100 hours, Losova is occupied.

10 March 1944: Five operational Tigers guard the division command post near Vojtovszy.

11 March 1944: Two Tigers advance toward Hill 338.7 north of the Vojtovzy Railway Station and knock out several enemy tanks.

12–14 March 1944: Operational tanks: 2.

14 March 1944: The armored group of the 1. SS-Panzer-Division "Leibstandarte SS Adolf Hitler," including SS-Rottenführer Warmbrunn's Tiger, clears up the eastern part of Petrovka; one tank and four antitank guns are destroyed.

15 March 1944: Two Tigers operational; the western part of Petrovka is cleared.

16–21 March 1944: Operational tanks: 3.

17 March 1944: Operational tanks: 3. The Kampfgruppe starts its advance east from Ssolomno to establish contact with the 7. Panzer-Division.

19–20 March 1944: No operations.

21 March 1944: SS-Rottenführer Warmbrunn knocks out an antitank gun.

22 March 1944: During the evacuation of a casualty clearing station at Kopytschinzy (45 kilometers southwest of Ssolomno), 1 Tiger knocks out three T-34s.

24 March 1944: Struggle to maintain contact; some aerial re-supply. In the days that follow, there are engagements to penetrate the enemy encirclement.

2 April 1944: Operational tanks: 3.

6 April 1944: First elements reach the Sereth River near Ulaskovcze.

7 April 1944: Two Tigers operational in the area southeast of Buczacz.

12 April 1944: Contact with the 10. SS-Panzer-Division "Frundsberg" is established.

14 April 1944: After establishing a base camp at Trybuchoce, the remaining tanks are handed over to the LIX. Armee-Korps.

16 April 1944: Remainder of personnel march off to Mons. SS-Rottenführer Warmbrunn continues to fight with the 10. SS-Panzer-Division "Frundsberg" and supports the elimination of the bridgehead near Bobulince. One T-34 and one Sherman are knocked out.

✙

The company knocked out more than 400 tanks within two years.

✙

COMPANY COMMANDERS

SS-Hauptsturmführer Kling	24 December 1942–30 December 1943
SS-Obersturmführer Wittmann	30 December 1943–1 February 1944
SS-Obersturmführer Wendorff	1 February 1944–5 March 1944

KNIGHT'S CROSS RECIPIENTS

SS-Unterscharführer Staudegger	10 July 1943
SS-Untersturmführer Wittmann	14 January 1944
SS-Rottenführer Woll	18 January 1944
SS-Obersturmführer Wittmann	30 January 1944 (380th Oak Leaves)
SS-Obersturmführer Wendorff	12 February 1944

The third train of the transport reached Poltawa during the night of 9/10 February 1943. In the morning, the crews attached the outer roadwheels prior to changing from the transport tracks to the wider combat tracks. WENDT

Field maintenance is conducted in March 1943. After removal of the gun tube, the mantlet is lifted using the portal crane. WENDT

Immediately after their arrival on the Eastern front, the tanks received a coat of whitewash. This photograph shows the unique way that space was left around the turret numerals and the divisional insignia on the hull front, exposing the original color beneath the whitewash. Company numbering initially started with three-digit numerals starting with 4. In this photograph, we see SS-Sturmmann Schön von Wildeneg, SS-Sturmmann Büvenich and SS-Sturmmann Reimers posing on their Tiger 411. WENDT

At the end of March 1943, the maintenance platoon obtained an ideal work setting in Kharkov. These two photographs show the initial phase of the maintenance work performed on the tank of SS-Untersturmführer Wendorf, which had bogged down in the Msha River on 6 March 1943. It remained there for several days before it could be recovered.

Generaloberst Guderian visited the 13./SS-Panzer-Regiment 1 in his capacity as Inspector General of the Armored Forces in mid-April 1943. The company commander's tank—Tiger 405—is displayed for Guderian. The officer in the cupola is SS-Untersturmführer Wittmann.

WENDT

Related to their original role as the guardians of the Reich Chancellery, it was obligatory for the division to celebrate Hitler's birthday on 20 April. In front of the Tiger are SS-Untersturmführer Wendorf, SS-Obersturmführer Schütz and SS-Untersturmführer Wittmann.

OTT

Five new Tigers arrive by rail on 13 May 1943. SS-Sturmmann Heepe stands guard in front of one of the tanks. These tanks have already had the newly introduced yellow-olive base coat applied.

WENDT

During the spring, the unit conducted individual and crew-level training. Here we see Tiger 411 of SS-Obersturmführer Schütz approaching the camera of the war correspondent.

One of the older tanks, which still has the smoke-grenade launchers, has just received a set of additional track links on the front of the hull. The track pins still have to be hammered in; the crewmember assigned that task does not appear to be in too much of a hurry.

The company was assembled in a patch of woods north of Olschany during the final days of June 1943. This photograph shows Tiger 1312 with a dispatch rider's motorcycle in the foreground.

Prior to the movement to the area of operations for Operation "Citadel," the tanks receive a basic load of ammunition.

Nearly all of the SS Tigers photographed during Operation "Citadel" were taken in the sector of SS-Panzer-Grenadier-Division "Das Reich." As a result, photographs of the 13./SS-Panzer-Regiment 1 are rare. Here we see Tigers pass haystacks in an early phase of the fighting. Impacting artillery can be seen in the background.

After the fighting was over, the Soviets produced some "authentic" footage for propaganda purposes showing dozens of burning Tigers with heroic Red Army soldiers in the foreground.

Having left behind their Tigers in Russia, the company received new tanks in the division's reconstitution area in Italy.

Tank commanders and platoon leaders proudly pose in front of their newly painted Tigers (from left to right): SS-Oberscharführer Augst, SS-Untersturmführer Wittmann, SS-Unterscharführer Molly and SS-Oberscharführer Brandt.
HELMKE

Tiger 1334 shows many of the scars it received during Operation "Citadel" shortly after the fighting was over.

On 14 October 1943, the company was formed up to receive decorations earned during the fighting as part of Operation "Citadel." SS-Hauptscharführer Habermann, the company first sergeant, appears to be checking the books in order to determine whether his company commander, SS-Hauptsturmführer Kling, was actually awarded the Tank Assault Badge. SS-Rottenführer Tassler smiles in the background as this light-hearted moment takes place. The company's tanks are already prepared for a no-notice alert for movement back to the Soviet Union. The tank in the background is Tiger S33. WENDT

This photograph, which shows SS-Oberscharführer Kamrad next to his Tiger S14, gives a good impression of the unique camouflage pattern the "soon-to-be" battalion has chosen for its tanks. WENDT

The company first sergeant, SS-Hauptscharführer Habermann, poses in front of Tiger S32 along with SS-Rottenführer Tassler, SS-Rottenführer Jarusch and SS-Rottenführer Schmidt-Adolf. HELMKE

The tanks have arrived in the Berditschew area and await movement to the area of operations. WENDT

Due to the critical situation on the Eastern Front, SS-Panzer-Grenadier-Division "Leibstandarte SS Adolf Hitler" began railway transport to Heeresgruppe Mitte (Army Group Center) at the end of October 1943. MHF

Tiger S24 on 29 December 1943 during one of the company's numerous road marches from one crisis area to another.

Unceasing maintenance was a major prerequisite for maintaining operational readiness for the outnumbered tanks. The turret of battle-scarred Tiger S12 is lifted by means of the tried-and-true portal crane.

This tank has been towed to cover after suffering a mechanical failure. It still displays some camouflage. The single towing cable attached to the left-hand towing eye could only be used for a short distance. For longer distances, two tow cables were needed (crisscrossed) or an iron scissors tow bar. BOXBERGER

Winter has arrived and whitewashed Tiger S45 has picked up some supporting infantry prior to moving out for an immediate counter-attack. WENDT

SS-Sturmmann Bobby Warmbrunn, who was one of the leading "aces" of the company, poses on the main gun after having scored his 43rd "kill" on 22 November 1943.
WARMBRUNN

Terrain conditions during the late autumn worsened as a result of the heavy rainfalls. This impressive photograph shows a column of Tigers—with Tiger S23 in the lead—trying to refuel. The fuel truck is obviously going to need some recovery assistance. ROTTENSTEINER

This Tiger has been directed to support an unidentified combat-engineer battalion. The command pennant for the engineers—a white horizontal bar on a black background—can be seen in the right of the photograph.

At the end of February 1944, the operational tanks were employed in the area around the Lipowez Railway Station. The numeral 24 has been repainted in black without the S prefix.

SS-Untersturmführer Wittmann and his crew pose in front of Tiger S21 with its 88 "kill" markings. SS-Untersturmführer Wittmann was awarded the Knight's cross on 14 January 1944. His gunner, SS-Rottenführer Woll, has just received the Knight's cross as well. The date is 18 January 1944. BÜSCHEL

This sequence shows one of the new replacement tanks that were delivered in February 1944 in action near Petrovka. The tactical identifier—a small black 2 on the forward art of the turret and on the rear turret stowage box—is faintly visible.

During the withdrawal operations in March 1944, one tank after another was left behind, where they soon came under new ownership.

Another dilapidated wreck that had to be abandoned. ANDERSON

13./SS-PANZER-REGIMENT 1

Vehicles on Hand/Deliveries

Date	Tiger I	Tiger II	On hand	Remarks
December 1942	6		6	15 Panzer IIIs (Model J)
January 1943	4		10	
13 May 1943	5		13	
June 1943	1		14	From the schwere SS-Panzer-Abteilung
16 July 1943	5		17	
26 July 1943	-17		0	9 to the 8./SS-Panzer-Regiment 2 and 8 to the 9./SS-Panzer-Regiment 3
August 1943	27		27	Intended for schwere SS-Panzer-Abteilung 101
10 February 1944	5		8	
February 1944	6		6	
Grand Total	42	0		

Losses

Date	Losses	On hand	Remarks
5 March 1943	1	9	Self-ignition
12 March 1	1	8	Self-ignition
6 July 1943	1	13	Cannibalized
12 July 1943	1	12	Knocked out by tanks
15 November 1943	2	25	Destroyed by friendly fire
8 December 1943	1	24	Captured
19 December 1943	1	23	Knocked out by an antitank gun
24 December 1943	7	16	Destroyed by own crew
28 December 1943	1	15	Knocked out by tanks
29 December 1943	2	13	Destroyed by own crew
2 January 1944	5	8	Destroyed by own crew
19–21 January 1944	2	6	Evacuated for depot-level maintenance
14 February 1944	2	4	Destroyed by own crew
16 February 1944	1	3	Destroyed by own crew
19 February 1944	1	2	Destroyed by own crew
24 February 1944	2	0	Evacuated for depot-level maintenance
March 1944	5	0	?
March–April 1944	6	0	?
Grand total:	42		

Of the losses suffered by the company, 75% were due to self-destruction (to prevent capture), 15% were lost in combat operations and 10% were lost due to other causes.

4./ SS-Panzerregiment 1 – 1 February 1943

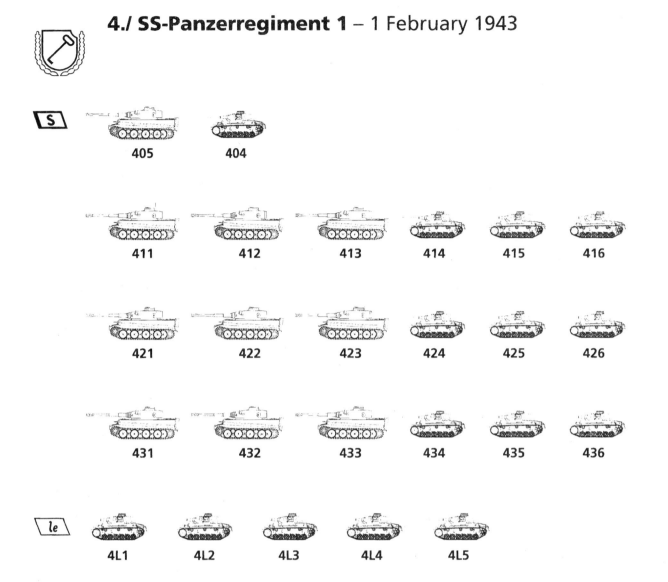

S

405   404

411   412   413   414   415   416

421   422   423   424   425   426

431   432   433   434   435   436

le

4L1   4L2   4L3   4L4   4L5

13./ SS-Panzerregiment 1 – 1 July 1943

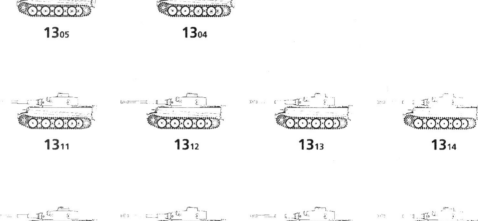

1305   **13**04

1311   **13**12   **13**13   **13**14

1321   **13**22   **13**23   **13**24

1331   **13**32   **13**33   **13**34

13./ SS-Panzerregiment 1 – 1 November 1943

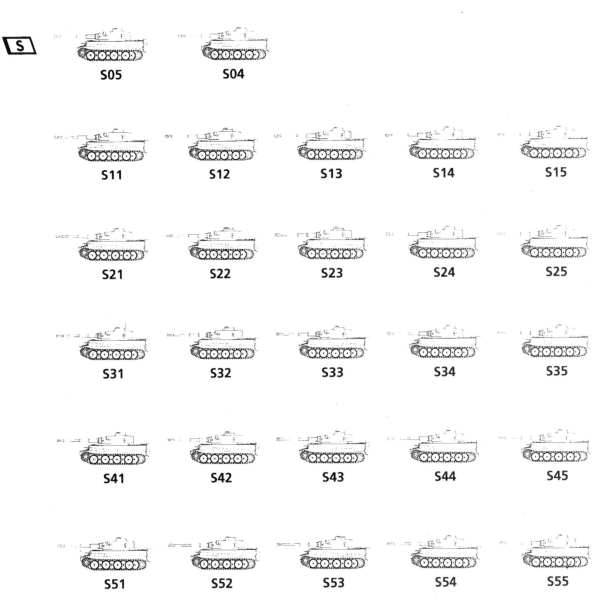

8./SS-Panzer-Regiment 2

With an effective date of 15 November 1942, a schwere Panzer-Kompanie was established for the SS-Panzer-Abteilung of SS-Panzer-Grenadier-Division "Das Reich" (KStN 1176d dated 15 August 1942) for the. It is activated in Fallingbostel beginning in early December 1942. The tank crews are trained in the production plants of Henschel und Wegmann in Kassel. The first company commander is SS-Hauptsturmführer Grader. The unit is soon redesignated as the 8./SS-Panzer-Regiment "Das Reich."

+

24–25 January 1943: Entrainment of the company.

1–2 February 1943: Detrainment near Kharkov. Some of the tanks are used as a covering force for the Kharkov Railway Station. Hazardous driving conditions due to extremely thick ice.

8 February 1943: During this covering-force mission, the company commander is killed in action; SS-Hauptsturmführer Kuhlmann takes over command. The company gets ice grousers for its tracks.

9 February 1943: Seven Tigers are entrained again. All Panzer IIIs stay with the tank regiment.

10 February 1943: The Kharkov elements withdraw to Merefa.

11 February 1943: Detrainment; one Tiger (SS-Obersturmführer Gerlach) is immobilized after running over a mine and is captured by the Soviets. Snow grousers (ice cleats) are finally fitted, considerably improving the driving capability.

Total tanks: 9.

12 February 1943: Kharkov is evacuated; march via the Donez Bridge to the main station.

14 February 1943: The road Merefa-Krasnograd is interdicted by the Russians; delaying actions start.

17 February 1943: Withdrawal to Poltava. The second command tank—Tiger 802—is delivered. SS-Hauptsturmführer Herzig becomes the new company commander because SS-Hauptsturmführer Kuhlmann receives a new duty assignment in SS-Panzer-Grenadier-Division "Leibstandarte SS Adolf Hitler." Operational Tigers: 3.

Total tanks: 10.

19 February 1943: Not being equipped with tank retrievers, the company has to ask for 18-ton prime movers from the corps' heavy tank maintenance company.

20 February 1943: Only one Tiger (SS-Oberscharführer Egger) is operational. This tank supports the attack of the II./SS-Panzer-Regiment 2 on Nowomoskowsk and destroys five antitank guns.

21 February 1943: Egger again spearhead the advance, this time on Pawlograd. Four T-34s and six antitank guns are destroyed.

22 February 1943: Several tanks (including Egger's Tiger) guard the bridge across the Woltschia on the western outskirts of Pawlograd (fifteen kilometers south of Kharkov), which has been taken by SS-Hauptscharführer Kloskowski's Panzer III 431. For his bravery, Kloskowski is awarded Knight's Cross in July.

25 February 1943: Operational Tigers: 3. During a party with Luftwaffe officers, the company commander makes a bet that his crew can move his Tiger across an ice-covered small river. The tank breaks through the ice and is almost covered with water. Several days later, it is recovered with the help of three tanks and two eighteen-ton prime movers; it has to be sent to Dnjepropetrowsk for depot-level maintenance; this has to be reported to the Führer Headquarters.

1 March 1943: A Kampfgruppe of SS-Panzer-Grenadier-Division "Das Reich" attacks in the area of Merefa. The Tigers knock out thirteen tanks. At the railway line Poltava-Kharkov, the Panzer III of SS-Untersturmführer Kalls is knocked out. The advance is continued with one Panzer III and two Tigers; one Tiger burns out due to self-ignition.

Total tanks: 9.

2 March 1943: Novabavaria is taken; then Jefremowka.

3 March 1943: The gepanzerte Gruppe of SS-Panzer-Grenadier-Division "Das Reich" heads for the Msha River Sector and establishes a bridgehead near Bachmetjewka. No Tigers are operational. The division is supported by SS-Panzer-Regiment 3.

4 March 1943: No Tigers operational.

7 March 1943: No Tigers operational.

8 March 1943: The company seizes Walki. Operational Tigers: 4.

9 March 1943: Two Tigers support the attack north from Walki to the northern outskirts of Kharkov to reach the main road to Belgorod (attack via Olschanny and Dergatschi); thirteen tanks are knocked out. The road is taken and blocked for the retreating Soviets.

10 March 1943: No Tigers operational.

11 March 1943: Early in the morning, march to the jump-off position before starting the attack on Saljutina. The attack stalls in front of an antitank-gun belt.

12 March 1943: Start of the counterattack on Nowa Barawa in the direction of Kharkov with three Tigers; one Panzer III knocked out, killing the radio operator.

13 March 1943: Advance through the northern part of Kharkov; engagements around the tractor factory northeast of Lossewo. Operational tanks: 5.

14 March 1943: Attack from the Rogan Railway Station to the railway embankment northwest of Ternowoje. Operational tanks: 4.

15 March 1943: Osnowa is taken. Operational Tigers: 3.

16 March 1943: Further advance to the north towards Wesseloje. Operational tanks: 2.

17 March 1943: Nepokrytoje is taken. Operational tanks: 2.

18 March 1943: The southern part Bjelgorod is taken after a road march of 80 kilometers; several mechanical failures.

19 March 1943: The Donez River is reached. Operational tanks: 2. US air raids on Belgorod.

20–21 March 1943: Covering positions occupied along the Donez River. Tiger 801 (formerly Tiger 802) knocks out three tanks. US air raids on Belgorod continue on 20 March 1944.

22 March 1943: The company marches back to Kharkov (one Tiger lost). It starts maintenance work at the gas station on the west end of the city.

24–26 March 1943: Operational tanks: 4.

27 March 1943: Six tank crews are sent to Paderborn.

28 March 1943: No tanks operational.

29 March 1943: The company commander is relieved of duty and transferred to a training course in Berlin for disciplinary reasons.

1 April 1943: The II./SS-Panzer-Regiment 2 is designated a ready-reaction force under command of SS-Obersturmbannführer Kumm (SS-Panzer-Grenadier-Regiment "Der Führer").

10 April 1943: SS-Hauptsturmführer Zimmermann becomes the new company commander. No tanks operational; still seven Panzer IIIs in the company's inventory.

20 April 1943: The company is relocated to the area of Peresetschnaja (eight kilometers west of Kharkov). Operational Tigers: 7.

24 April 1943: Visit of Reichsführer-SS Heinrich Himmler. A small field exercise is conducted for his benefit.

30 April 1943: Operational Tigers: 6.

7 May 1943: March to an assembly west of Belgorod.

10 May 1943: March back to Peresetschnaja.

13 May 1943: Six new Tigers are delivered. This transport was delayed when the train derailed after a sabotage action.

Total tanks: 14.

20 May 1943: Operational Tigers: 9. The tanks receive the S markings. The company turns in its remaining Panzer IIIs during this period.

30 May 1943: Operational tanks: 8.

10 June 1943: Operational tanks: 8.

20 June 1943: Operational tanks: 8.

30 June 1943: Operational tanks: 12.

1 July 1943: Operational tanks: 12.

2 July 1943: Operational tanks: 12.

3 July 1943: Assembly area 20 kilometers west of Tomarowka.

4 July 1943: Operational tanks: 12. During the night, positions occupied south of the road Tomarowka-Bykowka near Point 222.3 (later near Point 228.6).

5 July 1943: The company knocks out 23 tanks near Beresoff, Hill 233.3 and north of Hill 233.3. Two tanks are immobilized by mines.

6 July 1943: Twelve T-34s are knocked out by the Tiger company near Lutschki. An armored train joins the fight, causes some losses and is then set ablaze by the Tigers.

10 July 1943: Operational tanks: 9.

11 July 1943: The company commander is wounded in the arm; SS-Hauptsturmführer Lorenz assumes acting command. Ten enemy tanks are knocked out. At 1200 hours SS-Hauptsturmführer Lorenz is killed in action, and the Tiger is destroyed. SS-Obersturmführer Theiss assumes acting command.

Total tanks: 13.

12 July 1943: No tanks operational.

13 July 1943: Breakthrough to Winogradowka-Iwanowka.

14 July 1943: Assault of the armored group to the east; Iwanowka is taken. Attack continues towards Hill 234.9. Operational tanks: 4. Firefight with enemy armor south of Hill 242.1. This hill is later captured (two kilometers northeast of Leski).

15 July 1943: Continuation of the attack to the northeast in order to take Hill 242.7 as a prerequisite for further advance to the south. The latest acting company commander is killed when the commander's cupola is hit by an antitank gun. SS-Obersturmführer Reininghaus takes over acting command. Operational tanks: 8.

16 July 1943: Operational tanks: 5. Operation "Citadel" is terminated by the Germans. Relief-in-place by the 167. Infanterie-Division and redeployment of the division to Jakowlewo, Pokrowka and Beregowoj.

17 July 1943: Operational tanks: 9.

20 July 1943: Operational tanks: 8. Heavy air raid on the assembly area of the regiment.

24–25 July 1943: Entrainment at Ssossnowka; rail transport to Barwenkowo via Losowaja.

26 July 1943: Detrainment at Barwenkowo.

28 July 1943: Nine Tigers are received from the 13./SS-Panzer-Regiment 1. The company is entrained again.

Total tanks: 22.

28 July 1943: Detrainment in Lissitschansk.

29 July 1943: Arrival in Makejewka. Bivouac area in a balka two kilometers northeast of Petrowsky.

30 July 1943: Start of Operation "Roland" (neutralization of the enemy penetration along the Mius River Front). Attack south of Stepanowka is initially stopped in front of Hill 230.9 by an antitank-gun belt. Several tanks run over mines. After capture of this hill, further attack on the Doppelkopfhöhe ("Two-Headed Hill"). Order is given for subsequent attack on Marinowka.

31 July 1943: Operational tanks: 3. An attack starts at 0100 hours; engagements around Stepanowka. At noon, a very strong rainfall stops all movement on both sides.

1 August 1943: Two tanks—Tiger S02 of SS-Oberscharführer Hellwig and Tiger S24 of SS-Obersturmführer Tensfeld)—attack Hill 202. Tiger S02 is immobilized after being hit by an antitank gun; a short while later, the other tank is also hit and immobilized. Three operational Tigers assemble for an attack on Hill 203.4. Further advance to the Olchowtschik River Sector; seizure of Fedorowka.

2 August 1943: Enemy resistance is broken; the previous Mius fighting positions are taken in conjunction with SS-Panzer-Grenadier-Division "Totenkopf." Relief-in-place and assembly in the area of Charzyssk.

4 August 1943: Entrainment and transport to the west. Detrainment in Jassinowataija.

8 August 1943: A single Tiger (Tensfeld) stops an enemy armor attack with seventeen T-34s, knocking out ten of them.

10 August 1943: Operational tanks: 3.

13 August 1943: An attack starts at 0730 hours towards the woods north of Nikitowka and Miroljubowka.

14 August 1943: Railway transport from Jassinowataija in the direction of Kharkov. Concentration in Kijany as a ready-reaction force for use against enemy attacks

15 August 1943: Detrainment in Ljubotin. SS-Obersturmführer Matzke becomes the new company commander.

17 August 1943: Attachment to the division's combat-engineer battalion; the company assembles west of Scharowski-Sanat. An attack starts at 1500 hours on Hill 1811 north of Mirnoje; it then proceeds to Hill 196.0.

19 August 1943: Attachment to SS-Panzer-Grenadier-Regiment "Der Führer"; covering positions occupied three kilometers north of Kryssino. Three Tigers are knocked out during these two days of fighting.

Total tanks: 19.

21 August 1943: Relief-in-place of the division; the tank regiment starts marching with small march serials at 1400 hours into the new rest area (via Alexandrowka-Kowjagi-Ogulzy Railway Station).

22 August 1943: Operational tanks: 5. German forces abandon Kharkov.

23 August 1943: The Tiger company is used in support of the defensive operations of SS-Panzer-Grenadier-Regiment "Der Führer."

27 August 1943: Operational tanks: 6.

29 August 1943: Defense of the Merefa Position.

31 August–1 September 1943: Operational tanks: 2.

Early September 1943: The company stays in the area of Walki.

10 September 1943: Operational tanks: 5.

14 September 1943: Two Tigers under the command of SS-Hauptscharführer Soretz counterattack towards the important high ground near Kolomak; several T-34s and two antitank guns destroyed.

17–21 September 1943: All attacks on the high ground are repelled, however, twelve enemy tanks are knocked out. The tanks form a covering force for the withdrawal of the division to the E Line (Worskla River Sector).

18 September 1943: Three Tigers, still under the command of SS-Hauptscharführer Soretz, relieve trapped forces of SS-Panzer-Grenadier-Regiment "Der Führer" west of Tschutowo. The company is relocated to the Dnjepr River Sector. During several covering-force missions, two Tigers bog down and cannot be recovered. They have to be blown up several days later after being cannibalized for parts.

Total tanks: 17.

20 September 1943: Operational tanks: 7.

22 September 1943: Assembly as part of Kampfgruppe Schulze with the II./SS-Panzer-Grenadier-Regiment "Der Führer" near the road Poltava-Sabrodki. The company covers the withdrawal to the K Line. March to the reconstitution area southeast of Koselschtschina. In the days that follow, urgently needed maintenance is performed. Only the division's tank regiment remains in this area; the rest of the division relocates for the operation against the Grebeni Bridgehead.

30 September 1943: No tanks operational.

5 October 1943: Still no operational tanks.

20 October 1943: Operational tanks: 4. Entrainment in Kirowograd and transport to Znamenka-Bobruisk. Base camp at Pji.

Mid-October 1943: The company commander is wounded and relieved by SS-Obersturmführer Tensfeld.

29 October 1943: The Tigers support the attack of Grenadier-Regiment 80 on Hill 166.9; four tanks and several antitank guns are destroyed.

30 October 1943: Three Tigers take part in an immediate counterattack to Hill 103 along the Dnjepr River; four tanks and four antitank guns destroyed. After the loss of this hill, the attack is repeated; five dug-in tanks and assault guns are knocked out. 1 Tiger is a total loss.

Total tanks: 16.

31 October 1943: Operational tanks: 3.

1 November 1943: Tiger S11, (Soretz) knocks out the 2000th tank for the division. Operational tanks: 10.

5 November 1943: Covering positions occupied during the day. During, the night march to the depot at Bobruisk.

6 November 1943: The company is entrained during the night in Mnowka and relocated by railway from Bobruisk into the area of Bjelaja-Zerkwa (eighty kilometers southwest of Kiev). It moves via Wladislawka and Rakitno.

7 November 1943: The Tiger company destroys six T-34s five kilometers north of Grebeniki on the road to Kiev (six operational tanks). It is under command of SS-Obersturmführer Kalls, who has replaced the wounded SS-Hauptsturmführer Paetsch. During the movement to contact, one Tiger burns out after self-ignition. In the afternoon, four more tanks are knocked out in the area south of Grebeniki.

Total tanks: 15.

8 November 1943: The six Tigers are relieved by three other ones and stay in Grebeniki as a reserve. On the days that follow, covering-force operations around Grebeniki. Several enemy attacks are pushed back.

10 November 1943: Operational tanks: 5.

11 November 1943: The Tiger company knocks out twelve tanks east of Slavia.

12 November 1943: Shortly after midnight, an attack to the railway line Bjelaja Zerkow-Fastov, reestablishing the lines and contact with the twenty-five. Panzer-Division. Return to Slavia; tanks refueled and rearmed at 0300 hours. One hour later, the company is alerted and employed to clear an enemy penetration in Grebenki. Three enemy tanks are knocked out.

13 November 1943: Tiger S12 of SS-Schütze Skerbinz, a demoted former officer's candidate who is still the a platoon leader, knocks out five T-34s and one T-60.

16 November 1943: SS-Obersturmführer Tensfeld is killed; two days later, SS-Obersturmführer Kalls assumes command. In the days that follow, the company is employed in a counteroffensive in the Berditschew that advances in the direction of Kiev. Shitomir is retaken. The company suffers three total losses.

Total tanks: 12.

21 November 1943: Operational tanks: 7.

22 November 1943: Seventy kilometer road march to Kornin-Skotschischtsche.

23 November 1943: Entrainment at 0300 hours; railway transport back to Shitomir.

24 November 1943: Assembly in the bays of a field landing strip on the northern edges of Shitomir; towards noon, a road march of more than to seventy kilometers in the area Korosten-Radomichl.

25 November 1943: Departure at 0500 hours to the front and start of a counterattack. An enemy night attack that was supported by tanks is crushed after dawn breaks.

26 November 1943: One defective Tiger with its sight out of alignment fires in vain at three T-34s. Operational tanks: 2.

27 November 1943: An enemy infantry attack is mowed down. In the days that follow, defensive operations against sporadic enemy encounters; several "kills."

30 November 1943: Operational tanks: 3. 1 total loss.

Total tanks: 11.

31 November 1943: Operational tanks: 3.

1 December 1943: Operational tanks: 3.

2 December 1943: A single Tiger supports a counterattack. A strong infantry assault is repelled; after several hits from an antitank gun, the tank withdraws.

6 December 1943: Attachment to the 2. Fallschirmjäger-Division. After assembling in Garboroff, six Tigers under the command of SS-Oberscharführer Baumann are employed with a gepanzerte Kampfgruppe east of the road south of Radomichl. They attack the high ground west of the forester' s building at Schumowa; six antitank guns are destroyed. The infantry does not maintain contact; the tanks assume an all-round defense and withdraw during the night.

7 December 1943: Attack towards Beresizy. The attack has to be stopped because the accompanying infantry fails to maintain contact. The tanks pull back to the line of departure. Several bunkers and 6 antitank guns are destroyed. Tiger S04 is immobilized after several hits and faces capture by the Soviets. Two Tigers—the Tiger of SS-Unterscharführer Eichler and Tiger S34 under the command of SS-Oberscharführer Baumann—attack during the night and manage to recover it. Four Tigers operational.

8 December 1943: Two Tigers and several Panzer IVs and Panzer Vs attack via the sawmill to the right of the main road to Radomichl and take Hill 153; one antitank gun is knocked out. One Tiger runs over a mine. The planned attack on Radomichl is suspended; the company marches back to the former assembly area. Only one Tiger operational.

9 December 1943: Attack of five Tigers and one Panzer IV company on Radomichl. During the march to the line of departure, three Tigers bog down but manage to arrive in time for the attack. The armor moves into a defended wooded area, where the attack stalls. Two Tigers throw tracks and get bogged down due to tight curves. One tank can be recovered on the next morning and leaves under its own power; the other one is towed during the subsequently ordered withdrawal.

10 December 1943: Operational tanks: 3. One total loss.
Total tanks: 10.

11 December 1943: Operational tanks: 3. March to the south to the main route Kiev-Shitomir; one Tiger burns out due to self-ignition.
Total tanks: 9.

15 December 1943: The divisions begins preparations for movement to France for ·reconstitution. A Kampfgruppe with the Tigers stays in Russia.

16 December 1943: Entrainment in Shitomir. Attack of five Tigers towards the Shitomir airfield together with a paratrooper company.

17 December 1943: Formation of SS-Panzergruppe "Das Reich"—an ad hoc formation established out of the elements of the division that remaining the Soviet Union—under command of the division operations officer, SS-Obersturmbannführer Sommer. It includes the rest of the division's tank regiment. Two tank companies are formed. The five Tigers (and four Panthers and six Panzer IVs) are under command of SS-Obersturmführer Kloskowski. The main body of the division starts railway transport to France on 20 December 1943.

19 December 1943: Four Tigers under SS-Untersturmführer Tegethoff destroy one antitank gun near Jelnich.

20 December 1943: Operational tanks: 4. One total loss; one is sent to factory maintenance.
Total tanks: 7.

21 December 1943: Operational tanks: 4. Several enemy attacks in the Predm. Rudnaja Sector against the right flank are repelled, also on the following day.

23 December 1943: Five Tigers destroy three antitank guns and push back two infantry assaults on the road to Rudnja. The town is finally taken.

24 December 1943: The Russian offensive breaks loose; defensive operations around Radomichl. Operational tanks: 4. The tank engines will not start as a result of the low temperatures and have to be started manually. The Kampfgruppe knocks out sixty tanks. During the withdrawal, one Tiger is immobilized by a mine and another one gets bogged down in a large bomb crater.
Total tanks: 5.

25 December 1943: After crossing an engineer bridge across the Teterew River, all remaining Tigers break down during the subsequent retreat (some run out of fuel) and have to be abandoned. Only the two that had been evacuated for depot-level maintenance survive.

Total tanks: 0.

29 December 1943: A detail departs for Burg to pick up new tanks. It is under the command of SS-Untersturmführer Tegethoff.

2 January 1944: The remaining tank crews of the company are alerted and their leaves cancelled. They move back to the rally point at Schepetowka.

5 January 1944: The Kampfgruppe (without any tanks) moves via Staro Konstantinow and into the area around Proskurow, where it waits for new tanks.

22 January 1944: Several crews are dispatched to Proskurow, where the new tanks are supposed to arrive.

31 January 1944: Redeployment to a new base camp northeast of Staro Konstantinow.

10 February 1944: Five new Tigers arrive in Proskurow.

Total tanks: 5.

11 February 1944: March with the tanks to the assembly area.

12 February 1944: Two Tigers move sixty kilometers to the north to the frontlines there. No engagements; after midnight, they march back.

14 February 1944: The five Tigers under the command of SS-Untersturmführer Tegethoff are ordered to the sector of the 19. Panzer-Division in the area around Liubar (near the Slutsch River) and remain there as a divisional reserve.

20 February 1944: Operational tanks: 4. One tank suffers a broken final drive.

27 February 1944: The Tigers are relieved from their attachment to the 19. Panzer-Division and march back during the night (eighty kilometers) into the area southwest of Schepetowka.

29 February 1944: All five Tigers operational.

1 March 1944: An assembly area east of Semjelintzy is occupied.

2 March 1944: Counterattack against the Horyn Bridgehead is stopped; two disabled Tigers are recovered to the maintenance facilities.

3 March 1944: Employment of three Tigers and eleven Panzer IVs on both sides of the Semjelintzy Railway Station, where a large infantry assault is crushed. The Kampfgruppe knocks out twenty-eight tanks west of Semjelintzy. Withdrawal across the Horyn River proves impossible.

The Tiger of SS-Standartenjunker von Einböck bogs down in a swamp and has to be abandoned; it is destroyed by friendly gunfire. The tank of SS-Untersturmführer Tegethoff is knocked out by antitank guns, killing the driver and the radio operator. The third Tiger (Streng) transports the survivors outside of the tank, but they are all killed.

Heavy shelling on the very last Tiger, which starts burning in the engine compartment. The fire is extinguished by the fire-suppression system. A hit entering the turret rips off the loader's left hand.

At a brook south of the Horyn River, the engine catches fire again. The order to bail out is given, and the crew crosses the ice-cold water trying to escape. Those who do not keep up are immediately killed by the pursuing Russians. Contact with German forces is made east of Semjalintzki. In the evening, redeployment to Staro Konstantinow.

Total tanks: 2.

4 March 1944: March to Proskurow via Matrunki. The surviving crews wait to be transported back to France.

8 March 1944: All the remaining elements of the division are concentrated into a so-called SS-Regimentsgruppe "Das Reich" (SS Regimental Group "Das Reich"). The last tanks are consolidated to form a mixed tank company that consists of a platoon each of Panzer IVs, Panthers, Tigers, and Sturmgeschütze.

13 March 1944: Two tanks—Tiger 01 and Tiger 02—return from the maintenance facility and arrive at Arkadijew. An antitank-gun position north of the town is destroyed in a two-hour firefight (nine guns are destroyed). Afterwards, the enemy infantry is pushed back. Tiger 01 withdraws after having used up all its gun ammunition and being hit and penetrated by a sub-caliber armor-piercing round. Tiger 02 remains in position and knocks out two T-34s and one KV-85 later on.

16 March 1944: Road march to the south (two Tigers left).

18 March 1944: Kamenez-Podolsk is transited.

20 March 1944: Tiger 01 is repaired and sent to Bar.

21 March 1944: By order of the local commander, Generalmajor Nentig, Tiger 01 and 5 Panthers remain in Proskuroff to stiffen the local defense. Tiger 02 (chassis number 250 729) breaks through the Sinkoff Bridge (east of Jarmolinzy) at 0920 hours and falls four meters.

24 March 1944: The march is continued via Przemysl. Tiger 01 (chassis number 250 722) is blown up in Proskuroff.

Total tanks: 1.

25 March 1944: All remaining tanks except one Panzer IV and Tiger 02 have to be blown up in Bar. March on foot to Wonkowzie via Daschkowzie.

26 March 1944: Sinkowze-Strichkowze. Tiger 02 is blown up (see 21 March 1944).

Total tanks: 0.

27 March 1944: Gortschitschnaja-Ruda Gortschitschnaja-Iwankowzy. Contact with the 101. Jäger-Division. In the days that follow, movement via Sariza-Sipowze-Nowosiolka Jaztowiecka. Order for withdrawal of the Kampfgruppe on 14 April 1944. Railway transport to the west.

19 April 1944: Arrival in Paris (after short home leave had been granted). Rail movement to Bordeaux, then to Montauban.

27 April 1944: Movement to Amsterdam, then to the Zwolle Training Area.

✠

The Tiger company destroyed more than 250 tanks and assault guns during the time of its existence.

COMPANY COMMANDERS

November 1942–8 February 1943:	SS-Hauptsturmführer Grader (killed in action)
8–17 February 1943:	SS-Hauptsturmführer Kuhlmann
17 February 1943–29 March 1943:	SS-Hauptsturmführer Herzig
10 April 1943–11 July 1943:	SS-Hauptsturmführer Zimmermann (wounded)
11 July 1943:	SS-Hauptsturmführer Lorenz (killed in action)
11 July 1943–15 July 1943:	SS-Obersturmführer Theiss
15 July 1943–15 August 1943:	SS-Obersturmführer Reininghaus
15 August 1943–October 1943:	SS-Obersturmführer Matzke (wounded)
October 1943–16 November 1943:	SS-Obersturmführer Tensfeld (killed in action)
16 November 1943–December 1943:	SS-Obersturmführer Kalls

The road conditions in the first week of February 1943 were made extremely difficult by the heavy ice. Despite the layman's perception of the cross-country mobility of fully tracked vehicles, they often become virtually uncontrollable "bobsleds" under icy conditions. This Panzer III took a tumble into a body of water. It appears, however, that some or all of the crew managed to escape through the emergency hatch in the hull bottom.

Like the other three heavy tank companies that were formed during this period, the 8./SS-Panzer-Regiment 2 also had Panzer III's in its inventory. Due to the weather conditions, these tanks were equipped with the so-called Ostketten ("Eastern tracks"), which helped lower the ground pressure of the normal small-width tracks and prevent the tanks from bogging down in the snow. HASELBÖCK

Immediately after the 8./SS-Panzer-Regiment 2 arrived in Kharkov, its Tigers were involved in the defense of the city in Mid-February 1943. Here we see Tiger 811. SCHWEIGERT

The Tigers were equipped with ice cleats, which considerably improved their traction in ice and snow. They can be seen here on the Tiger of SS-Hauptscharführer Ott. HASELBÖCK

The company had to evacuate Kharkov on 12 February 1943. Panzer III 864 was still in operational condition. HASELBÖCK

After the withdrawal from Kharkov, the 8./SS-Panzer-Regiment 2 gathered in Poltawa and prepared for the recapture of the Ukrainian city. These three photographs show the crew of Tiger 832 performing maintenance on its vehicle on 26 February 1943. MITTELSTAEDT

This photograph was taken during the assault towards Olschany and shows a Tiger crossing a shallow stream that was formed by the recent thaw.

On 10 March 1943, the company prepared for a counterattack on Olschany I the small village of Walki. Tiger 821 of SS-Obersturmführer Theis is the first vehicle visible in this column.

Once Kharkov had been recaptured, the company had several days to restore the recovered Tiger and also apply a neat coat of whitewash to its vehicles, as can be seen here on the company commander's tank, Tiger 801.

Two other types of vehicles from the 8./SS-Panzer-Regiment 2 can be seen here: an Sd.Kfz. 251/1 of the scout platoon and a Büssing truck with crane.

During the recapture of Kharkov, the company recovered its first "near loss." This disabled Tiger had to be abandoned in February. STÜMKE

158B Two junior officers of the company—SS-Untersturmführer Schienhofen and SS-Untersturmführer Ebeling—pose from vantage points on Panzer III 854. EBELING

Some successful crewmembers received the iron cross, Second Class. FINK

In late March 1943, the company moved back to Kharkov and had some time to recover from its most recent fighting. Crewmembers of Panzer III 851—SS-Rottenführer Kempf, SS-Sturmmann Freiberger and SS-Sturmmann Holzer—lost their tank commander, Walter Tessmann, on 14 March 1943, as indicated on the turret memorial. KEMPF

On 17 March 1943, the offensive in the direction of Bjelgorod commenced. Tiger 821 is pictured near Nepertyaja.
GREVAUßMÜLLER

In contrast to the other tanks, Tiger 812 had solid white numerals painted on the turret. SS-Obersturmführer Schienhofen has gathered other leaders in the unit for a "photo opportunity." It is unknown why the army armor officer (far left) is in the group photo.
SCHIENHOFEN

At the fueling point established in Kharkov, the crews found ideal conditions for maintaining their vehicles. The whitewash was removed and the dark gray tanks received yellow-olive stripes. Because the tank losses had necessitated a reorganization of the company, the tanks received new identification numbers. The habit of painting individual markings and letters on the tanks began, as can be seen on Tiger 833. TiKi is an acronym for a girlfriend's name that stands for either Theresa-Katrin or Theresa-Kristine. In the top photograph, "Mr. Muscles" tries to demonstrate his strength in "punching" the gun tube all by himself. The rest of the crew looks on in amusement.

On 20 April 1943, the company relocated to Pereserschnaja (20 kilometers west of Kharkov). These aerial photographs show the initial movements of the tanks to seek concealment beside buildings in the village. RESTAYN

In early May 1943, a train carrying six replacement Tigers had difficulties making it through. Between Brest-Litowsk and Gomel, the train hit a mine placed by saboteurs and was derailed. These four photographs were taken prior to the day-long recovery operation. SCHWEIGERT

The time was used for individual and crew-level training in preparation for Operation "Citadel." KESSELS

Shortly after they finally arrived, the new tanks were viewed by some army personnel.

Tiger 802 during field training on 1 May 1943. HASSELBÖCK

In these two photographs, we see that the new alphanumeric system of vehicle identification has been applied. The tanks are zeroing their guns on a field range. SCHWEIGERT

Four images documenting one of the main threats to the tanks—mines! Tanks that ran over mines were to be recovered as quickly as possible, before the enemy artillery could range in on the stranded steel monsters. A common practice was to shorten the damaged track to allow the damaged tank to assist in the recovery effort (first image). If no power was applied to the tracks or a track was missing, it was very difficult to recover the vehi-

cle, if not impossible in difficult terrain. Sometimes, it was possible for the tank to limp back under its own power as well, depending on where the damage to the suspension was located. This can be seen in the case of Tiger S02 (second image), which has lost several roadwheels and suffered several broken torsion bars. The last two images show Tiger S02 after having been repaired and while it was being worked on. FINK

A common occurrence can be seen during this exercise: One of the Tigers has turned too sharply, causing it to "throw" its track off of the drive sprocket. The crew then had to "break" track, realign it and then reconnect it. RESTAYN

The tanks suffered numerous hits during the fighting, as can be seen on Tiger S24, which was photographed on 10 July 1943.

In many instances, the Tigers had to be towed to cover. Although the practice was officially forbidden, the only way to save a tank from further battle damage in may instances was to tow it out of harm's way with another tank. The "correct" way to recover the vehicle was with three 18-ton prime movers. It was possible to move the Tiger with only two of the prime movers, but the "school" solution was to employ three of them. FINK

The departing 13./SS-Panzer-Regiment 1 handed over nine of its tanks to the 8./SS-Panzer-Regiment 2. The photograph above shows one such tank after it had been handed over. The new owners have not had time to paint their markings over the old ones of Tiger 1334. Another view of the same tank several days later is seen below. The "new" Tiger S22 forms a backdrop for some of its crew, which has just been awarded the Iron Cross (both First and Second Class). FINK

There was only one week of rest after Operation "Citadel" was called off. The time was used to effect urgently needed maintenance and repair to the battle-damaged tanks.

Operation "Citadel" was followed by fighting along the Mius River line. These two photographs were taken during the rail journey to the new area of operations. The picture above shows a Tiger whose entire main gun and gun mantlet have been removed. The invaluable portal crane has also been loaded aboard the train; the tactical and divisional insignias have been neatly stenciled on to it. FINK

These photographs demonstrate the often chaotic conditions during the (final) German withdrawal from the city and the enormous variety of equipment (and horsepower!) that was employed by the Wehrmacht. Many of the vehicles were not really fit for use on the unimaginably bad road conditions of the Eastern Front. The bus was used by the company's maintenance platoon.

A few days later, Tiger S02 looks even worse than it did before and is out of action for some time. FINK

A detail view of Tiger S02 showing the numerous hits it had received from both antitank rifles and small-caliber antitank guns (4.5-centimeter?). These have caused heavy damage to the running gear. FINK

In October, the 8./SS-Panzer-Regiment 2 was transported by rail to Znamenka. Our good friend Tiger S02 can be seen loaded on the rail car with its combat tracks still on. FINK

The five replacement tanks delivered in February 1944 were used up in the battles around the Horvn bridgehead.

FINK

FINK

During the withdrawal, several Tigers had to be towed by the 18-ton prime movers before they could be rail-loaded and moved to another sector of the front.

8./SS-PANZER-REGIMENT 2

Vehicles on Hand/Deliveries

Date	Tiger I	Tiger II	On hand	Remarks
December 1942	2		2	
January 1943	8		10	12 Panzer IIIs (Model J)
February 1943	1		10	
May 1943	6		14	1 from the schwere SS-Panzer-Abteilung
27 July 1943	9		22	From the 13./SS-Panzer-Regiment 1
10 February 1944	5		5	
Grand Total	31	0		

Losses

Date	Losses	On hand	Remarks
11 February 1943	1	9	Abandoned
1 March 1943	1	9	Self-ignition
22 March 1943	1	8	Knocked out
11 July 1943	1	13	Knocked out
19–21 August 1943	3	19	Knocked out
28 September 1943	2	17	Destroyed by own crew
30 October 1943	1	16	Knocked out
7 November 1943	1	15	Self-ignition
Early December 1943	1	10	Knocked out
11 December 1943	1	9	Self-ignition
December 1943	3	6	Evacuated for depot-level maintenance
December 1943	6	0	Destroyed by own crew
3 March 1944	3	2	1 destroyed by own crew, 1 knocked out and 1 captured
24 March 1944	1	1	Destroyed by own crew
26 March 1944	1	0	Destroyed by own crew
Grand total:	31		

Of the losses suffered by the company, 32% were due to self-destruction (to prevent capture), 49% were lost in combat operations and 19% were lost due to other causes.

8./ SS-Panzerregiment 2 – November 1942 - May 1943

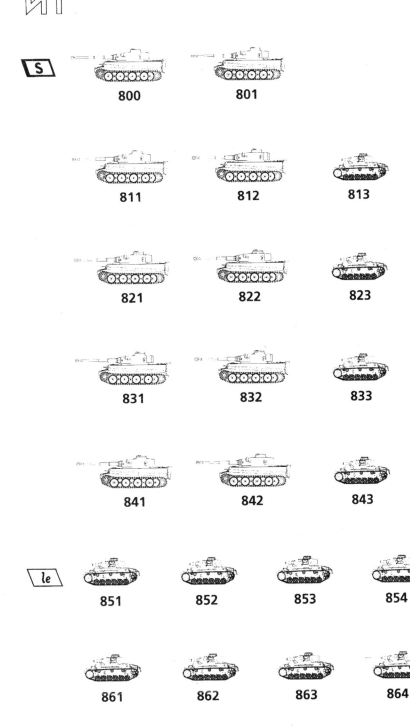

Schwere Panzerkompanie
SS-Panzerregiment 2 – 1 July 1943

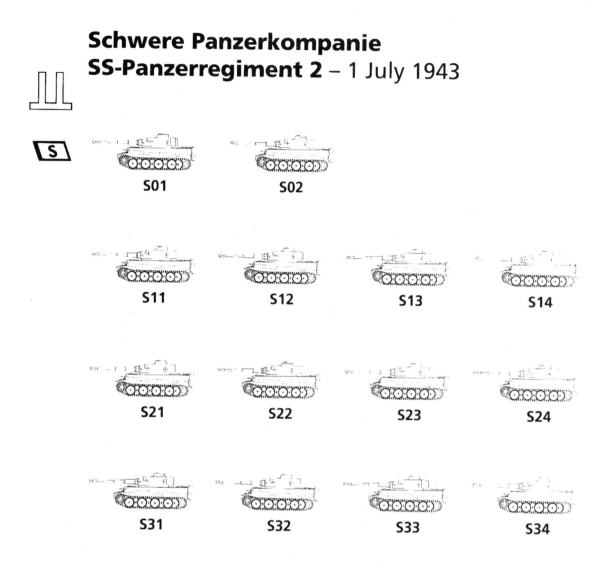

S01   S02

S11   S12   S13   S14

S21   S22   S23   S24

S31   S32   S33   S34

Schwere Panzerkompanie
SS-Panzerregiment 2 – Early August 1943

S01 S02 S03 S04 S05

S11 S12 S13 S14 S15

S21 S22 S23 S24 S25

S31 S32 S33 S34 S35

9./SS-Panzer-Regiment 3

The schwere Panzer-Kompanie for SS-Panzer-Abteilung "Totenkopf" is established effective 15 November 1942 in accordance with KStN 1176d dated 15 August 1942 (order: SS-Führungshauptamt Tgb.Nr. 7288/42 GEHEIM dated 13 November 1942). The company is activated at the Fallingbostel Training Area. SS-Hauptsturmführer Kanth is the first company commander. Besides its ten Tigers and ten Panzer IIIs, the unit has an oversized maintenance platoon (under SS-Untersturmführer Greisinger) consisting of a maintenance platoon and a recovery platoon. The personnel come primarily from the activation details responsible for the heavy companies of the two sister divisions, SS-Panzer-Grenadier-Division "Leibstandarte SS Adolf Hitler" and SS-Panzer-Grenadier-Division "Das Reich." Personnel are also provided from the reconnaissance platoons of the I. and the II./SS-Panzer-Regiment 3.

✚

January 1943: Delivery of nine Tiger Is.

10 February 1943: Entrainment and transport to the Eastern Front.

14 February 1943: Track change in Kowel.

16 February 1943: Arrival of the first transport train in Poltava; detrainment during the night. The unit is put up in the former Soviet garrison in Poltava.

17 February 1943: Arrival of the second transport, with the third one arriving on 18 February.

19 February 1943: Operational tanks: 9.

20 February 1943: SS-Hauptsturmführer Mooslechner takes over command of the company; SS-Hauptsturmführer Kanth becomes the adjutant of SS-Panzer-Regiment 3. Night march from Poltava to Karlowka during a snowstorm.

21 February 1943: The company is assembled north of Pereschtschepino. One Tiger (SS-Obersturmführer Rinner) breaks into the ice over a river and cannot be recovered before 27 February 1943. It must be turned in for depot-level maintenance at Dnjepropetrowsk).

Total tanks: 8.

Division ordered to attack north of the Ssamara River Sector towards the area north of Pawlograd.

22 February 1943: The offensive initially gets stuck on the icy slopes near Krassnograd. An enemy counterattack is repelled near Pereschtschepino.

25 February 1943: Attack to the northeast on Alexejewka (via Kondratjewka) from the assembly area at Wjasowok.

26 February 1943: Enemy tanks are pushed back along the railway line Orelka-Losowaja. Attack westward from north of Strastnoj on Zaredarowka. Southwest of Panjutina, the attack comes to a halt in the face of strong enemy tank formations. The corps' order for the continuation of the advance in the direction of Smirnowka cannot be sent due to a missing radio relay. The division commander, SS-Obergruppenführer Eicke, who is on a flight in a Fieseler Storch in order to establish contact with the forward elements, is shot down; no survivors.

27 February 1943: Attack initiated from the west towards Zaredarowka that starts from the assembly area north of the railway line near Sacharjewsksij. Seizure of Panjutina. Operational tanks: 9.

28 February 1943: SS-Panzer-Regiment 3 moves to an assembly area around Barbaschewka and Michailowka.

2 March 1943: An enemy tank assault on Paraskoweja is repelled. The company advances as far as Medwedowka in the afternoon.

3 March 1943: Attack with SS-Panzer-Grenadier-Regiment "Der Führer" via Losowaja into the area of Berestowaja; encirclement of strong enemy forces in conjunction with elements of SS-Panzer-Grenadier-Division "Das Reich" in the area of Jeremejewka. Operational tanks: 6.

4 March 1943: The company continues to support SS-Panzer-Grenadier-Division "Das Reich" in the taking of Ochotschaje. Operational tanks: 6.

5 March 1943: Final destruction of the trapped enemy. Operational tanks: 6.

6 March 1943: Withdrawal of the division from the line; movement into the area around Tischinkowka as the corps reserve.

8 March 1943: Relocation to the area of Stary Mertschik. When crossing the frozen river near Grijekowo, the Tiger of SS-Untersturmführer Köhler breaks through the ice and is covered by the stream. It is not recovered until April, when it is towed to Dnepropetrowsk for long-term repair. Another Tiger (SS-Untersturmführer Rathsack) bogs down and suffers engine damage.

Total tanks: 7.

9 March 1943: The division is directed to the north for the counteroffensive against Kharkov. A bridgehead at Oltschany is established.

10 March 1943: Operational tanks: 6. The company commander, SS-Obersturmführer Richter, attacks together with the I./SS-Panzer-Grenadier-Regiment 1 from the Udy Bridgehead near Golowatschtschewka. The attack moves via Karobki towards the northern part of Dergatschi. After seizing the town, covering positions are established to the east. No Tigers are operational.

11 March 1943: The division forms a covering force for the corps attack on Kharkov.

13 March 1943: After crossing the main road Kharkov-Bjelgorod near Rogan, the attack makes progress towards Bolschaja Danilowka; the Kharkov River can be forded. Flanking enemy attacks near Zirkuny are repelled. Operational tanks: 3.

14 March 1943: Western outskirts of Jaruga are reached. Operational tanks: 3.

15 March 1943: Arrival at the Tschugujew Pass. Operational tanks: 3.

16 March 1943: Further advance towards Bjelgorod. Operational tanks: 3.

17 March 1943: Relieved from attachment and returned to SS-Panzer-Grenadier-Division "Totenkopf." Enemy attacks on Tschugujew are repelled. Withdrawal from the front sector near Saroshnoje after the 6. Panzer-Division conducts a forward passage of lines. The division reorganizes for further offensive action towards Bjelgorod.

18 March 1943: Attack on Ternowaya. Operational tanks: 3.

19 March 1943: Order is given to attack Iwanowka. The company commander is mortally wounded inside a Tiger due to a delayed explosion of a propellant charge.

20 March 1943: The enemy bridgeheads near Iwanowka are eliminated. SS-Panzer-Regiment 3 "Totenkopf" is assembled near Mikojanowka. SS-Hauptsturmführer Richter takes over command. Only one Tiger I is operational; one total loss.

Total tanks: 6.

21–22 March 1943: No engagements. One Tiger operational.

23 March 1943: No Tigers operational; maintenance is performed.

24–25 March 1943: Operational tanks: 2.

26 March 1943: One Tiger operational. Six tank crews are sent to Paderborn.

1 April 1943: Operational tanks: 2.

10 April 1943: Operational tanks: 1.

20 April 1943: Operational tanks: 4.

22 April 1943: Reorganization order received (KStN 1176e dated 5 March 1943).

29 April 1943: Relief and march into an assembly area around Gurjewski (northwest of Kharkov).

30 April 1943: Operational tanks: 4.

12–14 May 1943: Redeployment into a rest area in Jushny (southwest of Kharkov). The Panzer III's are handed over to the regiment.

10 May 1943: Three Tigers are delivered from the SS-Panzer-Korps; six tanks operational. The Tigers receive the 900-series turret numerals.

Total tanks: 9.

20 May 1943: Operational tanks: 11. One command tank and five standard Tigers are delivered. March to Budy.

Total tanks: 15.

Crew-level training in the days that follow.

30 May 1943: Operational tanks: 10.

1–2 June 1943: Gunnery training.

3 June 1943: The company is alerted; the alert is called off at 1500 hours.

6 June 1943: Driver training.

10 June 1943: Ten tanks operational

20 June 1943: Ten tanks operational.

22 June 1943: Equipment inspection.

28 June 1943: Departure to the assembly area near Udy for Operation "Citadel."

30 June 1943: The division's tank regiment is assembled in the area Strelezkoje-Kasazjoje-Bessonowka. Ten tanks operational.

1 July 1943: Operational tanks: 11.

2 July 1943: Operational tanks: 11.

3 July 1943: Jump-off position near Rakowo.

4 July 1943: Operational tanks: 11.

5 July 1943: Operation "Citadel" is launched. After crushing stiff enemy resistance around Beresoff, the Tiger company, SS-Obersturmführer Schröder, reaches Hill 216.5, turns east and continues movement to the Gonki-Bjelgorod main road. Hill 225.9 is captured there. After pushing forward along the main road, the Ssemelo K. Trudo farmhouse is seized at 1545 hours. Five tanks are immobilized by mines.

6 July 1943: The attack recommences at 0345 hours from the area around Hill 225.9 to the southeast. The road junction south of Point 225.9 is blocked. The company is in the area north of the bridge west of Schopino at 0740 hours. At noon, a new mission is received: Reconnoiter in the direction of Lutschki in conjunction with the division's armored group in order to establish contact with SS-Panzer-Grenadier-Division "Das Reich."

7 July 1943: Sixteen hours of attack east of the main road. Tiger 912 is destroyed by a direct artillery hit; the crew manages to bail out.

Total tanks: 14.

8 July 1943: The regiment is assembled near Gonki. At noon, an enemy tank counterattack through the ravines of Wissloje and Ternowka is repelled. SS-Obersturmführer Schröder is killed by a hit from an antitank rifle, when he tries to disperse enemy infantry by firing his submachine gun out of the open commander's hatch. SS-Untersturmführer Köhler assumes acting command. Operational tanks: 5.

9 July 1943: Advance via Wesselyj to the northwest; occupation of a ridge 2 kilometers east of Kotschetowka. A massive tank attack—24th Guards Tank Brigade—on Gresnoje is pushed back. Only one Tiger operational.

10 July 1943: Attack across the hillside of Gresnoje on Kljutschi. One kill. Operational tanks: 11.

11 July 1943: Eleven Tigers conduct a counterattack on Wasiljewka. They then assault towards a military bridge across the Pssel River west of Bogorodizkoje.

12 July 1943: Attack on a group of barracks west of Klutschi. After stopping an enemy counterattack, the Pssel River is crossed. The advance is continued via Hill 226.6 to the northeast into the area two kilometers northwest of Poleshajew. During the evening, the advance continues to the road Beregowoje-Kartaschewka (furthest advance to the north during Operation "Citadel"). SS-Untersturmführer Köhler is killed in action; SS-Untersturmführer Schüssler assumes acting command.

13 July 1943: Four Tigers in repair. The planned attack on the road Kartaschewka-Prochorowka in order to outflank an enemy force is called off. Evasive movement into an area behind Hill 226.6. In the afternoon, a counterattack is launched across the hill. Strong enemy counterattack forces are eliminated. All ten Tigers are non-operational.

14 July 1943: The operational tanks stiffen the defense against enemy counterstrokes.

16 July 1943: Operation "Citadel" is called off. Withdrawal to the southern bank of the Pssel River and employment in a blocking position. Operational tanks: 9.

17 July 1943: German offensive efforts do not make progress due to strong enemy artillery fire; Seven Tigers operational.

18 July 1943: Several attacks are pushed back. Operational tanks: 7.

19 July 1943: Retrograde movement into the area southwest of Lutschki (northern edge of the Michailowka collective-farm complex) starts during the evening hours.

20 July 1943: Operational tanks: 5. March order to Barwenkowa. Entrainment in Bjelgorod and in Ssossnowka is planned.

21 July 1943: Road march along the main road Jakowlewo-Gluschinskij towards Bjelgorod.

22 July 1943: Entrainment in Kharkov and start of transport to the Mius Front.

28 July 1943: Detrainment and march into the area of Ssnesnoje.

29 July 1943: Relocation to an assembly area west of the housing area for the Rmowskij pit mine. Orders received for the next day to advance on both sides of the mountain road Ssenesnoje-Marinowka towards Hills 213.9 and 191.3. From there, the company is to cover the flank to the east along the road to the south in order to establish contact east of Jelisawtinskij with the forces from the south. Eight Tiger Is are received from the 13./SS-Panzer-Regiment 1, which is heading for Italy.

Total tanks: 22.

30 July 1943: Operational tanks: 10. Attack on Hill 213.9. It proves to be a heavily fortified stronghold manned by an entire antitank brigade and surrounded by minefields. The fighting wages the entire day, but the hill line cannot be taken. Seven Tigers are put out of action.

31 July 1943: Further unsuccessful efforts to seize Hill 213.9. The Tiger of SS-Oberscharführer Lampert is knocked out; another Tiger cannot be recovered. Both tanks are blown up by German forces on 7 August 1943. Only one Tiger I operational.

Total tanks: 20.

1 August 1943: Hill 213.9 is stormed again during the afternoon and finally taken. Further attack to the east. Operational tanks: 10.

2 August 1943: Pursuit of the retreating enemy forces across Hill 191.3. Elimination of all opposing forces on the west bank of the Mius River and occupation of the former main line of resistance. Operational tanks: 3.

3 August 1943: The majority of the division's tank regiment is assembled in the area of Stepanowka-Perwomaisk and employed as a reserve.

4 August 1943: The company is relieved by elements from the 23. Panzer-Division. March into area of Ordshonikidsa. Transport back to Germany is announced.

6 August 1943: Instead of that, movement is ordered into the Kharkov area to close the gap between Field-Army Detachment "Kempf" and the 4. Panzer-Armee (4th Armored Army).

7 August 1943: Assembly in Makajewka.

8 August 1943: Railway transport from Jassno-Wadaya to Kharkov (via Stalino-Barwenko-Krassnograd).

9 August 1943: Six rail cars of one of the trains with two Tigers derail due to destroyed rails following partisan activities. Detrainment in Kharkov; road march to Walkij during the night.

10 August 1943: Arrival of the last transport. Operational tanks: 2.

11 August 1943: In the afternoon, attack with six Tigers under command of SS-Untersturmführer Quade in the direction of Kolomak; fleeing infantry is hammered with indirect gun fire at long ranges. Tschutowo is taken during the night.

12 August 1943: Counterattack near Kosliki. An antitank-gun belt is encountered in the course of the attack on the hills on the west side. SS-Unterscharführer Finn's tank—Tiger 913—is knocked out by a US nine-centimeter antitank gun. Four other Tigers suffer heavy damage from numerous hits; seven German tankers killed. The last operational tank (SS-Untersturmführer Quade) supports the seizure of the hill after heavy shelling by rocket launchers.

Total tanks: 19.

13 August 1943: Attack together with the 13./Panzer-Regiment "Großdeutschland" on Katschalowka. During the advance on Alexejewa, an enemy tank attack ensues; approximately thirty tanks are knocked out.

14 August 1943: The planned attack on Alexejewa does not take place.

15 August 1943: Early in the morning, the attack is continued with three Tigers; in the afternoon, the main road to the east near Alexejewa is reached, trapping strong enemy forces.

16 August 1943: The Mertschik-Merla sector is secured. Assembly area around Alexejewka.

17 August 1943: Advance across the Merla River west of Subebowka. In the evening, Karaiskasowka is captured. The Tiger company destroys forty tanks on this day; only six Tigers operational.

19 August 1943: Redeployment from the area of Konstantinowka. Movement across a bridge to the northern bank of the Merla approximately twenty kilometers downriver (southwest) near Ssolonizewka. Then movement as far as Kolontajew.

20 August 1943: Support of the attack on Kolontajew. After seizure of the town, further advance to the north. Contact with the elements of Panzer-Grenadier-Division

"Großdeutschland," which is closing in from Parchomowka. Strong enemy forces are encircled once again. Operational tanks: 5.

21 August 1943: In the early morning, an enemy attempt to break out is dispersed.

22 August 1943: Operational tanks: 5. Offensive action together with the II./SS-Panzer-Regiment "Totenkopf" from the area north of Ljubowka and east of Kotelewka to the north on the plateau south of Stepanowka. In the evening, the advance stalls southeast of the Pioner collective farm.

25 August 1943: Warning order is given for the withdrawal to the Merla River Sector.

26 August 1943: The withdrawal of Panzer-Grenadier-Division "Großdeutschland" and strong enemy pressure make any movement impossible. Three operational Tigers support German infantry against the massed infantry assaults, which are supported by heavy artillery barrages. During the days that follow, continuous employment to support the hard-fighting defense forces.

31 August 1943: Attack with two Tigers toward the high ground south of Kolontajew. The Tiger of SS-Unterscharführer Privatzki is knocked out by a direct artillery hit, killing the driver.

1 September 1943: Antitank-gun fire takes the tanks by surprise in their defensive positions. SS-Untersturmführer Quade is killed when the commander's cupola is sheared off. Only one Tiger operational. No officers left in the company; the company first sergeant is in charge.

3 September 1943: Employment near Kolontajew. The Tiger of SS-Oberscharführer Müller is knocked out; he is murdered by a Russian with a spade.

Total tanks: 18.

10 September 1943: Operational tanks: 4.

20 September 1943: Operational tanks: 5.

21 September 1943: The division finally receives the order to withdraw.

22 September 1943: Continuous engagements while fighting delaying actions to the south; fighting continued when moving west of Poltava.

25 September 1943: An enemy attack along the main road to Perepeliza and Point 102.3 is contained.

27 September 1943: Delaying operations across the Dnjepr near Krementschug.

28 September 1943: A detail is sent to Dnjepropetrowsk to pick up five new Tigers.

1 October 1943: Operational tanks: 5. Time for urgent repair and maintenance. The maintenance facility is established in Korissowka (northwest of Alexandrija).

3 October 1943: Arrival of the five new Tigers at Protopopowka.

Total tanks: 23.

5 October 1943: Operational tanks: 5. In the days that follow, the company is employed sporadically in screening positions along the main line of resistance.

7 October 1943: The company is assembled in Usbenskoje.

8 October 1943: Support of a counterattack through a side arm of the Dnjepr and capture of the Kolerda Peninsula. One Tiger suffers an internal main-gun explosion.

9 October 1943: An enemy penetration west of Tschikalowka is cleared.

10 October 1943: Operational tanks: 2.

17 October 1943: The division is directed into the area of Pawlysch-Onufrijewka as a reserve of the XI. Armee-Korps.

20 October 1943: Operational tanks: 4. A staging area around Iwanowka-Sybkoje-Losowatka is taken for a deliberate attack towards Popelnsatoje.

21 October 1943: The attack is postponed to the next day. Operational tanks: 6. The division forms an armored battle group because only a few tanks are available in the tank regiment.

22 October 1943: Assembly in Swerigorodka during the night. Starting at 1050 hours, assault across the Ingulez River near Alexandrowka with six Tigers. Advance to the area south of Iwanowka. At night, withdrawal via the Ingulez River near Tschetscheliwka. SS-Panzer-Grenadier-Division "Totenkopf" is redesignated as SS-Panzer-Division "Totenkopf."

24 October 1943: Mop-up of a previous day's penetration at Dewtschje.

26 October 1943: Some tanks receive new engines.

27 October 1943: The division is pulled out of the frontlines and assembled in the area of Protopopowka-Alexandrija. Operational tanks: 5.

28 October 1943: March via Alexandrija at 0300 hours. Contact is made with the enemy east of Alexandrija at 0800 hours. Counterattack at 09000 hours after Stuka preparation. Fighting positions occupied south and southwest of Golowkowka. Orders received to attack south the next day.

29 October 1943: The attack is launched at 0130 hours. Advance via Olimpiadowka on Malinowka (fourteen enemy tanks are knocked out). Subsequent attack on Woltschanka, where enemy advancing from Spassowo is dispersed.

30 October 1943: Advance on Nowo Petrowka via Woltschanka-Hill 181.7-Malaja-Wodjana. Operational tanks: 4.

31 October 1943: Departure from the area of Wodjana to the southeast toward Point 167.5 (via Werschino-Wlassjewka). Subsequent change of direction to the east against the ridge running from Hills 155.5 to 146.0 and to Graphit.

1 November 1943: Operational tanks: 4. SS-Obersturmführer Baetke becomes the new company commander.

2 November 1943: Attack on Marijampol (line of departure at Graphit).

3 November 1943: Advance continued from the area of Marijampol-Petropol to the northeast. Hill 138.8 is taken.

4 November 1943: A Kampfgruppe is formed in Krassno-Konstantinowka in reaction to strong enemy forces near Annowka and Iskrowka.

5 November 1943: Counterattack against the enemy east of Kopany. At sunset, only five Tigers operational.

6 November 1943: Covering positions occupied in the early morning.

7 November 1943: Relief by elements of the 76. Infanterie-Division and march into the area of Losowatka. At about 1600 hours, the company assembles at Bairak.

8 November 1943: March is continued.

10 November 1943: Operational tanks: 4.

11 November 1943: Company is given "decompression" time: Recreational activities, a movie performance and a sparkling-wine party.

13 November 1943: Assembly at Bairak again.

14 November 1943: Soviet counterattack across the main road Luganka-Wodjana to the west. At 1000 hours, the armored group, including five Tigers, counterattacks from the area of Baschtina-Bairak; nineteen tanks are knocked out. After destruction of the 32nd Guards Tank Brigade, withdrawal to Krassno-Konstantinowka. The commander of the armored group, SS-Hauptsturmführer Biermeier, is later awarded the Knight's Cross for this operation.

15 November 1943: In the afternoon, a counterattack is conducted north of Bairak; ten tanks are knocked out.

16 November 1943: Counterattack against enemy armor east of Krassno-Konstantinowka. In the evening, only one Tiger I operational.

17 November 1943: Artillery and mortar shelling into the base camp at Bairak.

18 November 1943: Two Tigers (one commanded by Weitner) are entrained for depot-level maintenance.

17–19 November 1943: No tanks operational.

20 November 1943: Only one Tiger I operational. Several enemy attacks are repelled near Krassno- Konstantinowka.

21 November 1943: One Tiger and three Panzer IVs support the 10./SS-Panzer-Grenadier-Regiment "Theodor Eicke" near Hill 164.9 in defending against enemy armor heading for Bairak.

22 November 1943: The two entrained tanks (see entry for 18 November 1943) open fire against approaching enemy tanks and force them to withdraw. Subsequently, they are transported to Snamenka.

24 November 1943: The division is ordered to keep its armor on alert as a mobile reserve (only one Tiger and three assault guns are available).

25 November 1943: Russian battalion-sized attack supported by eight tanks on Hill 168.4. The "mobile reserve" assembled near Baschtina counterattacks and destroys six tanks.

26 November 1943: Retaking of Krassno-Konstantinowk, which had been lost during the night.

27 November 1943: Support of a counterattack of the II./Grenadier-Regiment 203 on Owrag Baschtanka. At night, the company assembles behind Grenadier-Regiment 203 near the Gruska collective farm.

29 November 1943: Reserve in Nowo Gannowka.

30 November 1943: Only one Tiger I is operational. Counterattack with parts of Grenadier-Regiment 203 from Nowo Gannowka on Hill 151.7; 5 antitank guns destroyed.

1 December 1943: Still only 1 tank operational. Assembly area near Nowo Petrowka.

3 December 1943: The armored group—consisting of one Tiger, three Panzer IVs, and one Panzer III!—is located at Nowoyj, where it launches an immediate counterattack against a regiment-sized force south of Grigorjewka. After an abortive attack to retake Hill 179.7, an all-round defensive position is established near Hill 170.2.

7 December 1943: At noon, a counterattack is launched east from Dutschnyj as far as a hill 1,500 meters northwest of Petro-Nikolajewka. It advances against the flank of an attacking enemy force. Since the German infantry is unable to maintain contact, the assault is diverted to the southwest. A position in the Tschabanowka area is secured together with the rest of Grenadier-Regiment 534.

8 December 1943: Containment of strong enemy pressure from the VII Guards Mechanized Corps advancing from Scharowka south of the railway line and from the area southwest of Nowaja-Praga. Delaying actions conducted back to the area west of the Lenin collective farm.

9 December 1943: Delay to Woroschilowka.

10 December 1943: Operational tanks: 2. The company supports infantry elements in the area of Dolinskaja.

12 December 1943: Constant attacks by fighter-bombers. Seven Tigers depart for long-term maintenance and repair.

Total tanks: 16.

20 December 1943: Operational tanks: 2.

21 December 1943: Operational tanks: 2.

23 December 1943: Only one operational Tiger I.

24 December 1943: Rest in Gurowka. Christmas party at the Dolinskaja Railway Station.

31 December 1943: Operational tanks: 2. New Years costume party.

1 January 1944: Operational tanks: 2.

6 January 1944: The armored group—consisting of five Panzer IIIs, ten Panzer IVs, and three Tigers—receives orders from the field-army group to move to Ingulo-Kamenka to report to the LII. Armee-Korps. The armored group is attached to Kampfgruppe von Gusovius of the 13. Panzer-Division.

7 January 1944: Attack is started from the area north of Nikolajewka along the road to the north (passing Ribtschina in the west). It eliminates two antitank-gun-belt defensive positions to the northwest. At the third antitank-gun belt, the advance stalls. The Kampfgruppe transitions to the defense. 3 Tigers knocked out.

Total tanks: 13.

10 January 1944: No Tigers operational.

11 January 1944: Relocation to an assembly area near Bobrinez (arrival at about 1900 hours). The company is relieved from attachment to the LII. Armee-Korps.

13 January 1944: Arrival in Rownoje.

15 January 1944: March starts to an assembly area in Bolschaja-Wyka.

16 January 1944: Arrival at 0600 hours; attack with six Tigers towards Petrowka to Hill 215.6 at the southern corner of the woods north of Owskanikowka. Attack slows down in front of an antitank-gun position; four Tigers are knocked out by US antitank guns. Employment as a quick-reaction force of the XXXXVII. Panzer-Korps; assembly around the Petrowka collective farm.

Total tanks: 9.

17 January 1944: No operations; in the evening, sporadic artillery fire.

18 January 1944: Attack starting from Petrowka to retake the wooded area northwest of Wladimirowka fails.

19 January 1944: Redeployment to Nowo Ukrainka.

22 January 1944: Tanks stay at Bolinskaya.

25 January 1944: The springtime mud period starts; movement is nearly impossible.

29 January 1944: Counterattack with six Panzer IIIs, five Panzer IVs and three Tigers against Soviet shock forces approaching from area south of Petrowka and advancing against Hill 205.6 southeast of Wesselowka.

31 January 1944: Repeated attacks with four Tigers (line of departure at Petrowka). Contact is made with a T-34 company; nine tanks destroyed. One Tiger (Lachner) receives an artillery hit on the radio operator's hatch; the operator is badly wounded. Covering positions occupied in front of the town.

1 February 1944: Withdrawal early in the morning. Operational tanks: 4.

6 February 1944: No combat operations from 1-6 February. The company is alerted in response to an enemy threat. A crisis in the sector of the II./SS-Panzer-Regiment 3 is cleared up.

12 February 1944: No combat operations; strong snowfall hampers fighting actions on both sides.

19–20 February 1944: The Tigers are used to support adjacent elements.

25 February 1944: Redeployment to Wolschaja Wyka.

28 February 1944: Operational tanks: 4.

1 March 1944: Operational tanks: 4.

3 March 1944: The Russian main offensive is launched. The operational Tigers are sent to Iwanowka to form a Kampfgruppe. An immediate counterattack by four Tigers via Nowo Alexandrowka is launched in the direction of Wolschaja Wyka. The company commander's tank is hit in the gun tube; a "test" round ruins the tube. SS-Obersturmführer Baetke changes tanks. Despite orders to the contrary, he starts a relief counterattack towards Nowo Ukrainka and is killed by a hit to the cupola.

5 March 1944: Relief-in-place of the division and relocation into the area of Pleten Taschlyk-Slynka.

6 March 1944: The armored group (three Panzer IIIs, eight Panzer IVs, 4 Tigers) stays with the defending infantry until the last moment.

9 March 1944: The tanks are employed piecemeal and spread across the entire divisional sector (four Panzer IIIs, eight Panzer IVs and four Tigers).

10 March 1944: Employment near the Gurjewa collective farm and in the area around Alexejewka. Redeployment to Panzer-Grenadier-Division "Großdeutschland" in Iwanowka. The company moves there together with the I./SS-Panzer-Grenadier-Regiment "Thule" and the II./SS-Panzer- Regiment 3 (ten Panzer IIIs/IVs and four Tigers). Kampfgruppe Laavkmann is formed.

11 March 1944: Immediate counterattack with four Tigers into the Kwitka area contains an enemy penetration. Later on, blocking positions are occupied near Raskopana and Grab (North).

12 March 1944: Entrainment in Kapistino and Nowo Ukrainka and transport across the Bug River to Kriwoje Osero (via Perwomaisk).

14 March 1944: One transport is strafed by fighter-bombers in Pomoschnaja at 1400 hours during the movement; several tankers are wounded.

15–16 March 1944: Rerouting and detrainment in Balta.

17 March 1944: First employment of four Tigers in the new area.

21 March 1944: Several air raids on the rest area.

24 March 1944: The enemy crosses the Bus River, forcing the Tigers to pull back to Balta. A Kampfgruppe is formed under SS-Hauptsturmführer Pittschellis, which includes two Tigers. It forms the covering force.

25 March 1944: Skirmishes at the eastern outskirts of Balta. Kampfgruppe Pittschellis throws enemy elements back to Bendsari.

27 March 1944: Counterattack with three Tigers from the southern section of Balta and from the Balta Railway Station to the northwest.

29 March 1944: Another counterattack near Balta.

30 March 1944: Withdrawal to Kotowsk.

31 March 1944: Further withdrawal. Blocking positions occupied on both sides of the road to Jelissawetowka.

3 April 1944: Last elements of the division cross the Dnjestr River near Dubossary and reach Romania.

8 April 1944: The division receives the mission to assemble in the Roman area. It is attached to the LVII. Panzer-Korps.

14 April 1944: Railway transport in the direction of Tiraspol for battlefield reconstitution. All train traffic comes to a halt on the single-rail line; all tanks have to be blown up. The company assembles in the days that follow at Bacau.

Total tanks: 0.

30 April 1944: A detail is formed to pick up new tanks.

1 May 1944: Sixty men are air transported by a Junkers 90 aircraft to Belgrade; from there, they travel by rail to Magdeburg.

2 May 1944: New tanks that arrived for the II./SS-Panzer-Regiment 3—to include three Tiger Is—to reinforce a divisional Kampfgruppe near Costesti (northwest of Targul Frumos) in order to stop enemy assaults from Ruginoasa to the south. In the late afternoon, a counterattack is launched from out of the area south of Pietriscu and westward to the hills north of Helestieni. Defensive skirmishes until late at night. SS-Obersturmführer Neidthart takes over command of the company.

3 May 1944: Defensive operations against an enemy tank attack south out of Ruginoasa.

8 May 1944: Transport of new tanks departs Magdeburg and moves via the Carpathians through Transylvania (southeast Hungary). Delays due to rail line destructions caused by British bombers. The trains do not arrive until the end of the month.

20 May 1944: Panzer-Grenadier-Division "Großdeutschland" turns over two newly arrived Tigers to SS-Panzer-Regiment 3, as well as two others from its own inventory.
Total tanks: 7.

31 May 1944: The divisional armored group (twenty-four Panzer IVs and two Tigers) assembles northeast of Targul Frumos as a ready-reaction force. Six more Tigers are announced for delivery.

1 June 1944: Operational tanks: 2.

7 June 1944: By order of the LVII. Panzer-Korps, the division assembles the bulk of its tank regiment—twelve Panzer IVs and eight Tigers—and the III./SS-Panzer-Grenadier-Regiment 5 "Thule" near the main road to Jassy. The mission is to establish contact with Kampfgruppe von Knobelsdorff in the area of Sacra-Podul Iloaei. Two Tigers are delivered.
Total tanks: 9.

8 June 1944: After arrival, covering positions are occupied on Hill 173.0 south of Horlesti. Later on, the company is attached to the 24. Panzer-Division and blocking positions are occupied on Hill 177.0 northwest of Damian.

9 June 1944: The division is withdrawn from the bridgehead, but the armored elements are kept in position. Arrival of six new tanks from schwere SS-Panzer-Abteilung 103. The company stays in Bacau until late June.
Total tanks: 15.

1 July 1944: Operational tanks: 9.

7 July 1944: As a result of the disastrous developments in the area of operations of Army Group Center (Soviet's Operation "Bagration"), the division is ordered to move to the Brest area. Entrainment in Roman; transport via Radom-Warsaw.

16 July 1944: The company reaches Grodno with its ten tanks. After the detrainment in Osowice, it assembles in Mieleszkowce (southwest of Kuznica).

17 July 1944: Attack towards Grodno. 1 Tiger (SS-Untersturmführer Wenzel) is knocked out; the crew is killed except for the radio-operator. SS-Hauptsturmführer Fischer becomes the new company commander.
Total tanks: 14.

18 July 1944: Defensive positions occupied in Kilbaski in a bridgehead on the Njemen River. While recovering another Tiger with engine damage (SS-Unterscharführer Schulz), the company commander's tank is hit by a friendly antitank gun (4. SS-Polizei-Panzer-Grenadier-Division?); SS-Hauptsturmführer Fischer is killed.

19 July 1944: Support of the attack of SS-Panzer-Aufklärungs-Abteilung 3 on Sopockinie, which is captured in the late afternoon. One tank advances without cover into no-man's-land and is immobilized by several hits. The commander (SS-Untersturmführer Wessel) and crew are pulled out of the tank by the Russians and immediately shot. Operational tanks: 9.
Total tanks: 13.

20 July 1944: Counterattack on Kilbolki.

21 July 1944: Employment on the defense. Operational tanks: 2.

22 July 1944: No Tigers operational. Due to a crisis north of the 4. Panzer-Armee and the threat of a Soviet breakthrough to the Vistula River, the division is moved to the Siedlce area.

24 July 1944: Counterattack on Dubosna.

26 July 1944: Further counterattacks on the bridges at Harasimowitsche and Jazze. Five new tanks arrive.
Total tanks: 18.

28 July 1944: Entrainment of the heavy company in two train transports at Osowiec.

29 July 1944: Arrival in Sokolow.

30 July 1944: Some of the tanks are still defending against constant enemy attacks on Sielce. Elements not in direct contact with the enemy assemble east of Wyskow.

31 July 1944: Several crews pick up five repaired Tigers at the Prague Station in Warsaw and road march via the bridge over the Vistula to the Stauffer Caserne.

Total tanks: 23.

1 August 1944: Covering positions occupied at the east end of Milosna Street. Only one Tiger I operational. After the Warsaw uprising starts, the tank crews receive fire around 1700 hours and are issued orders to clear the way to the central military administrative offices near the city center. At the barricades, the tanks are pelted from all sides with Molotov cocktails, acid and handheld antitank weapons.

2 August 1944: The Warsaw Tigers break through to the airport, guarding a column of wounded personnel. During the ensuing street fighting, one Tiger is set aflame and another one is knocked out by a Panzerfaust. The remaining three tanks are sent back to the company and arrive there about one week later.

Total tanks: 21.

3 August 1944: Covering positions occupied west of Gozdziowka. Operational tanks: 2.

4 August 1944: Operational tanks: 3. SS-Obersturmführer Neidhardt becomes the new company commander.

5 August 1944: Two Tigers in covering positions south of Lesnogora; three T-34s are knocked out.

6–7 August 1944: No combat operations.

8 August 1944: Operational tanks: 4.

12 August 1944: Withdrawal in a westerly direction. Operational tanks: 2.

14 August 1944: No operations. Operational tanks: 4.

19 August 1944: Attack one kilometer southeast of Krusze.

20 August 1944: Operational tanks: 3.

26 August 1944: Defensive operations east of Radzymin. Soviets attacks on the salient near Klembow are hemmed in. During engagements around Radzymin, the Tigers of SS-Untersturmführer Neff and SS-Oberscharführer Weidner are knocked out; the latter Tiger is a total loss. While outside his tank, the company commander is killed during a mortar attack. SS-Untersturmführer Neff assumes acting command.

Total tanks: 19.

29 August 1944: Engagement near Dykow.

30 August 1944: Fighting along the road at Radzymin.

31 August 1944: Engagements near Ziende.

1 September 1944: Operational tanks: 6. Counterattack on Natna.

2 September 1944: Fighting near Czerne Struga.

10–11 September 1944: Employment at Hill 104.

15 September 1944: The company is attached to SS-Panzer-Jäger-Abteilung 3 near Josefow.

16 September 1944: Counterattack with elements of the III./SS-Panzer-Grenadier-Regiment "Theodor Eicke" and the 2./SS-Panzer-Jäger-Abteilung 3 on Rembelszczyzna and Hill 104. Heavy artillery shelling and the presence of strong enemy infantry renders any advance impossible.

17 September 1944: Early in the morning, the attack on Hill 104 is resumed; it is taken with numerous casualties to the accompanying infantry (only to be lost again).

18 September 1944: Heavy enemy artillery fire; the Tiger of SS-Untersturmführer Neff is destroyed by a direct hit (driver, radio operator and gunner are killed). Withdrawal behind the high ground.

Total tanks: 18.

19 September 1944: Third attack on Hill 104. In order to guarantee a swift retreat, the tanks climb to the top of the hill with turrets reversed to the six-o'clock position. At midnight, the tanks are withdrawn behind the hill.

20 September 1944: During the morning, the enemy infantry starts infiltrating the lines and outflanking the tanks; the company breaks out toward the German lines.

1 October 1944: Operational tanks: 6.

10 October 1944: The II./SS-Panzer-Grenadier-Regiment "Theodor Eicke" and six Tigers push back a Russian counterattack as far as Josefow.

11 October 1944: Counterattack with elements the I. and II./SS-Panzer-Grenadier-Regiment "Theodor Eicke" and six Tigers on Michalow-Grabina fails early in the morning. Four Tigers are damaged.

14 October 1944: Defensive operations between Lapigrosz and Kill 97. Operational tanks: 3.

15 October 1944: Engagements in the Josefow area; six enemy tanks knocked out.

22 October 1944: The company is relieved from attachment to SS-Panzer-Jäger-Abteilung 3; it returns to the tank regiment near Jablonna-Legjonowo.

30 October 1944: Operational tanks: 6.

31 October 1944: Operational tanks: 6.

1 November 1944: Operational tanks: 8.

4 November 1944: Operational tanks: 8.

5 November–24 December 1944: No combat operations.

17 November 1944: Operational tanks: 10.

1 December 1944: Operational tanks: 10.

24 December 1944: Movement order to Hungary.

25 December 1944: Movement to Osowice starts in the morning.

26 December 1944: Entrainment in Nasielsk/Zichenau and transport via Bromberg-Posen-Breslau-Vienna into the staging areas between Raab and Komorn. Operational tanks: 11.

29 December 1944: First elements reach the railway station of Komorn (west of Budapest).

30 December 1944: Base camp established in a Hungarian garrison near Komorn. Operational tanks: 11.

31 December 1944: Supplies received and whitewashing of the tanks. In the afternoon, orders are issued: An attack along the embankment road towards Nyergesujfalu is scheduled at 2100 hours on 1 January 1945. The company celebrates with a New Year's party.

1 January 1945: Operational tanks: 11. Assembly near Szöny. The attack is delayed but then commences, with the Tigers in the lead, on Dunaalmas, which is captured at midnight. The company commander's tank is hit; the commander has to change tanks. Due to minefields, further attack is impossible.

Total tanks: 17.

2 January 1945: The attack starts up again at 0200 hours. In a left pincer movement, the road behind Almasnesmely is reached at dawn. Sutö is taken afterwards. After crashing through enemy resistance in Labatlan, contact with the 96. Infanterie-Division is established in the early afternoon in Nyergesujfalu. After rearming and refueling, the Tigers follow the II./SS-Panzer-Regiment 3 in the direction of Bajot.

3 January 1945: Fighting around Bajna; several enemy tanks are knocked out. The Tiger of SS-Oberjunker Blau is also lost.

Total tanks: 16.

4 January 1945: After seizure of Bajna, the attack continues in the direction of Gyarmat Psz.

5 January 1945: Assault on Szomor in order to cover the eastern flank. Enemy counterattack is repelled after destruction of several tanks. 3 Tigers are lost.

Total tanks: 13.

6 January 1945: Operational tanks: 4. In the afternoon, a reconnaissance-in-force is conducted on Many. Two Tigers and a regimental Panzer IV are hit by antitank guns outside of Szomor north of the junction Many-Zsambek. All three tanks have to be blown up. Later on, in February, they are used as a squadron command post of the 3. Kavallerie-Brigade. Inside the company commander's tank, the left arm of the gunner (SS-Rottenführer Krippl) is pinned and has to be amputated without anesthesia by the battalion surgeon, all while under constant artillery fire. Tiger 901 is loaded on a rail car and transported to Vienna for depot-level maintenance.

Total tanks: 10.

7 January 1945: Operational tanks: 4.

12 January 1945: The offensive in the Pilis Mountains to relieve Budapest is suspended; movement into the area northeast of Veszprem (Berhida).

18 January 1945: The Budapest relief effort is renewed under overall command of the IV. SS-Panzer-Korps. The division moves with three Kampfgruppen from Küngos to the northeast. In addition to the nine Tigers of the 9./SS-Panzer-Regiment 3, schwere Panzer-Abteilung 509 is attached to the division's tank regiment. After a time-consuming clearance of several passages through the minefields, Sandorka is captured. Following this, defensive operations are conducted against enemy tank attacks south of the hills around Felsösomlyo up to the road to Szabadbattyan.

19 January 1945: The attack stalls in front of the Sarviz Canal after all attempts to seize a suitable bridge fail. A ford is found east of the Szabadbattyan Railway Station in the afternoon. Darkness and dense snowfall stop every offensive movement.

20 January 1945: Two Tigers operational. In the morning, the divisional armored group is diverted to the north near Seregelyes; it arrives in Dinnyes at noon and continues its movement towards Gardony using the southern embankment road.

21 January 1945: What remains operational of SS-Panzer-Regiment 3—six Panzer IVs, two Panthers, and one Tiger I—assemble southeast of Kisvelencze together with the I. and III./SS-Panzer-Grenadier-Regiment "Theodor Eicke." This Kampfgruppe attacks along Lake Velencze (via Kapolnasnyek) in the direction of Baracska with the I./Panzer-Regiment 24. Fierce resistance in Kapolnasnyek that cannot be broken completely. During the night, covering positions are occupied along the road to Baracska.

22 January 1945: Operations around Kapolnasnyek. All Tigers in Veszprem are in the battalion's maintenance facility.

25 January 1945: The attacks across the Vali River Sector are stopped; instead, a new offensive out of the Pettend area on Acsa is planned in order to destroy enemy concentrations north of Lake Velencze. This is to be done in conjunction with the III. Panzer-Korps. The rest of SS-Panzer-Regiment 3, the I./Panzer-Regiment 24 and schwere Panzer-Abteilung 509 assemble near Sz. Pettend as Kampfgruppe (Obersturmbannführer) Kleffner (commander of SS-Panzer-Grenadier-Regiment "Theodor Eicke"). Start time for the attack is 2200 hours.

26 January 1945: After midnight, Pazmand is captured despite strong enemy resistance. The attack is continued into the area northeast of Vereb and south of Val. Later on, defensive operations against persistent enemy assaults. The tank regiment commander, SS-Sturmbannführer Pittschellis, is mortally wounded during an attempt to enter another tank. Disagreement between the Commanding General (SS-Obergruppenführer Gille) and the Commander-in-Chief (Generaloberst Balck) about the continuation of the offensive in the presence of superior enemy armor. The regiment itself has only 1 Panzer IV, 1 Panther and 1 Tiger I operational.

27 January 1945: Transition to the defense; containment of a Soviet counterattack (XXIII Tank Corps), which is totally destroyed. At night, a withdrawal order to the railway line Baracska-Pettend-Kapolnas Nyek is issued.

29 January 1945: The planned relief of the division cannot be realized due to constant enemy pressure. All repaired tanks of the regiment—including five Tigers—take up positions near Gardony and repel enemy penetrations from the northern outskirts of Agg. Szt. Peter-Kapolnas Nyek.

1 February 1945: Operational tanks: 2.

4 February 1945: Operational tanks: 2.

6 February 1945: The gap near Janos Mjr is finally closed by four Tigers and elements of the 5. SS-Panzer-Division "Wiking." Wimmer's crew is sent to Vienna to pick up a Tiger coming from depot-level maintenance; arrival is not before 5 March 1945.

12 February 1945: Operational tanks: 2.

13 February 1945: Operational tanks: 2.

Total tanks: 8.

15–19 February 1945: No combat operations.

19 February 1945: Only one Tiger I operational.

20 February 1945: Operational tanks: 6.

24 February 1945: New defensive positions on both sides of Zamoly.

1 March 1945: Operational tanks: 6.

4 March 1945: Operational tanks: 2.

6 March 1945: Start of Operation "Spring Awakening."

7 March 1945: Operational tanks: 6.

8 March 1945: Hillside three kilometers east-northeast of Degh is seized.

9 March 1945: Assault via Huszar Paz. to a position north of Simontor, where an anti-tank-gun belt s eliminated. During the night, Fanes Psz. is occupied.

10 March 1945: Four Tigers employed near Fanes Psz.

11 March 1945: Operational tanks: 7. New company commander is SS-Obersturmführer Wenke. Operations around Simontornya.

15 March 1945: Operational tanks: 7.

16 March 1945: The Soviet counteroffensive breaks loose. Enemy artillery shelling on the assembly area. Five Tigers are in Magyaralmas; the rest are located northeast of it.

17 March 1945: Trains elements that are partially bogged down in Mor are wiped out by enemy infantry. Huge masses of infantry start an assault on the two tanks in position in the north; both Tigers have to withdraw. The other five Tigers are held in reserve after completing gun zeroing in Magyaralmas. One Tiger bogs down in the marshy ground during evasive movement and has to be destroyed by friendly gun fire. Operational tanks: 7.

Total tanks: 7.

18–19 March 1945: Withdrawal in the direction of Mor.

21 March 1945: A local counterattack on Kete (in the area of Kisber) by a small Kampfgruppe under SS-Untersturmführer Heidbutzki succeeds on the second attempt. Heidbutzki's attack is supported by two Tigers and elements of the 6. Panzer-Division.

22 March 1945: Defensive operations 800 meters outside of Nagyesztergar in conjunction with the remnants of the II./SS-Panzer-Regiment 3.

24 March 1945: Blocking positions established along the line: southeast of Bakonybel-hills west of Borzar-east of Koppany-Papateszer. Two Tigers operational.

25 March 1945: Rest of the tank regiment evades encirclement by the enemy by moving on the road to Marczaltö via Papa.

30 March 1945: A single Tiger returning from the Maintenance Company in Ritzing makes contact in Neutal with enemy forces approaching from the direction of St. Martin. The tank is later abandoned.

Total tanks: 6.

Parts of the divisions withdraw during the night towards the line north of Groß Zinkendorf (Nagycenk)-Holling (Fertöboz). During the withdrawal at Peresteg, one Tiger is knocked out.

Total tanks: 5.

31 March 1945: Relief attack of an armored group of the division (five or six Tigers and two assault guns) under SS-Obersturmführer Wenke. The attack moved from the Ritzing area towards enemy-held Horitschon, which is finally taken; seventeen enemy tanks knocked out. Subsequent withdrawal to the north.

1 April 1945: The rest of the regiment assembles in the area southeast of St. Pölten.

3 April 1945: The company is in Tross (near Krems). The crews without tanks are transported to Vienna to be used as infantry.

4 April 1945: The last tanks of the regiment are in action north of Götzendorf and then around Pitschelsdorf. With them are two Tigers (SS-Oberscharführer Tassler and SS-Oberscharführer Wimmer). On 6 May 1945, these two tanks have to be blown up.

Total tanks: 3.

5 April 1945: Withdrawal via Deutschkreuz-Wiener Neustadt to Baden. One Tiger (without main-gun ammunition) that is coming from the maintenance facility is attached to the 2. SS-Panzer-Division "Das Reich" in the area of Baden. No combat operations. One Tiger lost.

Total tanks: 2.

One repaired Tiger (SS-Oberscharführer Wimmer) is transported by rail to the company and covers the approach road to Wiener Neustadt for about one week; it then returns to the company.

7–9 April 1945: Return march on Judenau via Klausen-Leopoldsdorf-Pressbaum-Sieghartskirchen.

10 April 1945: Tulln and Langenlois are reached.

What remains of the company stays in the area of Rechberg until early May. The maintenance facility repairs two Tiger Is and also one Army Tiger II (commanders: SS-Oberscharführer Tönges, SS-Unterscharführer van Kerkohm and SS-Unterscharführer Privatski in the Tiger II). No combat operations. During this time, several Soviet M-4s (without turrets) are equipped by the maintenance facility with quadruple Flak and are employed by an Army unit.

8 May 1945: The three remaining tanks are blown up.

Total tanks: 0.

Surrender to US forces for the majority of the division in the vicinity of Pregarten; subsequent handover to the Soviets! Only a few soldiers manage to escape.

✛

During its combat period, the company knocked out more than 500 tanks.

COMPANY COMMANDERS

15 November 1942–20 February 1943:	SS-Hauptsturmführer Kanth
20 February 1943–19 March 1943:	SS-Hauptsturmführer Mooslechner (killed in action)
20 March 1943–12 July 1943:	SS-Obersturmführer Schröder
8–12 July 1943:	SS-Untersturmführer Köhler (killed in action)
12 July–11 August 1943:	SS-Untersturmführer Schüssler
11 August–1 September 1943:	SS-Untersturmführer Quade (killed in action)
1 September–1 November 1943:	no officer in the unit
1 November–3 March 1944:	SS-Obersturmführer Baetke (killed in action)
2 May–17 July 1944:	SS-Obersturmführer Neidthardt
17–18 July 1944:	SS-Hauptsturmführer Fischer (killed inaction)
4–26 August 1944:	SS-Obersturmführer Neidhardt (killed inaction)
26 August–18 September 1944:	SS-Untersturmführer Neff (killed in action)
11 March–8 May 1945:	SS-Obersturmführer Wenke

On 10 February 1943, the company was moved by rail to the Eastern Front. The tanks received a coat of winter whitewash. Note the divisional insignia on the rear of the truck in front.

SCHULZE-BERGE

The company was activated at the Fallingbostel Training Area in late 1942. At the time of this photograph, the tanks still lacked turret numerals. The Panzer IIIs had the divisional insignia painted on the left front of the hull.

VON KERKOHM

Prior to the recapture of Kharkov, the tanks were assembled at Tischnonkowa in early March 1943.

Even the tanks had difficulties in mastering the terrain. Panzer III 403 appears to be in serious trouble. BARTH

Tiger 411 of SS-Untersturmführer Köhler failed to cross a frozen river near Grijenko. The tank could not be recovered until April 1943. HOFMANN

In Mid-May 1943, the company was relocated to Jushny and started preparations for Operation "Citadel." The tanks were concealed next to the buildings and houses, and the crews took the rare opportunity to "enjoy" a field shower.

These two photographs give a good impression of the adverse weather conditions in the Krassnograd Sector in February 1943. The supply trucks frequently bogged down and had to be recovered by tanks. HOFMANN

Having been successful in the fighting in and around Kharkov and Bjelgorod, the regiment assembled in Mikojankowka during the last week of March 1943. The whitewash was removed, and the crews had some time to rest and conduct maintenance. VAN KERKOHM

During this period of relative rest, the crews found time to conduct some military "sightseeing," such as this inspection of a captured Lend-Lease M3 Grant.

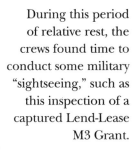

During the subsequent training period, many senior officers visited the Tiger units. This photograph shows the commander of SS-Panzer-Regiment 3, SS-Sturmbannführer Possmann, the future commander of the II./SS-Panzer-Regiment 3, SS-Hauptsturmführer Biermeier and the future commander of the Tiger company, SS-Obersturmführer Schröder, in conversation with two Tiger tank commanders, SS-Oberscharführer Baumann and SS-Oberscharführer Frank.

The Panzer IIIs were still with the unit, but the lead digit (indicating the company) has already been painted over. VAN KERKOHM

On 20 May 1943, the company road marched to Budy and continued preparations for the upcoming offensive. SCHULZE-BERGE

During the long railway journey to central Russia, SS-Unterscharführer Tassler and a crewmember make the best of their available time to operate the machine-gun ammunition belting device. HOFMANN

Nine brand-new Tigers were picked up in Germany to bring the company up to full strength.

There followed several days of rest at Budy. SS-Unterscharführer Lachner, standing next to SS-Sturmmann Molzschik, even found time for donning the correct physical-fitness uniform. HOFMANN

A strange way to conceal a Tiger! An Opel Blitz—a common two-ton supply truck—looks a bit different. Wooden signs like this were frequently used by advance parties to mark individual parking places for vehicles when entering an assembly area. HOFMANN

One of the company's Tigers after its arrival at Budy. The new tank still needs markings and camouflage paint. This is the Tiger of SS-Untersturmführer Kößler; it would become Tiger 911.

At the end of June 1943, the company relocated to its final assembly area before the offensive near Udy. All of the vehicles bear the divisional insignia used just for the offensive. The black triple bar has been painted on the right front of the upper hull of Tiger 923. BENEKE

A small net has been used by the crew of the Tiger 932 to aid in camouflaging the tank by breaking up its outline. BENEKE

The driver of Tiger 933 avails himself of a libation to lift his "spirits." VAN KERKOHM

A Tiger is a whole lot faster without its turret! The personnel of the maintenance platoon take a test drive after completing repair work. HOFMANN

Work on the tracks and the suspension was normally conducted by the crews during lulls in the fighting. HOFMANN

Working around the clock, the maintenance platoon managed to get most of the battle-damaged or mechanically disabled vehicles operational again for employment the next day. HOFMANN

Virtually every tank broke down during the fierce fighting, which meant that the maintenance platoon was constantly on the go. Within several days, these 18-ton prime movers had covered several thousand kilometers. BENEKE

The drum-shaped commander's cupola was a weak point in the design in the early versions of the Tigers. It was frequently sheared off when hit, since it was only attached to the turret roof with bolts. SS-Untersturmführer Quade points to a hit by an antitank rifle. The viewer is left wondering whether this hit occasioned a light wound and the eye patch he is wearing. HOFMANN

Shortly after the conclusion of Operation "Citadel," the company received eight Tigers from the 13./SS-Panzer-Regiment 1. Tiger 1313 is being inspected by its new owners.

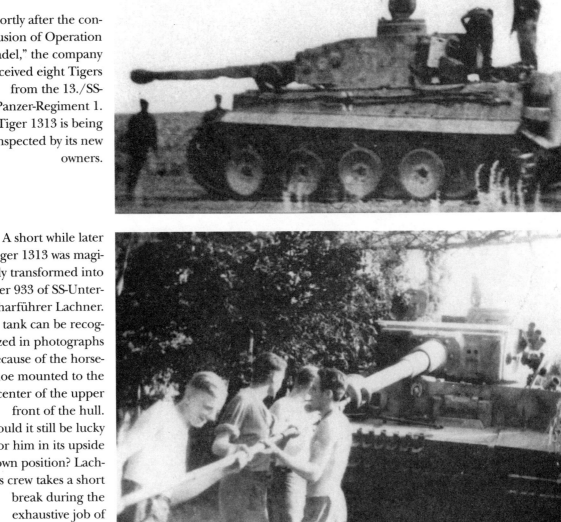

A short while later Tiger 1313 was magically transformed into Tiger 933 of SS-Unterscharführer Lachner. This tank can be recognized in photographs because of the horseshoe mounted to the center of the upper front of the hull. Would it still be lucky for him in its upside down position? Lachner's crew takes a short break during the exhaustive job of "punching" the gun tube. VAN KERKOHM

Several days later, SS-Unterscharführer Lachner's Tiger was in trouble. It was towed to a concealed position in a patch of woods, where it waited to be repaired. Maintenance personnel and crewmembers find time to pose for the camera. VAN KERKOHM

After Operation "Citadel," some of the crews had the opportunity to enjoy a short rest, such as this one awaiting maintenance personnel.

The operational tanks were then employed in the Bjelgorod Sector. The gun tubes have been marked with "kill" rings from Operation "Citadel."

SCHULZE-BERGE

Crews frequently placed shelter halves over gun tubes to form a tent to give them shade from the sun or to help keep inclement weather off them.

VAN KERKOHM

231M During the rest period, the crew finds time to enjoy the latest issue of "Ostfront" ("Eastern Front").

VAN KERKOHM

Tiger 924 also came from the 13./SS-Panzer-Regiment 1, as evidenced by the larger turret numerals. It was photographed in the Bjelgorod Sector on 20 July 1943. HOFMANN

The crews normally lived among the civilian populace. The primitive Russian huts were most welcome when the weather turned cold.

SCHULZE-BERGE

It looks as though something "fowl" is happening among this crew. Local foodstuffs were a welcome addition to the routine military fare.

VAN KERKOHM

SS-Unterscharführer Lachner seems to have retained his luck. His tank has been repaired and can be reported as operational again. VAN KERKOHM

At the end of July, the company was loaded on trains and relocated to the Mius Sector. The tanks kept their combat tracks on, speeding up the loading and detraining times considerably. MÜNCH

The 9./SS-Panzer-Regiment 3 was overstrength at the end of Operation "Citadel" and had twenty-two Tigers on its property book. A crew from the 4th Platoon can be seen enjoying lunch. VAN KERKOHM

Early autumn is always the harvest time. Being a farm worker back home, SS-Sturmmann Arthur seems pleased by the unique camouflage arrangement.

One of the two Tigers lost during the fighting along the Mius River. One of the crews inspects its burnt-out Tiger several days later. HOFMANN

A common sight after the heavy fighting in the Mius Sector: Tigers in a collection point for repair. Here we see SS-Untersturmführer Hadera, the platoon leader of the maintenance platoon, and SS-Oberscharführer Biermann, the leader of the recovery section, observing maintenance work on Tiger 922. The tanks still bear the triple-bar formation marking. HOFMANN

This Tiger negotiates a ford across the Bystraja River during the withdrawal to Krementschug in September 1943.

New Tigers arrived on 3 October 1943. They featured the new-style tank commander's cupola and were covered with the Zimmerit anti-magnetic coating.

SCHULZE-BERGE

This photograph of a new Tiger was taken at Protopopowka. The vehicles still need markings and camouflage finishes.

The early part of December 1943. The company, assembled at Nowo Petrowka, was surprised by the first snow and did not yet have its whitewash applied. KRIPPL

On 7 January 1944, the days of rest were over. During a counterattack north of Nikolajewka, the company lost three Tigers during the partially successful attempt to eliminate several antitank-gun belts.

The company bivouacked at Gurkowka in late December 1943. SS-Oberscharführer Lachner has decided to try out a new kind of "ride." KRIPPL

In the early days of March 1944, this crew found an easy, if messy way of obscuring its tank's whitewash - it simply covered the tank in mud.

VAN KERKOHM

In Mid-March 1944, the company was relocated to Balta as part of the operations to contain the Russian bridgeheads along the Bug River. This photograph was taken after the Tigers were rail loaded in Nowo Ukrainka, with the soldiers bundled up against the rain.

HOFMANN

During the rail movement, the weather improved somewhat, as did the mood of the crews. WAGNER

During this period, the company made the best of the alternating periods of freezing and thawing. They tanks received wooden placards, on which the turret identification numerals were painted. This eliminated the need for painting and repainting the numerals on the turret sides.

Another view of this rail movement. The crews were always finding inventive ways of finding cover from inclement weather. Here we see shelters at both ends of the tank.

This method of transporting a wheeled vehicle—straddling to flat cars—is quite astonishing. Any sharp bend would prove disastrous for the vehicle. HOFMANN

One of the Tigers employed in the Balta area in March 1944. HOFMANN

Pfiffi, the company mascot, appears to be intent on collecting hazardous-duty pay! HOFMANN

The company was assembled at Roman in early April 1944 and waited there for several days before being moved to Tiraspol.

During this period, the company renewed its camouflage schemes and vehicle markings. The Totenkopf (death's head) symbol of the division stands out on the side of this maintenance platoon halftrack. SCHULZE-BERGE

Even the mess truck has received a proper coat of camouflage.

BENEKE

The turret identification numerals were applied as white outlines, as seen here on the company commander's tank, Tiger 901.

SCHULZE-BERGE

Having lost all of the remaining tanks during the rail transport to Tiraspol, the crews were flown to Belgrade on 1 May 1944 on their way to pick up new vehicles. From there, the personnel moved to Germany by rail.

KRIPPL

Two sensational photographs show a broken-down Tiger in Warsaw during the time of the uprising. This Tiger was one of five picked up there at a maintenance facility on 31 July 1944. They were employed in operations directed against the Polish "Home Army" insurgents. ANDERSON

Several Tigers originally earmarked for the III./Panzer-Regiment "Großdeutschland" were received in May 1944. This photograph was taken during detraining operations. Of interest is the unique gun-tube rest on the rear deck that is fashioned out of wood. JAUGITZ

The majority of the new tanks arrived in June and July, such as this late-version Tiger with the cut-out front shackle arrangement. HOFMANN

An important part in the life of every soldier in the field: The company clerk has just arrived with mail for the crew of Tiger 911. VAN KERKOHM

During the following weeks, the company was employed in central Poland. These three photographs show Tiger 913 of SS-Unterscharführer Wimmer in an unknown assembly area. KRIPPL

The crew of SS-Oberscharführer Heimbruch maintains its two machine guns. KRIPPL

Tiger 923 undergoing maintenance in a small Polish village. SCHULZE-BERGE

9./SS-PANZER-REGIMENT 3

Vehicles on Hand/Deliveries

Date	Tiger I	Tiger II	On hand	Remarks
January 1943	9		9	10 Panzer IIIs (Model J)
10 May 1943	3		9	From the schwere SS-Panzer-Abteilung
20 May 1943	6		15	1 from the schwere SS-Panzer-Abteilung
29 July 1943	8		22	From the 13./SS-Panzer-Regiment 1
3 October 1943	5		23	From the 13./SS-Panzer-Regiment 1
2 May 1944	3		3	
20 May 1944	4		7	
7 June 1944	2		9	
June 1944	6		15	From schwere SS-Panzer-Abteilung 103
26 June 1944	5		18	
31 July 1944	(5)		23	
Grand Total	51	0		

Losses

Date	Losses	On hand	Remarks
21 February 1943	1	8	Evacuated for depot-level maintenance
8 March 1943	1	7	Evacuated for depot-level maintenance
20 March 1943	1	6	Knocked out
7 July 1943	1	14	Destroyed by artillery
31 July 1943	2	20	Destroyed by own crew
12 August 1943	1	19	Destroyed by own crew
30 October 1943	1	16	Knocked out by an antitank gun
3 November 1943	1	18	Knocked out
December 1943	?	?	Knocked out
1 January 1944	?	?	Knocked out
16 January 1944	4	?	Knocked out by antitank guns
14 April 1944	?	0	Destroyed by own crew
17 July 1944	1	14	Knocked out
2 August 1944	2	21	1 captured and 1 knocked out by a Panzerfaust

Losses

Date	Losses	On hand	Remarks
26 August 1944	2	19	Knocked out
18 September 1944	1	18	Destroyed by artillery
1 January 1945	1	17	Knocked out
3 January 1945	1	16	Knocked out
5 January 1945	3	13	Knocked out
6 January 1945	2	11	Knocked out by an antitank gun
6 January 1945	1	10	Evacuated for depot-level maintenance
February 1945	2	8	Evacuated for depot-level maintenance
17 March 1945	1	7	Destroyed by friendly fire
30 March 1945	2	5	1 destroyed by its own crew and 1 knocked out
4 April 1945	2	3	Destroyed by own crew
5 April 1945	1	2	Destroyed by own crew
8 May 1945	2	0	Destroyed by own crew
Grand total:	37		

Of the losses suffered by the company, 35% were due to self-destruction (to prevent capture), 55% were lost in combat operations and 10% were lost due to other causes.

4./ SS-Panzerregiment 3 – January 1943

S

401 **402** **403**

411 **412** **413** **414**

421 **422** **423** **424**

431 **432** **433** **434**

441 **442** **443** **444**

9./ SS-Panzerregiment 3 – 1 July 1943

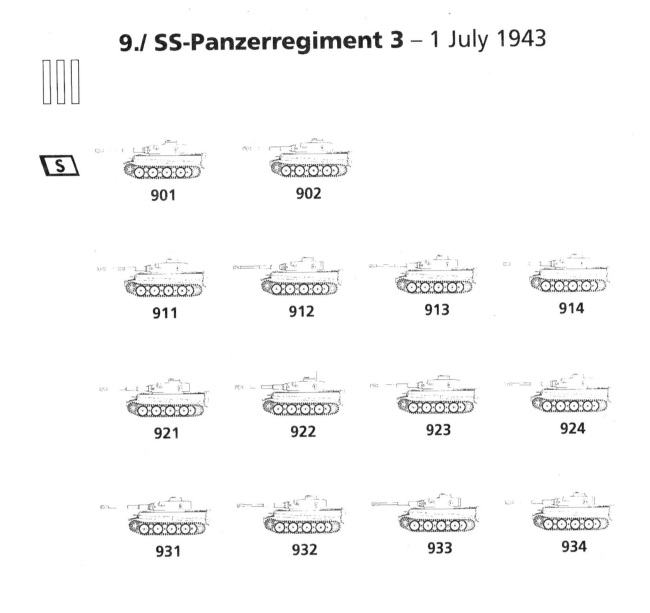

9./ SS-Panzerregiment 3 – 5 October 1943

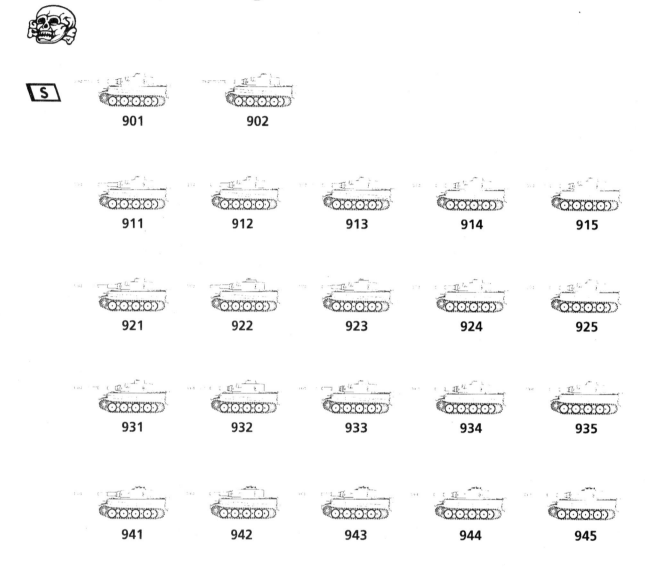

Schwere SS-Panzer-Abteilung 101
(Schwere SS-Panzer-Abteilung 501)

The SS main office issued orders for the establishment of a heavy tank battalion on 24 December 1942 (order: Org.Tgb.Nr. 8990/42 geh.). The two heavy tank companies of SS-Panzer-Grenadier-Division "Leibstandarte SS Adolf Hitler" and SS-Panzer-Grenadier-Division "Das Reich" were to be consolidated with the battalion to form two of its tank companies. The battalion was to be established at the Bergen-Fallingbostel Training Area.

Beside these two companies (KSt u. KAN 1176d dated 15 August 1942), the following units were to be formed:

- 1 heavy tank battalion headquarters (KSt u. KAN 1107 dated 1 November 1941)
- 1 heavy tank battalion headquarters company (KSt u. KAN 1150d dated 15 August 1942)
- 1 heavy tank battalion maintenance company (KSt u. KAN 1187b dated 25 April 1942)

The replacement battalion was to be SS-Panzer-Ersatz-Abteilung 1 in Weimar-Buchenwald.

The commander was designated as SS-Hauptsturmführer Laackmann.

✛

24 March 1943: The SS-Panzer-Korps receives orders from the SS Main Office to dispatch twenty tank crews to Paderborn (for five additional Tigers for each heavy SS-Panzer-Kompanie, three for the battalion headquarters and two reserve crews).

27 March 1943: SS-Panzer-Grenadier-Division "Das Reich" and SS-Panzer-Grenadier-Division "Totenkopf" each send 6 tank crews to Paderborn. The division commander of SS-Panzer-Grenadier-Division "Leibstandarte SS Adolf Hitler" refuses to carry out this order, because he prefers to keep his Tiger company. In response, the SS Main Office directs SS-Panzer-Ersatz-Abteilung 1 to provide the remaining crews.

April and May 1943: The SS-Panzer-Korps received fifteen Tiger I tanks earmarked for this battalion. The tanks were then divided among the three companies.

The original plans to employ this new battalion during Operation "Citadel" did not materialize. The three divisions retained their heavy companies. Later on, only the personnel of the Tiger company of SS-Panzer-Grenadier-Division "Leibstandarte SS Adolf Hitler" merged into this newly formed battalion, which was redesignated as schwere SS-Panzer-Abteilung 101.

✚

The battalion was established by order of SS Main Office on 19 July 1943 as a corps formation of the I. SS-Panzer-Korps. Two of the three companies needed to be established; the third company was formed from the 13./SS-Panzer-Regiment 1. The maintenance platoon of this company was merged into the battalion's Maintenance Company.

✚

19 July 1943: Establishment of the battalion starts at the Senne Training Area (South Camp).

5 August 1943: The new battalion commander, SS-Sturmbannführer von Westernhagen, is still absent on a training course and recovering from a severe injury.

23–27 August 1943: Relocation to the area of Verona (Italy).

15–25 August 1943: Twenty-seven new Tigers arrive, including two command tanks.

27 August-30 September 1943: Establishment continues in Reggio Nell Emilia.

6 October 1943: Establishment of the 3./schwere SS-Panzer-Abteilung 101 starts.

12 October 1943: Attachment to SS-Panzer-Grenadier-Division "Leibstandarte SS Adolf Hitler" and training in the area of Pontecurone (southwest of Voghera) with the assistance of personnel from SS-Panzer-Regiment 1.

27 October 1943: A detail is sent to Burg (Magdeburg) to pick up ten Tigers.

28 October 1943: The 1. and 2./schwere SS-Panzer-Abteilung 101 (SS-Hauptsturmführer Kling and SS-Untersturmführer Wendorff, respectively) are reassigned to the 1. SS-Panzer-Division "Leibstandarte SS Adolf Hitler," where they are consolidated and redesignated as the 13./SS-Panzer-Regiment 1. SS-Hauptsturmführer Kling is named the commander.

2 November 1943: Ten new Tigers that are already moving by rail to the Eastern Front are stopped in Lemberg (Lvov) and redirected to Paderborn.

5–11 November 1943: Movement of the 13./SS-Panzer-Regiment 1 to the Eastern Front, where it is allocated to the 4. Panzer-Armee (27 Tigers).

3–8 November 1943: The remaining elements—the battalion headquarters, the battalion headquarters company (SS-Hauptsturmführer Möbius), the 3./schwere SS-Panzer-Abteilung 101 and the battalion maintenance company (minus its 1st Platoon)—are transported to the Senne (North) Training Area near Augustdorf. Several Italian wheeled vehicles are now in the battalion's inventory.

9 November 1943: SS-Obersturmbannführer Leiner is designated the battalion commander until SS-Sturmbannführer von Westernhagen can arrive. SS-Hauptsturmführer Schweimert is given command of the 3./schwere SS-Panzer-Abteilung 101.

8 November–27 December 1943: Individual and crew-level training. SS-Panzer-Grenadier-Ausbildungs-Ersatz-Bataillon 1 provides the battalion with 120 soldiers. The misdirected ten Tigers finally arrive.

27 December 1943: Start of platoon- and company-level training. Due to the lack of special-purpose vehicles, full combat readiness cannot be established.

1 January 1944: The battalion's strength reaches only eighteen officers / eighty-three noncommissioned officers / / 365 enlisted personnel (full strength is twenty-seven officers /153 noncommissioned officers /419 enlisted personnel). Operational tanks: 9.

3 January 1944: A detail is sent to Burg to pick up another ten Tigers (of which two are command tanks).

9 January 1944: The detail arrives in Mons (Belgium). Due to a damaged railway car, one Tiger has to be left behind near the Belgium border and arrives several days later.

9–12 January 1944: Relocation to the Maisieres Training Area near Mons.

13 January 1944: Training is continued. The 3./schwere SS-Panzer-Abteilung 101 now has eighteen tanks (four platoons of four tanks each).

12 February 1944: Field-training exercise of the 3./schwere SS-Panzer-Abteilung 101, which is attended by SS-Obergruppenführer Dietrich.

13 February 1944: Arrival of SS-Sturmbannführer von Westernhagen.

20 March 1944: The crews of the 13./SS-Panzer-Regiment 1 return from the Eastern Front and join the battalion. Continuation of training and refitting. The 13./SS-Panzer-Regiment 1 is consolidated with the battalion and forms two companies: 1./schwere SS-Panzer-Abteilung 101 (SS-Hauptsturmführer Möbius) and the 2./schwere SS-Panzer-Abteilung 101 (SS-Obersturmführer Wittmann). The 3./schwere SS-Panzer-Abteilung 101 company transfers its 4th Platoon to the 1./schwere SS-Panzer-Abteilung 101 (as its 3rd Platoon).

3–4 April 1944: Relocation into the area of Gournay-en-Bray-Beauvais in expectation of an Allied invasion in the area of the Pas de Calais.

20 April 1944: Eighteen of twenty Tigers operational. Delivery of the rest of the vehicle inventory and twenty-five Tiger I tanks.

22 April 1944: Last elements of the 13./SS-Panzer-Regiment 1 that remained in Russia return to the battalion.

30 April 1944: Thirty-eight of forty-five Tigers operational.

10–17 May 1944: Live-fire exercise of the entire battalion east of Amiens. Redeployment to the former assembly area and continuation of the training.

1 June 1944: Operational tanks: 37.

7 June 1944: March on the D 316 to the road junction of St. Jean de Fronelles (via Gournay-en-Bray and Morgny. At Morgny, the 1./schwere SS-Panzer-Abteilung 101 is strafed by fighter-bombers. The march continues on the N 14 to Paris, passing the Arc de Triomphe to Versailles. The 2./schwere SS-Panzer-Abteilung 101 and the Maintenance Company are hit by a air strike near Versailles.

8 June 1944: The 1. and 2./schwere SS-Panzer-Abteilung 101 continue to road march via Verneul-l'Aigle. From there the 1./schwere SS-Panzer-Abteilung 101 proceeds via Vimoutiers to the area south of Caen. The 2./schwere SS-Panzer-Abteilung 101 moves via Argentan to Falaise. The 3./schwere SS-Panzer-Abteilung 101 returns to Paris and starts single tank movement to the west on the next day. Numerous strafing attacks by fighter-bombers.

9 June 1944: During the next few days, road marches are conducted only during the night due to the Allied air threat.

10 June 1944: The 2./schwere SS-Panzer-Abteilung 101 is strafed by fighters in Argentan. A short while later it is hit from the air again at Occagnes. 1 aircraft is shot down by SS-Unterscharführer Warmbrunn with antiaircraft machine-gun fire. The 2./schwere SS-Panzer-Abteilung 101 arrives in Falaise during the night.

12 June 1944: During the night, the battalion completes arrival in its designated assembly area, experiencing many mechanical problems and failures during the road march. The 1./schwere SS-Panzer-Abteilung 101 (eight Tigers) assembles eight kilometers northeast of Villers-Bocage on the N 175; the 2./schwere SS-Panzer-Abteilung 101 (six Tigers) assembles in a defile south of Montbrocq (two kilometers northeast of Villers-Bocage). The battalion is immediately ordered to cover the left flank of the I. SS-Panzer-Korps. Because of incessant heavy naval shelling, the crews cannot rest.

13 June 1944: In the morning, the 2./schwere SS-Panzer-Abteilung 101 (six Tigers; Lötzsch's Tiger has track damage) is assembled at Point 213 northeast of Villers-Bocage in a defile south of the road Villers-Bocage-Caen.

A detachment of the British 22nd Armoured Brigade approaches Point 213 and stops there. The British element is moving in column along the road and not deployed for combat. This element was attempting to exploit a gap between the 352. Infanterie-Division and the Panzer-Lehr-Division.

SS-Obersturmführer Wittmann attacks the enemy—a Squadron of the 4th City of London Yeomanry and parts of the 1st Battalion of the Rifle Brigade—ahead of his company, which is not yet ready for action. He uses Tiger 222 of SS-Unterscharführer Sowa. First, he knocks out a Cromwell and a Firefly of A Squadron, which had already nearly reached Point 213.

Afterwards, he advances parallel to the road towards Villers-Bocage. Passing within a short distance of the enemy, he destroys the majority of the 1st Rifle Brigade: thirteen M-3 halftracks, three Stuart light tanks, two Sherman artillery observer tanks, the Daimler Scout Car of the brigade's Intelligence Officer, the M-3 of the brigade surgeon, and more than one dozen Bren and Lloyd carriers (some from the antitank-gun battery).

At the outskirts of the town, he knocks out three of the four Cromwells of the regimental headquarters section of the City of London Yeomanry. Still alone, he enters Villers-Bocage, pursued by the fourth Cromwell, which intends to hit the Tiger from the rear. Inside the town, Wittmann's forward progress is stopped by tanks of B Squadron (including one Sherman Firefly). He turns around and rushes back along his route of advance. On his way back, he knocks out the Cromwell, whose two armor-piercing rounds fired at a distance of only fifty meters fail to penetrate the Tiger. After several hundred meters, the tank becomes immobilized from an antitank gun hit damaging the left front drive sprocket. The crew bails out and leaves the tank. It sneaks through to the command post of the Panzer-Lehr-Division at Orbois-Sermentot, which directs offensive action towards Villers-Bocage with fifteen Panzer IVs.

The remaining tanks of the 2./schwere SS-Panzer-Abteilung 101 occupy position east of Villers-Bocage (south of the road) and knock out two more Cromwells (SS-Unterscharführer Sowa) and three Shermans (SS-Oberscharführer Brandt). Approximately 230 British soldiers surrender and are taken prisoner. Eight Tigers of the 1./schwere SS-Panzer-Abteilung 101 (SS-Hauptsturmführer Möbius) attack at 0800 hours along the N 175 towards Villers-Bocage. Five Cromwells positioned farther north are damaged and abandoned by the crews. Several Panzer IVs of the Panzer-Lehr-Division positioned at Parfouru-sur-Odon join the attack. Two Tigers and one Panzer IV advance along the main road (Rue Pasteur).

The rear tank—Tiger 112 of SS-Oberscharführer Ernst—is knocked out by a Firefly of B Squadron, which fires through two corner windows of a building. After changing positions, a Panzer IV is knocked out by an antitank gun. The leading tank—Tiger 121 of SS-Obersturmführer Lukasius—is hit from the rear by a Firefly. These tanks are then set on fire by the British.

Five more Tigers advance forward on roads farther south. One Tiger is knocked out by an antitank gun in the Rue Emile Samson. Two more Tigers are immobilized by antitank-gun fire. Tiger 132 of SS-Unterscharführer Wendt remained at the outskirts of the village. During the night, Tiger 132 is in position on Hill 213. Four Tigers of the 1./schwere SS-Panzer-Abteilung 101 are positioned south of Villers-Bocage; the 2./schwere SS-Panzer-Abteilung 101 assembles again in the defile parallel to the N 175.

The 3./schwere SS-Panzer-Abteilung 101 reaches Falaise. The casualties of the battalion on this day amount to three tank commanders and seven other crew members. Three

Tigers of the 1./schwere SS-Panzer-Abteilung 101 are lost, whereas the British lose twenty-six tanks, fourteen M-3s, eight Bren Carriers, and eight Lloyd Carriers.

Total tanks: 42.

For his decisive influence on the course of the day's events, SS-Obersturmführer Wittmann is recommended for the Swords to the Knight's Cross.

14 June 1944: In an assault into the area of Villers-Bocage-Cahagne, the 1./schwere SS-Panzer-Abteilung 101 is tied down by concentrated enemy artillery fire.

15 June 1944: The 3./schwere SS-Panzer-Abteilung 101 moves into the assembly area near Evrecy. During the night, the 3./schwere SS-Panzer-Abteilung 101 (four Tigers) is hit by a heavy air strike. Almost all the Tigers are inoperative. The tank of SS-Untersturmführer Günther and another one burn out completely; another one attempting to evade the air attack tumbles into a defile, killing the crew. The turret of the company commander's tank is blown off. Altogether, there are eighteen dead and eleven wounded soldiers; among the civil population, 138 persons are killed.

Total tanks: 38.

In the morning, the 1./schwere SS-Panzer-Abteilung 101 launch an attack with four Tigers (including Wendt's tank) right into British forces attempting to escape. Five enemy tanks are destroyed, as is Wendt's tank, whose crew bails out.

Total tanks: 37.

16 June 1944: Four Tigers of the 1./schwere SS-Panzer-Abteilung 101 start a counterattack near Cahagnes; the leading tank—Tiger 111 of (SS-Obersturmführer Philipsen)—is set on fire by an antitank gun. After bailing out, the platoon leader is killed.

Total tanks: 36.

18 June 1944: The battalion is kept in reserve on both sides of the road Caen-Villers-Bocage; urgent needed maintenance is performed.

21 June 1944: The battalion commander is promoted to SS-Obersturmbannführer.

22 June 1944: SS-Obersturmführer Wittmann is awarded the Swords to the Knight's Cross and promoted to SS-Hauptsturmführer. (The award is presented on 29 June 1944 at Berchtesgaden).

23 June 1944: Several tanks of the 3./schwere SS-Panzer-Abteilung 101 under SS-Untersturmführer Amselgruber are positioned along the Route Nationale and repulse the British advance. They knock out five enemy tanks.

24 June 1944: Tiger 332 of SS-Unterscharführer Wanecke knocks out seven enemy tanks. Two tanks cannot be repaired.

Total tanks: 34.

26 June 1944: The 3./schwere SS-Panzer-Abteilung 101 parries the British thrust at the forest near Tessel and near Rauray (Operation "Epsom").

SS-Untersturmführer Amselgruber with another Tiger of the 3./schwere SS-Panzer-Abteilung 101 knocks out three enemy tanks near Grainville and stops the advance of the British infantry. Near Mouen, a single Tiger knocks out several enemy tanks of the 23rd Hussars. New positions are taken along the line Marcelet-high ground southeast of Cheux-Rauray-Vendes. Eighteen Tigers operational.

27 June 1944: On a reconnaissance mission, the tank of SS-Unterscharführer Warmbrunn is knocked out by an enemy antitank gun. The eighteen operational tanks of the battalion are scattered along the corps frontline.

Total tanks: 33.

28 June 1944: In the eventually futile attempt to repulse the enemy assault at Grainville, the tank of SS-Untersturmführer Amselgruber (Tiger 331) is finally knocked out after eliminating two Shermans on this day. The commander, in spite of a severe leg wound, stays with his men. SS-Hauptsturmführer Möbius knocks out six enemy tanks and is then knocked out himself. The remaining Tigers block further enemy advances at Verson and on Hill 112. In Rauray, one Tiger is knocked out.

Total tanks: 30.

29 June 1944: In the afternoon, a counterattack is conducted in the area of Hill 112.

30 June 1944: Hill 112, temporarily lost to the enemy, is recaptured.

1 July 1944: Eleven Tigers operational. From 1-12 July, the remaining operational tanks are employed west of Maltot. The companies have the following tanks: seven in the 1./schwere SS-Panzer-Abteilung 101, eight in the 2./schwere SS-Panzer-Abteilung 101, and ten in the 3./schwere SS-Panzer-Abteilung 101. In addition, the battalion headquarters has three Tigers.

2 July 1944: Immediately after arriving at the location of the 2./schwere SS-Panzer-Abteilung 101, the new company commander, SS-Obersturmführer Wendorff (Tiger 205), is knocked out near Hill 112. This tank is later recovered.

3 July 1944: The 1./schwere SS-Panzer-Abteilung 101 hands over its last three Tigers to the 3./schwere SS-Panzer-Abteilung 101 and moves back to Paderborn to be re-equipped with Tiger IIs.

5 July 1944: No tanks operational.

7 July 1944: None of the thirty Tigers operational. Two Tigers cannot be repaired.

Total tanks: 28.

8 July 1944: Operational tanks: 21.

9 July 1944: Operational tanks: 19.

10 July 1944: Assault northwest from St. Martin towards Baron. Operational tanks: 15 Tigers.

11 July 1944: Operational tanks: 13. Operations near Maltot-Eterville.

12 July 1944: Operational tanks: 13. Operations near Maltot-Eterville.

13 July 1944: The battalion is moved into the area around Grainville. The battalion commander, in a state of complete physical exhaustion, is ordered by SS-Obergruppenführer Dietrich to go on convalescent leave. Wittmann, back from leave, takes over acting command of the battalion.

14 July 1944: Five Tigers under SS-Obersturmführer Wendorff start a counterattack at Maltot. Three Cromwells are knocked out; one Tiger is damaged.

15 July 1944: Operational tanks: 20.

16 July 1944: Operational tanks: 19.

17 July 1944: SS-Unterscharführer Warmbrunn knocks out three enemy tanks.

18 July 1944: Start of the British "Operation Goodwood" offensive. The Tigers are concentrated around Bourguebus. In a counterattack west of Hubert-Folie and north of la Guinguette, several enemy tanks are knocked out. South of Soliers, a Firefly of the 5th Royal Tank Regiment knocks out a Tiger by firing right through a haystack.

Total tanks: 27.

19 July 1944: Scattered operations by the operational tanks. The commander of the 3./schwere SS-Panzer-Abteilung 101 is knocked out by friendly antitank gun and is killed.

Total tanks: 26.

The battalion maintenance officer, SS-Hauptsturmführer Heurich, takes over the command of the 3./schwere SS-Panzer-Abteilung 101, which is committed near Chichebouille.

20 July 1944: One Tiger of the 2./schwere SS-Panzer-Abteilung 101 is knocked out by the City of London Yeomanry. The 3./schwere SS-Panzer-Abteilung 101 is employed near the Ferme Beauvoir.

Total tanks: 25.

21 July 1944: Operational tanks: 6.

22 July 1944: Operational tanks: 7. The former frontline near the Ferme Beauvoir is re-established.

23 July 1944: Operational tanks: 10.

24 July 1944: Fourteen operational Tigers are attached to Kampfgruppe SS-Obersturmführer Wünsche south of Imont. The 3./schwere SS-Panzer-Abteilung 101 is in position near Garcelles-Sequeville with six tanks.

25 July 1944: Operational tanks: 14.

26 July 1944: In the morning, 4 Tigers employed against the 1st Royal Tank Regiment.

27 July 1944: Operational tanks: 14.

28 July 1944: Operational tanks: 20.

29 July 1944: Operational tanks: 21.

30 July 1944: Operational tanks: 20.

31 July 1944: Operational tanks: 19.

1 August 1944: Operational tanks: 20. Three tanks of the 2./schwere SS-Panzer-Abteilung 101 (SS-Obersturmführer Wendorff) in action near Grimsbosq. The tanks of the battalion headquarters and the 3./schwere SS-Panzer-Abteilung 101 are employed along the N 158. According to the monthly strength report of the I. SS-Panzer-Korps, the battalion has the following tanks: ten Tigers each in the 2. and 3./schwere SS-Panzer-Abteilung 101 and five tanks in the Headquarter Company.

2 August 1944: Operational tanks: 19.

3 August 1944: Defensive operations between St. Sylvain and Cintheaux. Operational tanks: 20.

4 August 1944: Operational tanks: 20.

7 August 1944: The 2./schwere SS-Panzer-Abteilung 101 is attached to the 12. SS-Panzer-Division "Hitlerjugend" to support it in defensive operations against the British Operation "Totalize" (employed near Grimsboq). Twenty-one Tigers operational. Grimsboq and Brieux are captured. The remaining ten operational tanks stay as a corps reserve in the area south of Caen.

8 August 1944: An attack of the 2./schwere SS-Panzer-Abteilung 101 is stopped by massive shelling. The tank of SS-Obersturmführer Wendt is knocked out, but it is recovered afterwards. The operational Tigers take up positions near Potigny and block the bottleneck Laize-Laison.

Kampfgruppe Waldmüller—consisting of the II./SS-Panzer-Regiment 12 with thirty-nine Panzer IVs, 1./SS-Panzer-Jäger-Abteilung 12 with ten Panzer IVs and ten Tigers—assembles near Retteville-Rabet for a counterattack on the Canadian II Corps.

Wittmann (in headquarters Tiger 007) and six other Tigers (SS-Untersturmführer Dollinger, SS-Untersturmführer Ihrion, SS-Hauptscharführer Höflinger, SS-Hauptscharführer Kisters, SS-Oberscharführer von Westernhagen (the battalion commander's brother) and SS-Hauptsturmführer Heurich) road march north as the spearhead along the N 158.

Several Canadian Shermans are knocked out. Right outside of Gaumesnil, the 3rd Platoon of A Squadron of the 1st Northamptonshire Yeomanry open fire from the flank. The only Sherman Firefly knocks out five Tigers and sets them on fire, there are but a few survivors. SS-Hauptsturmführer Wittmann and his crew are killed. About 1,500 meters north of this location, 1 Tiger of the 2./schwere SS-Panzer-Abteilung 101 is abandoned.

East of St. Aignan, three Tigers stop the advance of the Polish 1st Armoured Division; seven tanks are knocked out. Tiger 214 is knocked out near the Bois du Quesnay. *Total tanks: 18.*

9 August 1944: Operational tanks: 8. Assault of the British Columbia Regiment (Canadian 28th Armoured Regiment) from the area south of Cintheaux in the direction of Bretteville is crushed by Kampfgruppe Wünsche (reinforced by Tigers) near Estrees-la-Campagne in the morning: forty-four Shermans, two Stuarts, and one Crusader are knocked out. Among the dead are the Regimental Commander and 2 Company Commanders.

10 August 1944: Operational tanks: 17. Several Tigers of the 3./schwere SS-Panzer-Abteilung 101 repulse the renewed Canadian tank attacks and knock out a further thirty-eight tanks.

11 August 1944: Operational tanks: 11. The tanks are in an assembly area south of Quesnay as the corps reserve. The 2./schwere SS-Panzer-Abteilung 101 is employed north of des Laison near le Bu-sur-Rouvres.

12 August 1944: Three Tigers of the 2./schwere SS-Panzer-Abteilung 101 knock out seven Canadian tanks before noon. After nightfall, a counterattack is started against the enemy lines to relieve pressure on the defensive positions. This results in completely surprising an enemy tank company while refueling; it is completely wiped out.

13 August 1944: During the night, six Tigers of the 2./schwere SS-Panzer-Abteilung 101 move into an orchard southwest of Assy.

14 August 1944: In the morning, SS-Obersturmführer Wendorff is surprised by two Shermans on the march from Assy to Maizieres (to support the 85. Infanterie-Division), He manages to knock out one of them, but the other one fires at the Tiger and sets it on fire. The commander and loader are killed; the radio operator (Zimmermann) shoots himself when he is trapped in the burning tank and cannot get out.

Total tanks: 17.

SS-Oberscharführer Brand takes over the command of the company and destroys nineteen Shermans of the Canadian 6th Armoured Regiment (1st Hussars) attempting to cross the Laizon River near Rouvres.

15 August 1944: SS-Oberscharführer Brand and another Tiger are positioned on Hill 160 east of the road Caen-Falaise. The enemy takes the accompanying infantry by surprise and outflanks the Kampfgruppe. The Tigers knock out twelve enemy tanks and break out. SS-Oberscharführer Brand takes the disabled second one in tow. Six Tigers of the 3./schwere SS-Panzer-Abteilung 101 (SS-Hauptsturmführer Heurich) are in position southeast of Hill 180 and knock out several enemy tanks.

16 August 1944: A damaged tank of the 3./schwere SS-Panzer-Abteilung 101 cannot be ferried across the Seine River at Rouen and is set on fire by the crew. (It suffered engine damage on 9 August near Cintheaux.)

Total tanks: 16.

17 August 1944: The remaining Tigers assemble near l'Abbaye. After shooting down a Spitfire, the Flak platoon is destroyed on the road Vimoutiers-Orbec.

18 August 1944: One Tiger with track damage is abandoned in Livarot.

Total tanks: 15.

19 August 1944: Two Tigers support the breakout of the 3. Fallschirm-Jäger-Division from the Falaise Pocket. Two more Tigers detached to Kampfgruppe Olboeter knock out eight enemy tanks and clear a path by fire. In an assault of the South Alberta Regiment at St. Albert, one Tiger is knocked out by infantry in close combat. Three Tigers stop the attack of the 1/7th Queens Own.

Total tanks: 14.

20 August 1944: Six Tigers are employed with elements of the 12. SS-Panzer-Division "Hitlerjugend" south of Lisieux.

23 August 1944: The 2./schwere SS-Panzer-Abteilung 101 is committed west of Vernon.

24 August 1944: One Tiger is knocked out by an M 10 of the Norfolk Yeomanry eight kilometers north of Montfort-sur-Risle .

Total tanks: 13.

25 August 1944: Approximately ten Tigers of the 2. and 3./schwere SS-Panzer-Abteilung 101 reach the Seine River; two have to be blown up after final drive or engine damage (among them, the Tiger of SS-Unterscharführer Warnecke). While conducting reconnaissance, the commander of the 3./schwere SS-Panzer-Abteilung 101 is taken prisoner by the Americans.

Total tanks: 11.

Several Tigers are ferried over the Seine River at Rouen and Elbeuf and evade towards Songeons, but three of them have to be abandoned there later on.

Total tanks: 8.

27 August 1944: Three Tigers in action with Kampfgruppe (Oberst) Schrader of the 49. Infanterie-Division along the road Tilly-Vernonet. Tiger 221, in the lead, is knocked out from behind a bend in the road at close distance by a six-pounder antitank gun with the new sub-caliber armor-piercing rounds. It catches fire, which results in a total loss. A short time later, the second Tiger follows up, destroys the antitank gun and wipes out D Company of the 1st Worcestershires. The remaining British escape, panic-stricken. Because the German infantry does not follow up, the Tiger withdraws and is later abandoned.

Total tanks: 6.

28 August 1944: Counterattack by two Tigers of the 2./schwere SS-Panzer-Abteilung 101 (SS-Oberscharführer Brandt) at the Vernon Bridgehead; two enemy antitank guns destroyed.

29 August 1944: Both Tigers cover the retrograde movements of German ground forces and eliminate an enemy infantry battalion. One Tiger (ex-Kampfgruppe Schrader) is knocked out south of Tilly.

Total tanks: 5.

30 August 1944: In the morning and in the evening, both Tigers stop an enemy advance at Brunehamel, seven kilometers northeast of Rozoy. They knock out 8 tanks; lack of fuel causes both Tigers to be blown up.

Total tanks: 3.

During a march break, one Tiger of the 3./schwere SS-Panzer-Abteilung 101 is taken by surprise behind St. Quentin by a US Sherman and set on fire.

Total tanks: 2.

One Tiger I (old suspension) is abandoned at Marle.

Total tanks: 1.

One Tiger I is abandoned near the Bois Bourdon (north of Maubeuge).

Total tanks: 0.

+

THE CONCURRENT OPERATIONS OF
THE 1./SCHWERE SS-PANZER-ABTEILUNG 101

4 July 1944: The remaining three Tigers are handed over to the 3./schwere SS-Panzer-Abteilung 101.

5 July 1944: Road march to Paris, then to Strasßburg (Strasbourg).

9 July 1944: Arrival in Paderborn. Training on the Tiger II.

12–19 July 1944: Training given to commanders and drivers on the Tiger II at the Henschel Works in Kassel.

28 July–1 August 1944: Fourteen Tiger II tanks are in the Senne Training Area.

5 August 1944: Entrainment at the Senne Training Area and movement to the Western Front.

18 August 1944: Detrainment thirty kilometers northeast of Paris.

20 August 1944: The 1./schwere SS-Panzer-Abteilung 101 arrives northwest of Paris.

23 August 1944: Four Tiger IIs support a counterattack of Luftwaffen-Feld-Regiment 33 and Luftwaffen-Feld-Regiment 36 (33rd and 36th Luftwaffe Field Regiments) starting at

0600 hours near Guitrancourt; two Tigers attack south along the N 190 towards Issou; they then move in the direction of Limay. Porcheville is taken, and one M-4 is knocked out. Some time later, a Tiger is knocked out by the 749th Tank Destroyer Battalion. Two other Tigers attack Melier; one is knocked out by an antitank gun.

Total tanks: 12.

25 August 1944: Air strikes in the area of St. Souplettes; several dead and wounded. Two Tiger II tanks (with the Porsche turret) of schwere Panzer-Abteilung 503 are integrated with the company.

Total tanks: 14.

26 August 1944: The 1./schwere SS-Panzer-Abteilung 101 supports the counterattack of the 18. Luftwaffen-Feld-Division (18th Luftwaffe Field Division) west of Sailly against the Seine Bridgehead of the US 79th Infantry Division near Limay. After passing Vexin and assembling in the De la Montcient Valley, the attack starts at 1630 hours with two battalions of Luftwaffe soldiers (via Montgison). The 1st platoon advances via the Maison Blanche crossing near the Du Mesnil Castle; the 3rd platoon moves along the road Montgison-Fontenay St. Pere; and the 2nd Platoon along the road at Meulan. One of the Porsche Tigers has to be abandoned 200 meters in outside of Meulan after being hit continuously. Because of the heavy casualties sustained by the accompanying infantry, the Kampfgruppe has to withdraw.

The attack is resumed in the evening. The Tiger of SS-Untersturmführer Stamm is knocked out from the flank by an antitank gun at the D 913 when attempting to cross the road ditch; the commander is killed. One M-4 is knocked out near the Bois Claire. Further to the northeast, the last tank—Tiger 124—is attacked by fighter-bombers on the road Sailly-Fontenay St. Pere and tips over after two bomb near misses.

Total tanks: 11.

28 August 1944: Several Tiger IIs attack from Sailly towards Montgison; total loss of the leading tank after numerous hits. During the withdrawal east of Sailly, the Tiger of SS-Hauptscharführer Hibbeler is abandoned after being hit twice.

Total tanks: 9.

29 August 1944: Under the command of SS-Hauptsturmführer Möbius, the 1./schwere SS-Panzer-Abteilung 101 takes part in the counterattack of a Luftwaffe field division west of Magny-en-Vexin. An antitank-gun belt not identified in time immobilizes several Tiger IIs on the right flank. Two tanks cannot be recovered and have to be blown up. Tiger 104 of SS-Oberscharführer Franz gets in an engagement with some Shermans west of Magny-en-Vexin and suffers slight hits to the tracks. After targeting a farm house from a turnip field, the vehicle turns too tightly and the final drive is broken. The crew blows the tank up. While bailing out, the crew is fired at by French Marquisards, and two crewmembers are killed. Sergeant Roberts of A Squadron of the 23rd Hussars fires at the abandoned tank afterwards and reports the "kill." (This tank was evacuated to Great Britain and has been on display ever since at Shrivenham.)

Total tanks: 6.

30 August 1944: Tiger II 111 is knocked out by some British Shermans on the D 981 leading to Gissors.

Total tanks: 5.

31 August 1944: Operations near Lamecourt.

2 September 1944: Tiger 113 runs out of fuel and is abandoned in Jemappes in the evening along the Avenue Foch.

Total tanks: 4.

3 September 1944: Two Tiger IIs knock out several US tanks, forcing the rest to withdraw, near Brunehamel (seven kilometers northeast of Rozoy).

4 September 1944: SS-Hauptsturmführer Möbius gets as far as Huy (on the Neuse River) with 2 Tiger II's.

Total tanks: 2.

5 September 1944: Tiger 121 of SS-Oberscharführer Zahner is abandoned on the roadway near la Capelle due to a lack of fuel. The crew demolishes the gun, ignites the demolition charges in the engine compartment and abandons the vehicle. US troops push the obstacle from he road, and the tank topples over. (Today, it is on display in the armor museum at Munster.)

Total tanks: 1.

Only one Tiger II survives the Normandy Campaign. It was later entrained in Siegburg and transferred to the SS-Panzer-Ersatz-Abteilung at Augustdorf.

✚

In the fighting in Normandy, the battalion suffered more than 300 killed and missing soldiers.

✚

10–17 September 1944: Assembly in the area of Düren

18 September 1944: Movement into the area of Meschede.

22 September 1944: The company is relieved from attachment to the General der Panzertruppen West and then attached to the 6. Panzer-Armee. Consequently, it ends its habitual relationship with the I./SS-Panzer-Korps, thus resulting in its redesignation as schwere SS-Panzer-Abteilung 501.

The battalion personnel are moved into the Bielefeld area. SS-Hauptsturmführer Möbius assumes acting command of the battalion (the commander requires convalescence for an illness).

23 September 1944–30 November 1944: The battalion is reconstituted in a designated area southwest of Bielefeld. The Battalion Headquarters and the Headquarters Company are located at Schloß Holte; the 1./schwere SS-Panzer-Abteilung 101 at Oerlinghausen; the 2./schwere SS-Panzer-Abteilung 501 at Eckardsheim; the 3./schwere SS-Panzer-Abteilung 501 at Verl; the Supply Company at Wilhelmsdorf; and the Maintenance Company at Stukenbrock.

17 October 1944: Four Tiger IIs delivered.

18 October 1944: Six Tiger II's delivered.

12 November 1944: Fourteen Tiger IIs received at the Senne Training Area.

14 November 1944: The battalion surgeon, SS-Hauptsturmführer Dr. Rabe, is awarded the German Cross in Gold for exhibiting gallantry in battle.

17 November 1944: Temporary consolidated with SS-Panzer-Regiment 1 as its 2nd Battalion.

21 November 1944: SS-Obersturmbannführer von Westernhagen rejoins the battalion. SS-Hauptsturmführer Möbius commands the 2./schwere SS-Panzer-Abteilung 501; SS-Hauptsturmführer Wessel the 1./schwere SS-Panzer-Abteilung 101; and SS-Hauptsturmführer Birnschein 3./schwere SS-Panzer-Abteilung 501.

26 November 1944: Ten Tiger IIs delivered.

30 November 1944: Military District IX orders the creation of another armored Flak platoon for the battalion.

2 December 1944: Start of entrainment in Gütersloh, Arsemissen, Brackwede and Schloß Holte. Prior to the rail movement, schwere Panzer-Abteilung 509 had to hand over eleven Tiger IIs to the battalion.

Start of movement into the region Münstreifel-Zingsheim-Tondorf for the Ardennes offensive.

5 December 1944: Beginning of detraining in Zülpich-Euskirchen; base camps established to the south.

9 December 1944: The last elements of the battalion detrain at Liblau and Euskirchen.

13 December 1944: During the night, movement into an assembly area on both sides of the road Zingsheim-Engelgau; the headquarters is located in Tondorf.

14 December 1944: Briefing at SS-Panzer-Regiment 1, to which the battalion is attached.

15 December 1944: Briefings in the regimental command post and afterwards at the battalion command post.

16 December 1944: The start time is delayed; the battalion follows to the rear of Kampfgruppe Peiper and experiences numerous stops.

17 December 1944: At about 0900 hours, the junction of the R 265 in the direction of Losheimergraben is reached while moving on the R 421. Towards noon, Honsfeld is transited. A short while later, so is Büllingen. After passing Büllingen, the column is attacked by eleven Thunderbolts from the IX Tactical Air Command. One immobilized Tiger is later abandoned (25 December 1944). Because of bad road conditions, several tanks suffer final-drive damage. The march is continued to Thirimont via Schoppen, Faymonville-Ondenval into the evening. Some Tigers try to avoid the heavily damaged road and take the road to Engelsdorf (Ligneuville) via Heppenbach-Born-Kaiserbarracke.

18 December 1944: In the morning, the 2./schwere SS-Panzer-Abteilung 501, which is the lead company, reaches the crossroads of Baugnez. After dawn, it transits Engelsdorf.

About noon, the 2. and 3./schwere SS-Panzer-Abteilung 501 and the battalion command group pass through Stavelot. The 2./schwere SS-Panzer-Abteilung 501 participates in the attack at Chauveheid. In the afternoon, four Tigers of the 1./schwere SS-Panzer-Abteilung 501 are attacked by fighter-bombers when crossing the bridge over the Ambleve River at Stavelot. The company commander's tank—Tiger 105—is forced to take evasive maneuvers in Stavelot, when it is fired on by two antitank guns from the US 526th Infantry. While rolling backward, it gets stuck in a building and has to be abandoned. SS-Hauptsturmführer Wessel changes to the tank of SS-Oberscharführer Franzel and moves in the direction of Trois Ponts.

Total tanks: 44.

The other tanks remain at Stavelot; the spearhead reaches Trois Points and then heads north because of the blown-up bridge there. It transits Coo and La Gleize. As a result of mechanical damage, Tiger 332 has to be abandoned on the road Trois Points-La Gleize at the junction to Coo (See also the entry for 25 December 1944.)

Tiger 008 has to be abandoned near Trois Points at the St. Antoine farmhouse and is later rendered inoperable by the crew.

Total tanks: 43.

The march towards Cheneux is continued; due to the weather clearing up, a series of Thunderbolt air raids recommence.

The bridge across the Lienne River near Neucy is reached via Bahier. When the tanks approach, the bridge is blown up. The leading element has a short encounter with the US 199th Infantry at Oufni and is ordered to pull back to La Gleize after loss of several SPWs.

Due to the lack of fuel, several tanks have to have fuel siphoned off and are then taken in tow.

19 December 1944: Both tanks in Stavelot—Tigers 132 and 133—move in the direction of Trois Points and are attached to SS-Panzer-Aufklärungs-Abteilung 1 in Coreux. They take part in another unsuccessful assault at Stavelot; afterwards, they guard the battalion command post.

Kampfgruppe Peiper assembles for the assault at Stoumont and leaves the Tigers behind to screen at La Gleize. Tiger 104 is immobilized outside of La Gleize while engaging some US tanks; it knocks out one Sherman.

Tiger 222 of SS-Oberscharführer Sowa is knocked out in front of the approach to the bridge in Stavelot. The crew bails out.

Total tanks: 42.

Two Tigers of the 3./schwere SS-Panzer-Abteilung 501 are positioned on the high ground outside of Stavelot; both are hit by tanks of the US 823rd Tank Destroyer Battalion. One of the Tigers receives a hit to the turret, but it knocks out a tank destroyer on the opposite bank. Both tanks are recovered some time later.

20 December 1944: Several enemy assaults at La Gleize are repulsed. Elements of Task Force Lovelady (US 2-33 Armor Battalion), approaching from Roanne towards the junction of the N 33, manage to pass the position of one Tiger (SS-Untersturmführer Handtusch), one Panzer IV (SS-Hauptsturmführer Klingelhöfer) and three Puma armored cars at Moulin Marechel. The German elements were supposed to block the Trois Ponts approach; this worsened the situation of Kampfgruppe Peiper decisively. SS-Untersturmführer Handtusch was later accused of not having opened fire on the US task force, even though it passed within 600 meters of his position.

One Tiger supports the II./SS-Panzer-Grenadier-Regiment 1 in its attempt to cross the Salm River near Trois Ponts, but it has to withdraw after being hit by a phosphorus mortar round from a 505th Parachute Infantry Regiment element.

Tiger 133 of SS-Oberscharführer Wendt again supports the ultimately unsuccessful assault of the 2./SS-Panzer-Aufklärungs-Abteilung 1 outside of Stavelot. About noon, the second tank—Tiger 132 of SS-Oberscharführer Brandt—and some antitank guns beat back an enemy tank attack near Petit Spa; one enemy tank is destroyed.

21 December 1944: The defensive positions are pulled back to La Gleize. The bridge across the Ambleve River near Petit Spa—important as a supply route—collapses under the weight of a Sturmgeschütz IV.

22 December 1944: Towards noon, Tiger 334 and two Panzer IVs of the 6./SS-Panzer-Regiment 1 make contact with advancing enemy troops on the road to Borgoumont at Les Tcheus. After knocking out a Sherman, the Tiger is hit by a nine-centimeter antiaircraft gun, damaging the right drive sprocket. The crew bails out and escapes to La Gleize.

Total tanks: 41.

The tanks in La Gleize repel a series of enemy assaults, but they are fixed in place by superior enemy forces. Tigers 211 (Hantusch) and 213 (taken over by SS-Obersturmführer Dollinger) are knocked out after numerous hits. (Tiger 213, whose muzzle brake was shot off, has remained at La Gleize ever since as an exhibit.)

Total tanks: 39.

Tiger 133 advances toward the western edge of Stavelot in order to relieve encircled parts of SS-Panzer-Aufklärungs-Abteilung 1. During the second advance, this tank is accidentally hit in the turret ring. The driver's hatch is torn off, and the radio operator is killed. The driver, unable to communicate with the commander, turns the tank and backs up. The steering hydraulics lose pressure, and the tank is stuck in the road ditch. It is then abandoned.

Total tanks: 38.

23 December 1944: Since Kampfgruppe Peiper cannot be relieved and the tanks have neither fuel nor ammunition, the order to breakout that night is ordered.

24 December 1944: Beginning at 0200 hours, the members of Kampfgruppe Peiper move on foot to the German lines. In the village, two more tanks are abandoned—Tigers 204 and 231—on the road to Gue at Point K22. Tiger 104 is also lost.

Total tanks: 35.

25 December 1944: Tiger 332 is "knocked out" by a Sherman of the US 740th Tank Battalion, even though it had been abandoned by its crew some days earlier (see entry for 18 December). The tank was later recovered and shipped to the US Army's Aberdeen Proving Grounds. (It is now in the possession of the Patton Museum of Armor and Cavalry at Fort Knox KY.).

Total tanks: 34.

SS-Oberscharführer Wendt blows up his disabled tank and retreats across the Ambleve River near Petit Spa. SS-Oberscharführer Brandt, the commander of Tiger 132 is mortally wounded outside his tank by an artillery shell at Petit Spa. SS-Unterscharführer Otterbein takes command of the tank and fords the Ambleve River.

During the preceding days of the offensive, all the damaged vehicles had been collected at Engelsdorf. Tigers 111 of SS-Untersturmführer Henniges and Tiger 312 are abandoned. One of these two tanks was hit by a bomb from a P-38 near the Antoine Farm at the Petit Spa bridge.

Total tanks: 32.

26 December 1944: The battalion assembles in the area Petit Their-Burtonville. All the damaged vehicles are collected at Engelsdorf.

28 December 1944: The operational tanks (approximately 14–16) are moved into the area of Arloncourt-Harzy-Schimpach-Longvilly and are pooled as Kampfgruppe Möbius.

30 December 1944: The 1./schwere SS-Panzer-Abteilung 501 hands over all the tanks it still has and is moved to Oerlinghausen.

Counterattack of the 1. SS-Panzer-Division "Leibstandarte SS Adolf Hitler" with two Kampfgruppen (Kampfgruppe Möbius in the north) towards Bastogne. After reaching the road Bastogne-Martelange, the assault is stopped between Sainlez and Point 535.

3 January 1945: Repeated attacks against the Bastogne corridor. Elements of the 6th US Armored Division take flight. Due to lack of forces, this favorable situation cannot be exploited.

8 January 1945: The German front line is withdrawn. A Kampfgruppe that includes two Tigers remains behind to support the 340. Volks-Grenadier-Division.

Total tanks: 30.

10 January 1945: Withdrawal from the area Lutremange-Villers La Bonne Eau into the area east of St. Vith. Running engagements from Malmedy to St. Vith.

13 January 1945: SS-Oberscharführer Brandt is posthumously awarded the German Cross in Gold for fifty-seven kills.

15 January 1945: Operational tanks: 10. March into an assembly area around Blankenheim.

16–24 January 1945: The remaining tanks reach Brühl (mostly moving individually).

20 February 1945: The I. SS-Panzer-Korps is ordered to be immediately transported via Berlin to a yet unknown detrainment location.

24 January 1945: Entrainment of the operational elements in Brüggen and Brühl.

31 January 1945: Operational tanks: 19.

1 February 1945: Operational tanks: 23. The battalion (minus the 1./schwere SS-Panzer-Abteilung 501) is entrained at Brühl. As part of a deception campaign, it is transported to the area of Cottbus before moving on to Vienna and then Hungary.

8 February 1945: Operational tanks: 15. Detrainment near Raab (Györ).

10 February 1945: Beginning of the assembly for the elimination of the Gran Bridgehead. 6 Tigers of the 1./schwere SS-Panzer-Abteilung 501 and the trains rejoin the company.

Total tanks: 36.

12 February 1945: Operational tanks: 19. Detrainment near Raab.

14 March 1945: SS-Untersturmführer Amselgruber is awarded the German Cross in Gold.

17 February 1945: Panzergruppe "Leibstandarte SS Adolf Hitler"—including nineteen Tigers of schwere SS-Panzer-Abteilung 501—starts its attack at the Parisky Canal. Though the thaw causes the ground to be soft, the day's objective is taken towards evening after an antitank-gun belt is eliminated.

18 February 1945: A bridgehead is established on both sides of Gywa (Sarkan); after crossing the river, an attack is started via Sarkanyfal towards the high ground northwest of Muzsla.

19 February 1945: The southward attack is continued in the direction of Parkany, which is captured in the evening. Several enemy tanks are knocked out.

23 February 1945: The forces are reorganized for the elimination of the rest of the bridgehead.

24 February 1945: After a strong antitank-gun belt is pierced, Kemend can be captured and the rest of the bridgehead is eliminated. Operational tanks: 4.

25 February 1945: Start of the movement into the area of Komorn (Kamarom); the tracked elements are moved by rail to Veszprem.

3 March 1945: The main body of the battalion arrives in the new assembly area. Operational tanks: 4.

4 March 1945: During the night, road march into an assembly area southeast of Polgardi for the relief attack on Budapest.

6 March 1945: Operation Frühlingserwachen starts slowly due to the soaked ground.

7 March 1945: Assembly northeast of Ödön Puszta; advance past Kaloz towards the road Kaloz-Simontornya; Kaloz is captured.

8 March 1945: Assault continued; in the evening, the high ground north of Nagyhörcsök Psz is occupied.

9 March 1945: The advance gets stalled by an antitank-gun belt near Janos Mjr. The attack is then shifted towards the high ground north of Simontornya. Two Tigers are sent back for depot-level maintenance.

10 March 1945: Four Tigers operational (in support of the 1. SS-Panzer-Division "Leibstandarte SS Adolf Hitler").

11 March 1945: Operational tanks: 8.

11–14 March 1945: Engagements at the bridgehead established on the far side of the Sio River near Simontornya. (The Tigers were not ferried over the river). During the evening of 14 March, assembly in the area of Deg.

15 March 1945: Operational tanks: 8.

16 March 1945: Soviet main offensive in the direction of the narrow passage between Lake Balaton and Lake Velencese.

17 March 1945: Nine Tigers operational (in support of the 1. SS-Panzer-Division "Leibstandarte SS Adolf Hitler").

18 March 1945: The I. SS-Panzer-Korps is ordered to move into the area north of Varpalota and join Armeegruppe Balck. During the night, the march into the area east of Inota is started. Nine Tigers are operational.

19 March 1945: The assembly area is reached in piecemeal fashion. Several tanks have to be blown up because recovery vehicles are not available.

20 March 1945: Defensive fighting along the road Stuhlweißenburg-Veszprem not far from Inota. On the road to Varpalota, one Tiger knocks out fifteen enemy tanks.

The 3./SS-Panzer-Regiment 1, supported by two Tigers of the 3./schwere SS-Panzer-Abteilung 501 (SS-Obersturmführer Wessel), is involved in skirmishes east of Inota. Before midnight, a dash is conducted through the enemy-occupied village of Inota in order to break out towards Varpalota. Other elements are committed near Peremontor-Berhida.

The battalion commander, who has been worn down by illness, is relieved from his command. During the procedure of transferring command, there is an enemy air raid. According to the official statement, SS-Obersturmbannführer von Westernhagen is killed by an aircraft bomb. In fact, he shoots himself with his own pistol. SS-Sturmbannführer Kling is appointed the new commander.

21 March 1945: One Tiger II (SS-Hauptsturmführer Birnschein) is in action on the road Öskü-Hajmasker (oriented towards Veszprem). With the support of two Panthers, seventeen enemy tanks are knocked out. Initiation of delaying actions.

22 March 1945: Heavy fighting near Veszprem; the town finally has to be abandoned.

24 March 1945: Two Tigers of the 1. and 2./schwere SS-Panzer-Abteilung 501 (Staudegger and Stadler, respectively) are committed in the area around Marko; several enemy tanks are knocked out.

25 March 1945: In an air raid, Birnschein and Kling are wounded. Encounters with the enemy along the line Kislöd-Ajka-Urkut.

27 March 1945: Withdrawal into the area around Felsösog.

28 March 1945: N. Lozs is transited.

29 March 1945: March through Ödenburg (Sopron)

30 March 1945: Assembly in the area Hainfeld-St. Veit. During the retreat, many tanks have to be blown up. The surplus crews of the tanks are then employed as infantry.

Two Tigers under SS-Unterscharführer Eser remain behind in Neudörfl without fuel and ammunition. Two days later, the crews are shot after the Russians march in. The corpses were not allowed to be buried.

31 March 1945: Three Tigers of the 3./schwere SS-Panzer-Abteilung 501 reach the Reich border near Deutschkreuz.

1–3 April 1945: Defensive fighting in the bottleneck near Ödenburg. South of Mattersburg, several T-34s are knocked out.

3–15 April 1945: Withdrawal via Wiener Neustadt through the Traisen Valley into the area of Lilienfeld. The remnants of the battalion are consolidated with SS-Panzer-Regiment 1 as the II./SS-Panzer-Regiment 1. Crews having lost their tanks are engaged as infantry in the area of Wilhelmsburg.

5 April 1945: Five tanks left behind are taken over by schwere Panzer-Abteilung 509.

11 April 1945: Kampfgruppe Peiper is formed out of the remnants of SS-Panzer-Regiment 1 and schwere SS-Panzer-Abteilung 501. It is ordered to protect the Traisen Valley near Wilhelmsburg from Soviet assaults from the direction of St. Pölten and attacks into the flank of the corps in the Gölsen Valley along the line Hainfeld-Wilhelmsburg.

15 April 1945: Counterattack of Kampfgruppe Kling in the Traisen Valley. St. Georgen is taken back.

16 April 1945: Soviet assault originating from the recaptured St. Georgen at Wilhelmsburg is repelled; two Shermans are knocked out. A further assault from the direction of Ochsenburg is also repulsed; two more enemy tanks are knocked out.

17 April 1945: Kampfgruppe Kling wipes out enemy troops that had infiltrated Wilhelmsburg. Eleven enemy tanks are knocked out.

18 April 1945: Soviet forces outflank Wilhelmsburg on both sides. The encircled Kampfgruppe Kling breaks out and assembles near Rotheau. One Tiger (Staudegger) crashes through a bridge and has to be abandoned.

21 April 1945: Eschenau is recaptured.

19–23 April 1945: Engagement as infantry on Hill 621 near Plambach.

24–26 April 1945: Operations near Klein Zell.

27 April 1945: Infantry skirmishes near Klein Zell, Kalte Kuchl and Kirchberg.

29 April 1945: The remnants of the battalion assemble in the area of Scheibss, St. Anton and Neubruck.

2 May 1945: Approximately forty soldiers are sent to the Nibelungen works at St. Valentin with the mission of making six Jagdtigers operational.

5 May 1945: Two Jagdtigers march along the road Linz-St. Pölten.

7 May 1945: Both Jagdtigers reach the divisional command post at Scheibss. They are ordered committed in an advance towards Enns with some Panzer IVs. During the night, Waidhofen an der Ybbs is reached.

8 May 1945: The tanks are called back to cover the retreat from the Soviet forces. When crossing a bridge, one of the Jagdtigers loses a track and its skews off the road. The other tanks take positions at the edge of Waidhofen. From there, they can overwatch Weyer Markt.

9 May 1945: The Jagdtiger is placed right in the middle of the narrow street; it is blown up to barricade the road to Soviet armor. Disengagement operations across the Enns River near Losenstein. Surrender to the US Army in the area of Steyr.

✚

Operations of the elements of the 1./schwere SS-Panzer-Abteilung 501 that stayed behind at Schloß Holte.

30 December 1944: The 1./schwere SS-Panzer-Abteilung 501 is ordered out of the area of operations in the Ardennes.

31 December 1944: Oerlinghausen is reached.

6 January 1945: The company is ordered to pick up six Tigers at the Senne Training Area. The company commander, about half the crews, the field mess, the maintenance platoon and the trains head in this direction.

8 January 1945: The other half of the company moves to Schloß Holte. The palace has served as a base camp for the battalion since November. The rear-area commander is SS-Obersturmführer Schierke, who is no longer fit for frontline service due to the amputation of a leg.

19 January 1945: A few days after the tanks are picked up, they are entrained at Senne Training Area. They then have to spend several days in the Brilon Forest because of air raids.

Several days later, rail movement east begins: Dresden-Cottbus-Breslau. The entrained tanks and crews spend several days there. At the beginning of February, the transport to Hungary is continued; detrainment in Raab, where these elements rejoin the battalion.

Half the contingent that stays behind at Schloß Holte (and the recruits) starts training on the Tiger II. (This is the only tank that had made it back from France the previous September.)

9 February 1945: The tank crews are sent to pick up new equipment at the Senne Training Area. The battalion surgeon, SS-Hauptsturmführer Dr. Rabe, functions as the company commander while the tanks are picked up.

February–3 March 1945: Delivery of 13 Tigers. Entrainment and rail transport to Dresden—and then back! SS-Hauptsturmführer Dr. Rabe and some other officers join the battalion in Hungary.

12 March 1945: The tanks are handed over to schwere Panzer-Abteilung 506. The crews return to Oerlinghausen.

30 March 1945: US attacks reach the area as far as Beckum.

31 March 1945: The company is relocated back to Schloß Holte.

1 April 1945: A bicycle reconnaissance group with Panzerfäuste locates several enemy tanks and knocks out one of them. The Tiger II used for training purposes is made operational and moves under command of SS-Untersturmführer Henniges in the direction of Sende. At the railway station at Kraks, he is mistakenly fired at by an Army soldier with a Panzerfaust. Henniges and three members of the crew are killed. The rifleman deserts, and he is shot by order of the local commander several days later when he is found.

The knocked out Tiger II is made operational again and SS-Untersturmführer Buchner takes command with a new crew. It moves toward US tanks on the Autobahn. Some 500 meters east of the Elbrechter Farmhouse, he is fired at by a US tank and set on fire.

With the Americans approaching, the base camp at Schloß Holte is evacuated. The soldiers fight their way through as far as Seesen in the Harz Mountains.

Some even manage to get back to the battalion and participate in the final fighting.

+

In the one and a half years of its existence, the battalion knocked out more than 500 tanks.

BATTALION COMMANDERS

SS-Sturmbannführer von Westernhagen	19 July 1943–8 November 1943
SS-Obersturmbannführer Leiner	9 November 1943–13 February 1944
SS-Obersturmbannführer von Westernhagen	13 February 1944–20 March 1945
SS-Sturmbannführer Kling	20 March 1945–8 May 1945

KNIGHT'S CROSS RECIPIENT

SS-Hauptsturmführer Wittmann	Swords to the Knight's cross (22 June 1944)

TOP SCORERS

SS-Hauptsturmführer Wittmann	121
SS-Obersturmführer Wendorff	95
SS-Oberscharführer Brandt	57
SS-Unterscharführer Warmbrunn	57
SS-Sturmbannführer Kling	51

The crews of schwere SS-Panzer-Abteilung 101 waited for their tanks for a long time, Crew training started in December 1943 and continued into January 1944 after relocation to Mons in Belgium. The tanks still feature bright, solid-white numerals. WENDT

The 3./schwere SS-Panzer-Abteilung 101 had 18 tanks and used the overstrength vehicles to form a fourth platoon. In this photograph, we see Tiger 342 after it has broken down with a mechanical problem. The yellow flag on the top of the radio antenna makes it easier for the maintenance personnel to find the vehicle. WENDT

In the early days of April 1944, the tanks were prepared for rail shipment to Beauvais. Worn-out drive-sprocket rings were replaced and the transport tracks were mounted. WENDT

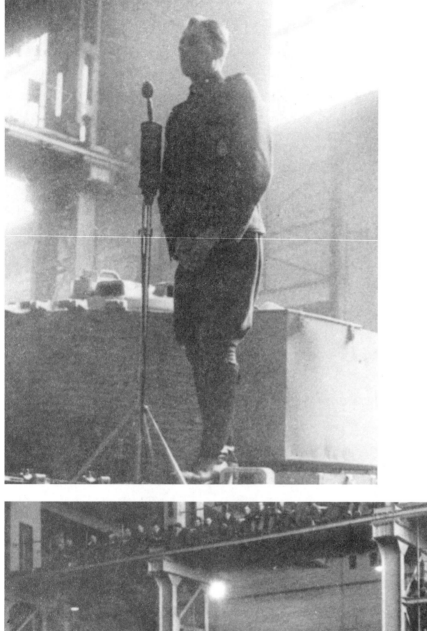

During this period, SS-Obersturmführer Wittmann performed some temporary duty in Germany and visited the Tiger production plant at the Henschel facilities in Kassel. Standing on top of a new Tiger, he addresses the workers and praise the superiority of this outstanding weapons system. HELMKE

This photograph was taken on 6 April 1944 and shows the tanks being rail loaded in Mons. These tanks were loaded with their combat tracks. WENDT

Despite the threat from the air, the tanks made several dangerous attempts to approach the front lines during daylight hours. STÜMKE

Operation "Overlord" started and the battalion was alerted.

Normally, however, the tanks "hid" during the day, usually using patches of woods as concealment against acquisition from the air. These unassuming photographs are interesting because they were personally taken by SS-Obersturmführer Wittmann. The author obtained them from his former wife, who now lives in northern Germany. HELMKE

The 3./schwere SS-Panzer-Abteilung 101 moves through Paris on 7 June 1944, arousing a great deal of interest on the part of the local populous.

This photograph shows Tiger 121 after Allied airpower had taken care of this small village some weeks later. IMPERIAL WAR MUSEUM

This photograph was taken just after the arrival of the 2./schwere SS-Panzer-Abteilung 101 at the front. The tanks are in good shape, a situation that would soon change. WENDT

Hill 112 in Normandy got the same reputation as Longstop Ridge in Tunisia. The fighting there raged with intense ferocity for numerous days. This photograph of SS-Untersturmführer Günther's Tiger 311 is certainly one of the most-published images of this theater of operations.

On 27 June 1944, the Tiger of the youngest tank commander, SS-Rottenführer Bobby Warmbrunn, was knocked out near Cheux. BTM

Two Tigers of the battalion headquarters section. Tigers 008 and 009 tried to remained concealed from aerial observation in a patch of woods.

This nice sequence tells of an action on 28 June 1944. Tiger 334 was knocked out at Raury. The Durham Light Infantry inspect the "beast." The wooden sign in the background—Achtung! Feindeinsicht! (Careful! The Enemy can observe!)—should have warned the tank commander. Below, a German sniper is being taken to the rear after capture. IWM

The British infantry advance with caution and seek cover behind the hull of the knocked-out Sherman in front of the Tiger. Its turret had been ripped off by a direct hit from the 8.8-centimeter main gun of the Tiger. The intact Shermans continue their movement towards Tilly sur Seulles, while covering each other. Bren carriers of the 2nd Battalion Kensingtons join in the movement. IWM

Several days later, the knocked out Tiger is inspected by senior officers. Later on, it was collected with other captured vehicles, such as this Panther. IWM

By early July 1944, the 1./schwere SS-Panzer-Abteilung 101 was combat ineffective. Its remaining tanks were taken over by the 3./schwere SS-Panzer-Abteilung 101. This French woman is perhaps astonished by the fact that the crew did such a sloppy job in changing the turret numerals from 121 to 324. RESTAYN

This heavily battered Tiger of the 2./schwere SS-Panzer-Abteilung 101 was towed into a concealed position behind a building, but it finally had to be abandoned. BTM

This Tiger, formerly of the 1./schwere SS-Panzer-Abteilung 101—the small rhomboid on the right front hull has been painted over—tows a fellow tank through a small village scattered with debris.

An indispensable photograph—the wreck of Tiger 007, which became the fiery grave of SS-Hauptsturmführer Wittmann near Gaumesnil on 8 August 1944.

Many tanks suffered mechanical failure due to the long periods of combat operations and the resulting lack of maintenance. They were often simply abandoned, such as Tiger 211 seen here.

Only a few tanks made it to the Seine River. Tiger 332 is seen at Elbeuf at the end of August 1944. Since no bridge was available, the tank had to be blown up.

Tiger 221 was knocked out by a 6-pounder antitank gun probably firing sub-caliber munitions on 27 August 1944, while supporting a counterattack near Gisors. GRUBB

The 1./schwere SS-Panzer-Abteilung 101 was reequipped with Tiger II tanks. This photograph is of Tiger 105, which never did reestablish contact with the battalion. BOXBERGER

Only a few tanks managed to cross the river. This Tiger of the 2./schwere SS-Panzer-Abteilung 101 moves through Rouen, still burning from the recent bombing.

Tiger 104 was abandoned by its crew west of Magny en Vexinon 29 August 1944. It was recovered by the British and is now on display at Shrivenham.

Tiger 111 was knocked out by British Shermans on the D981 near Gisors. After a short inspection and "photo opportunity" by the victors, the tank's tracks were removed and the road obstacle was pushed (or pulled) out of the way. GEMOB

The tanks saw only limited action during the final days of August 1944, when they were employed in an effort to eliminate the US bridgeheads over the seine River in the vicinity of Limay. This tank was knocked out by a hit through the gun mantlet. The hull proved impervious to the preceding hits.

GEMOB

Tiger 113 passing through Beauvais at the end of August 1944. It ran out of fuel at Jemappes and was abandoned there on 2 September 1944. GEMOB/DE MEYER

This is the Tiger that managed to get the furthest east of all the battalion's tanks. The location is the Bois Bourdon in southwest Belgium. DE MEYER

The roads in northern France and Belgium were littered with the abandoned vehicles. This Tiger of the 3./schwere SS-Panzer-Abteilung 101 remained at this spot at Marle for a long time. Note the absence of markings!

The location of this Tiger II, which still has tow cables attached to it, is unknown.

The initial attacks fared well, and long columns of demoralized GIs were passed by the Tigers.

The reconstituted and redesignated battalion—schwere SS-Panzer-Abteilung 501—took part in the Ardennes Offensive. Tiger 008 is seen entering Tondorf on 13 December 1944. The letter G painted on the front slope of the tank indicates that this vehicle was only allowed to use March Route G. This was a common method of controlling traffic flow in the rear combat zone.

Tiger 105 was the battalion's first loss (18 December 1944). It got stuck in debris on the Rue St. Emilon at Stavelot. BOTH—DE MEYER

Tiger 008—still with the G route marking on the front hull—got as far as Born, where it suffered final-drive problems and was abandoned by the crew. They chose the simple way of disabling the main gun. They opened the air-bleed valve of the recuperator and fired a final round. DE MEYER

This Tiger, also marked with a G on its front slope, still seems to be in running order.

Despite early setbacks, the German forces had high hopes, like these paratroopers catching a ride on the rear deck of a Tiger II.

The following sequence of photographs shows the fate of Tiger 332, which was abandoned near Bourgoument. The first image shows a member of the ordnance evacuation team posing in front of the tank. The vehicle has been prepared for recovery. The shackles have been removed, and the towing cables of the retriever will be used in stead. The tank was then winched onto the low boy, which almost wrecked it due to the tank far exceed-

ing the rated carrying capacity. Several tires blew out due to the stress, but the transporter finally arrived at Spa, where the Tiger II awaited shipment to the USA. After its arrival, it was cut open and put on display. It was later returned to Germany, where it is currently on display at the Panzermuseum at Munster. PATTON MUSEUM OF ARMOR AT FORT KNOX, KENTUCKY

SS-Oberscharführer Sowa's Tiger 222 was knocked out just in front of the bridge over the Amblève at Stavelot. DE MEYER

Tiger 204 ran out of fuel and was then driven for several miles by US soldiers until the engine overheated on a steep hill outside of Ruy.

This grim shot shows the remains of SS-Oberscharführer Wendt's Tiger 133. It was blown up by its crew west of Stavelot.

DE MEYER

Tiger 334 knocked out an M4A1 (76) near Bourgemont and was them immobilized by a 9-centimeter hit to the right drive sprocket. This marks the most westerly advance by schwere SS-Panzer-Abteilung 501.

DE MEYER

This photograph shows the "US crew" during the tank's short movement uphill. PATTON MUSEUM OF ARMOR AT FORT KNOX, KENTUCKY

Two Tigers remained at the center of La Gleize. This series tells the story of Tiger 213, which was commanded by SS-Obersturmführer Dollinger. The tank was positioned beside a building, where it was hit several times. One of the hits sheared off the forward end of the gun tube, which put an end to the tank's combat career. The vehicle remained in the village for several years before it was towed in front of a World War II museum. Later on, it received a new "main gun" made out of wood. Its tracks were also fixed, but the vehicle received a terrible paint job.

Tiger 211 of SS-Untersturmführer Hantusch lost its right track after numerous hits. The GI's who were passing by on 23 December 1944 were still wary and tossed in a hand grenade. Several days later, it was pulled up the steep road and then used as a target for bazooka training. In the springtime, the vehicle was still an attraction for the local populace.

DE MEYER

Tiger 211 was knocked out by a Sherman at the Wérimount Farm near La Gleize on 22 December 1944.
DE MEYER

Tiger 312 was abandoned in late December 1944 west of Engelsdorf. The tank was claimed as a "kill" by the US 628th Tank Destroyer Battalion.

Tiger 312 seen in the springtime of 1945.

This rusting Tiger of schwere SS-Panzer-Abteilung 501 rested somewhere near a small town in northwest Hungary. PAPENFUß

There are only a few photographs available of the final employment of the Tigers in Hungary and Austria. This abandoned or knocked out Tiger is being photographed by Soviet propaganda personnel. PAPENFUß

In mid-January 1945, the battalion was assembled near Blankenheim, where this winter scene with the Tiger of SS-Unterscharführer Markewitz (2./schwere SS-Panzer-Abteilung 501) was photographed. WENDT

This photograph shows one of the Jagdtiger tank destroyers that was manned by crews from schwere SS-Panzer-Abteilung 501. It was abandoned at Strengberg, where Soviet and US soldiers established contact. DE MEYER

SCHWERE SS-PANZER-ABTEILUNG 101 (501)

Vehicles on Hand/Deliveries

Date	Tiger I	Tiger II	On hand	Remarks
29 October 1943	10		10	
January 1944	10		20	1 from the Japanese purchase that could not be delivered
April 1944	25		45	
28 July 1944		5		1./schwere SS-Panzer-Abteilung 101
31 July 1944		2		1./schwere SS-Panzer-Abteilung 101
1 August 1944		7	14	1./schwere SS-Panzer-Abteilung 101
17 October 1944		4	4	
18 October 1944		2	6	
11 November 1944		8	14	
26 November 1944		8	22	
28 November 1944		4	26	
1 December 1944		5	31	
3 December 1944		3	34	
4 December 1944		11	45	
26 January 1945		6	36	
3 March 1945		13		
12 March 1945		-13		To schwere Panzer-Abteilung 506
5 April 1945		-5		To schwere Panzer-Abteilung 509
5 May 1945				2 Jagdtigers
Grand Total	45	60		

Losses

Date	Losses	On hand	Remarks
13 June 1944	3	42	1 knocked out by a Firefly; 2 knocked out by antitank guns
15 June 1944	4	38	Air raid
15 June 1944	1	37	Knocked out
16 June 1944	1	36	Knocked out by an antitank gun
24 June 1944	2	34	Cannot be repaired
27 June 1944	1	33	Knocked out by an antitank gun
28 June 1944	3	30	Knocked out
7 July 1944	2	28	Cannot be repaired
18 July 1944	1	27	Knocked out by a Firefly
19 July 1944	1	26	Knocked out by a Pak
20 July 1944	1	25	Knocked out
8 August 1944	7	18	5 knocked out by a Firefly; 1 abandoned; 1 ?
14 August 1944	1	17	Knocked out by a Sherman
16 August 1944	1	16	Destroyed by own crew
18 August 1944	1	15	Abandoned
19 August 1944	1	14	Destroyed by infantry
24 August 1944	1	13	Knocked out by an M 10
25 August 1944	5	8	Destroyed by own crew
27 August 1944	2	6	1 knocked out by a 6-pounder antitank gun and 1 abandoned
29 August 1944	1	5	Knocked out
30 August 1944	5	0	Destroyed by own crew (1 knocked out)

1./schwere SS-Panzer-Abteilung 101

Date	Losses	On hand	Remarks
23 August 1944	2	12	1 knocked out by an M 10 and 1 knocked out by an antitank gun
26 August 1944	3	11	Knocked out (1 by a fighter-bomber)
28 August 1944	2	9	Knocked out
29 August 1944	3	6	Destroyed by own crew
30 August 1944	1	5	Knocked out by Shermans
2 September 1944	1	4	Abandoned
4 September 1944	2	2	Destroyed by own crew
5 September 1944	1	1	Destroyed by own crew

Losses

Date	Losses	On hand	Remarks
schwere SS-Panzer-Abteilung 501			
18 December 1944	2	43	1 knocked out and 1 destroyed by own crew
19 December 1944	1	42	Knocked out
22 December 1944	4	38	Knocked out
24 December 1944	3	35	Destroyed by own crew
25 December 1944	2	30	Destroyed by own crew
8 January 1945	2	30	Destroyed by own crew
February–May 1945	32		Details unknown
Grand total:	107		

Of the losses suffered by the battalion, 31% were due to self-destruction (to prevent capture), 67% were lost in combat operations and 2% were lost due to other causes.

Schwere SS-Panzerabteilung 101 – 9 January 1944

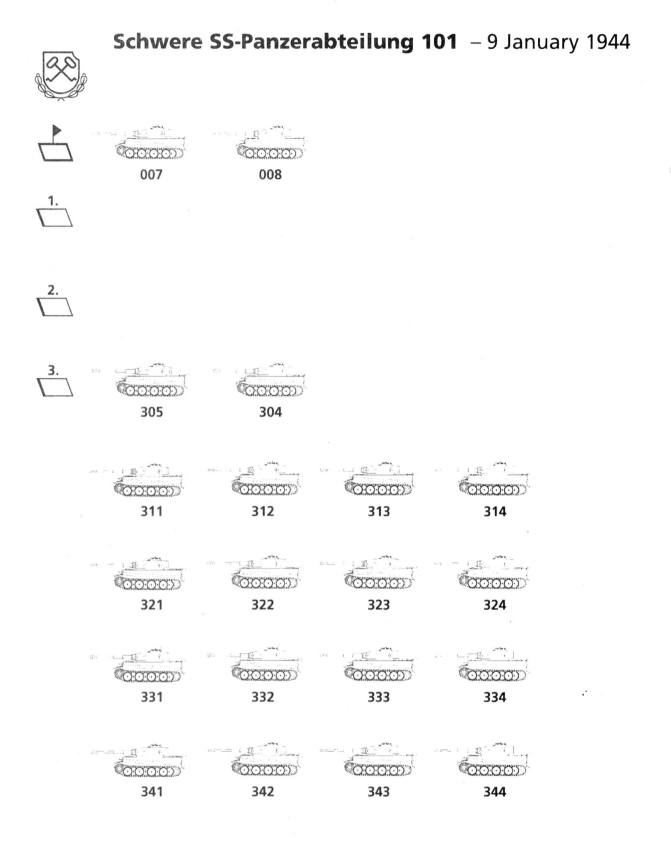

Schwere SS-Panzerabteilung 101 – 1 May 1944

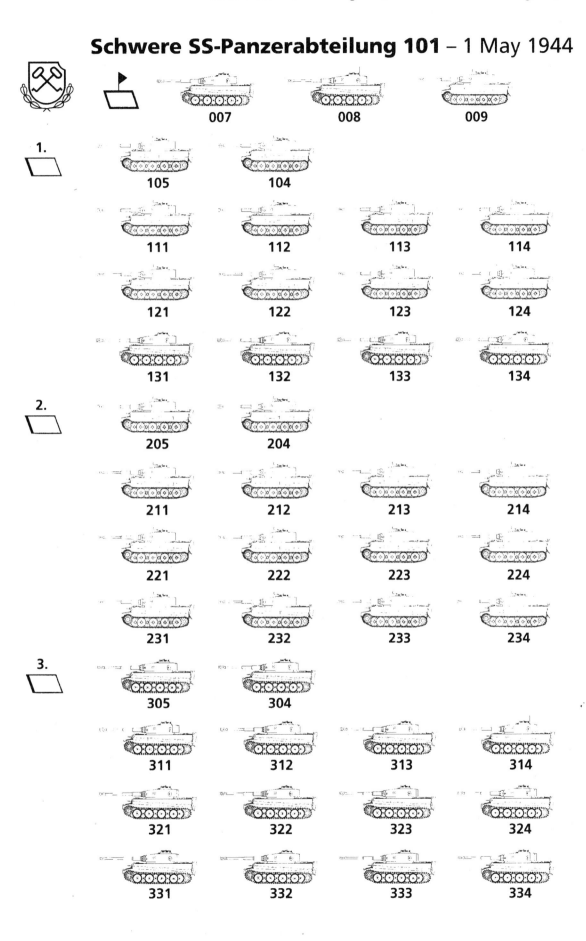

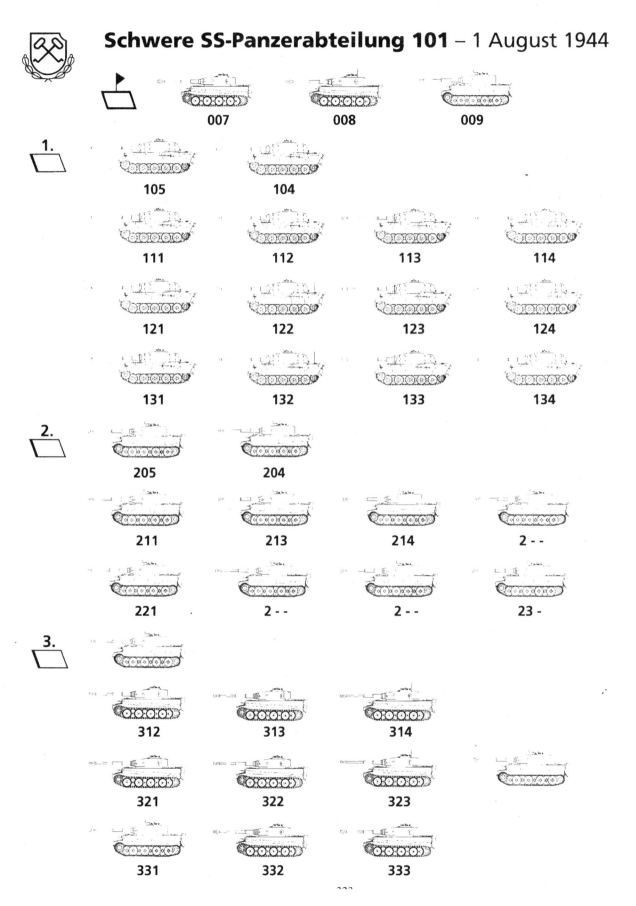

Schwere SS-Panzerabteilung 101 – 1 August 1944

007   008   009

1.

105   104

111   112   113   114

121   122   123   124

131   132   133   134

2.

205   204

211   213   214   2 - -

221   2 - -   2 - -   23 -

3.

312   313   314

321   322   323

331   332   333

Schwere SS-Panzerabteilung 501 – 2 December 1944

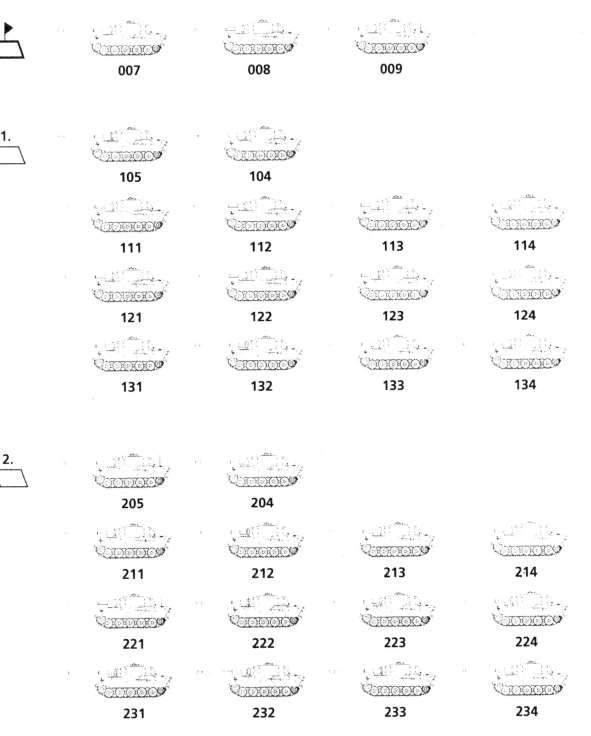

007   008   009

1.

105   104

111   112   113   114

121   122   123   124

131   132   133   134

2.

205   204

211   212   213   214

221   222   223   224

231   232   233   234

3.

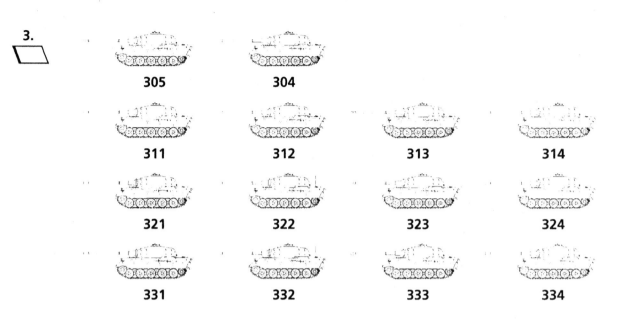

305   304

311   312   313   314

321   322   323   324

331   332   333   334

Schwere SS-Panzer-Abteilung 102 (Schwere SS-Panzer-Abteilung 502)

19 July 1943: A Tiger battalion is ordered established as corps troops for the I. SS-Panzer-Korps. A cadre of about 120 men was already assembled for this purpose in Augustdorf in April 1943. Training starts in early May 1943 with three Tiger I tanks in Senne Training Area (South) under command of SS-Untersturmführer Schienhofen.

July 1943: Movement to Walki (near Kharkov) with the intent of continuing the establishment of the battalion in the rear combat zone!

August 1943: Attachment to SS-Panzer-Grenadier-Division "Das Reich." Sporadic operations, with parts of the battalion also serving as infantry.

October 1943: Redeployment to Augustdorf for reconstitution. Continuation of the establishment under command of SS-Hauptsturmführer Fischer.

4 November 1943: By order of the SS Main Office (order: II OrgAbt IA/II TbNr 1574/43 gKdos dated 22 October 1943) the battalion is designated as schwere SS-Panzer-Abteilung 102.

January 1944: Railway transport to Argentan (France). SS-Sturmbannführer Laackmann becomes the battalion commander. Night employment and search-and-destroy operations against air-inserted sabotage parties.

February 1944: 201 recruits coming from SS-Panzer-Grenadier-Ausbildungs- und Ersatz-Regiment 2 (2nd SS Mechanized Infantry Training and Replacement Regiment) are incorporated into the battalion and trained.

Spring 1944: Redeployment to the Wezep Training Area in the Netherlands. The new commander becomes SS-Sturmbannführer Weiss in early March.

1 April 1944: Training and reconstitution continue.

21 April 1944: Six Tiger I tanks delivered.

8 May 1944: All six Tigers operational. The battalion continues its reconstitution in the Oldebrock section of the Wezep Training Area. Parts of the battalion stay in Paderborn, where they attend Tiger-related courses.

15 May 1944: Thirty-seven Noncommissioned officers and 231 enlisted personnel from schwere SS-Panzer-Abteilung 103 are transferred into the battalion. Due to shortage of personnel, the 3./schwere SS-Panzer-Abteilung 102 cannot be established.

21 April–29 May 1944: Delivery of forty-five Tiger I tanks.

1 June 1944: Operational tanks: 28.

6 June 1944: The Paderborn crewmembers are moved to the Wezep Training Area by bus. In a solemn ceremony, the tanks are issued to the individual crews.

11 June 1944: Entrainment of the battalion and transport via Tilburg and Breda to the west.

12 June 1944: Roubaix, Lille and Douai are transited. Detrainment near Arras followed by a forty-kilometer road march west via St. Pol to the southern area of Calais. Two days after arrival, the battalion marches back to Arras again, where it is loaded on trains.

13 June 1944: Air strike in Lens on the 3./schwere SS-Panzer-Abteilung 102; no casualties.

16 June 1944: Rail movement stops at Laon. The French railway personnel try to delay the transport. The tactical leaders speed things up by announcing the use of firearms to get the trains moving again.

18–19 June 1944: Halt in Reims.

21–23 June 1944: Arrival at the freight yard at Versailles. After detrainment, rest area in the castle gardens. A road march to the front is ordered. Initially, only the 2./schwere SS-Panzer-Abteilung 102 is available.

The transport of the 3./schwere SS-Panzer-Abteilung 102 is attacked by several fighter-bombers near Sees (several men dead). The locomotive derails, and the tanks are expeditiously removed from the rail cars. They subsequently starts a road march towards Joue-du-Bois; after halting there, they continue towards the front.

25 June 1944: Rambouillet is reached shortly after 0300 hours; the crews are allowed to rest.

26 June 1944: Night march via Epernon to Maintenon; rest in the wooded area. Numerous mechanical failures.

27 June 1944: March to Chateauneuf-en-Thymerais.

28 June 1944: March is continued via Senonches to Longny-au-Perche.

1 July 1944: The 2./schwere SS-Panzer-Abteilung 102 of SS-Hauptsturmführer Endemann rests at Neauphe sur Essai with eight tanks. Movement to Joue-du-Bois is continued during the night (via Sees and Carrouges). The battalion commander, Weiss, is promoted to SS-Obersturmbannführer.

2 July 1944: Night march via La Ferte-Mace and Briouze to Segrie Fontaine. Detrainment of the last transport in Versailles.

3 July 1944: Night movement via Rouvrou, St. Marc, Proussy and La Villette to Cauville.

4 July 1944: Maintenance halt in the area north of Cauville

5 July 1944: The maintenance halt continues.

6 July 1944: The road march starts towards the assembly area at Vacognes at 2300 hours.

7 July 1944: The 2./schwere SS-Panzer-Abteilung 102 reconnoiters the terrain near Evrecy, Hill 112 and the area north of it. Operational tanks: 28.

8 July 1944: Operational tanks: 15. March to the area of St. Honorine du Fay.

9 July 1944: The 1./schwere SS-Panzer-Abteilung 102 conducts a reconnaissance-in-force in the direction of Maltot with a platoon-sized element (SS-Untersturmführer Baral). Three Shermans are knocked out. At 2000 hours there is an attack on Hill 112.

The 2./schwere SS-Panzer-Abteilung 102 receives orders to move the northern outskirts of St. Martin (northeast of Vieux). At 2230 hours, the company moves out via Amaye-sur-Orne to the designated release point. Tiger 211 suffers a mechanical failure. Mission for the 2./schwere SS-Panzer-Abteilung 102: counterattack Hill 112. Operational tanks: 27.

3./schwere SS-Panzer-Abteilung 102 is still road marching.

10 July 1944: Air strike early in the morning; two Tigers are knocked out.
Total tanks: 43.

March via Maizet and Amaye-sur-Orne to an assembly area near Vieux. At 0530 hours, the 1. and the 2./schwere SS-Panzer-Abteilung 102 starts offensive operations. (Within the 2./schwere SS-Panzer-Abteilung 102 the 3rd Platoon of SS-Untersturmführer Rathmann is on left flank, the 1st Platoon of SS-Untersturmführer Schroif is on the right.) There is a meeting engagement with the 7th Royal Tank Regiment (northeast of Baron) and the 9th Royal Tank Regiment, which are both attacking simultaneously (on both sides of the road Fontaine Etoupfour-Maltot). The Wäldchen der halben Bäume (Half-Tree Woods) near Hill 112 is taken. Tiger 213 of SS-Unterscharführer Piller) is hit by an antitank gun. Three enemy tanks and one antitank gun are destroyed.

The company commander—SS-Hauptsturmführer Endemann in Tiger 221—takes a route too far to the right into the high brush and is subsequently missed. Strong enemy artillery fire, including smoke, forces the Tigers to leave the open terrain. The 1./schwere SS-Panzer-Abteilung 102 knocks out several tanks. During the attack of the 3./schwere SS-Panzer-Abteilung 102, Tiger 311 of SS-Untersturmführer Streu is knocked out; Streu is killed. Later on, two more tanks are knocked out—Tiger 312 of SS-Unterscharführer Richter, who losses one arm, and the tank of SS-Unterscharführer Novy, who is taken prisoner—are also knocked out.

During the night, a counterattack is launched near Maltot (north of the road to St. Martin) is supported.

Total tanks: 40.

11 July 1944: A counterattack starts at 0515 hours to restore the previously held main line of resistance near Hill 112. Three enemy tanks, four antitank guns, and fifteen armored vehicles are destroyed. Tiger 232 of SS-Unterscharführer Winter is hit by an antitank gun.

The 1./schwere SS-Panzer-Abteilung 102 attacks with six Tigers, taking a defile on the hillside facing towards Avenay. It is able to take advantage of the enemy's use of artificial smoke; seven enemy tanks and eight antitank guns are knocked out. One Tiger, that of SS-Oberscharführer Canesius, erroneously fires three rounds at a fellow tank (SS-Oberscharführer Knecht), but he misses since the main gun sights are out of adjustment.

The battalion is employed with the 10. SS-Panzer-Division "Frundsberg" around Maltot, Eterville and Fontaine. Another Tiger of the 3./schwere SS-Panzer-Abteilung 102 is knocked out. The acting company commander of the 3./schwere SS-Panzer-Abteilung 102, SS-Untersturmführer Klust, is relieved by the battalion commander, because he disobeys an order to advance into a terrain obscured by smoke grenades. Operational tanks: 16.

Total tanks: 39.

12 July 1944: Covering positions are occupied on Hill 112; Tigers 212 and 214 are in overwatch positions. The hill is captured again by the British. Operational tanks: 12.

13 July 1944: The mission remains the same; Tigers 212, 213 and 233 are committed.

The 1./schwere SS-Panzer-Abteilung 102, the friendly forces to the right of the 2./schwere SS-Panzer-Abteilung 102, again takes Hill 112. West of the hill, Tiger 321 of SS-Obersturmführer Schienhofen is employed in St. Martin along with two Tigers from the 2./schwere SS-Panzer-Abteilung 102. Operational tanks: 12.

14 July 1944: No change in orders: two tanks are in covering positions. A total of nine Tigers are operational. The 2./schwere SS-Panzer-Abteilung 102 redeploys to Amaye due to the constant air threat. Operational tanks: 22.

15 July 1944: The situation remains unchanged initially. Heavy artillery shelling all day long. At 2230 hours, an enemy attack is repelled. Tiger 212 of SS-Unterscharführer Kuhlemann has to be sent to the rear after receiving a direct artillery hit. Operational tanks: 8.

16 July 1944: The 2./schwere SS-Panzer-Abteilung 102 is in covering positions in an orchard south of St. Martin; a single tank is in a screening position on Hill 112. (Elements of the 10. Panzer-Division "Frundsberg" are in defensive positions there.) Operational tanks: 7. The 1./schwere SS-Panzer-Abteilung 102 is employed near Maltot; 4 Churchills are knocked out.

17 July 1944: The tanks remain in covering positions.

18 July 1944: The situation in the sector of the 2./schwere SS-Panzer-Abteilung 102 remains stable. Tiger 224 of SS-Unterscharführer Oberhuber) knocks out three tanks and one antitank gun. Operational tanks: 5.

The 3./schwere SS-Panzer-Abteilung 102 is hit by a heavy air strike; five out of its seven Tigers are damaged.

19 July 1944: Situation unchanged in the sector of the 2./schwere SS-Panzer-Abteilung 102; eight tanks operational.

20 July 1944: Two antitank guns are destroyed by the screening tanks. Relief at 2000 hours by the 1./schwere SS-Panzer-Abteilung 102. The 2./schwere SS-Panzer-Abteilung 102 marches via Amaye to the wooded area east of Lieu des Pres (11 Tigers operational).

21 July 1944: The 2./schwere SS-Panzer-Abteilung 102 conducts maintenance.

22 July 1944: The 2./schwere SS-Panzer-Abteilung 102 is put on alert and advances towards Amaye. It receives orders there to attack along the road to Maltot. It pulls back after being hit by fighter-bombers. The 2nd Platoon knock out three antitank guns at the northern outskirts of Feuguerolles-sur-Orne. Covering positions are occupied during the night 600 meters north of Feuguerolles-sur-Orne at the road junction 600 meters south of the church at Maltot. Seven Tigers operational.

23 July 1944: Defensive positions are established by the 2./schwere SS-Panzer-Abteilung 102 (8 Tigers) in captured terrain. A British tank assault is pushed back in the morning; six tanks are knocked out by the 2./schwere SS-Panzer-Abteilung 102. Two more are put out of action by the 1./schwere SS-Panzer-Abteilung 102 on the left flank. When the infantry closes up to the tanks, the Tigers occupy hide positions 200 meters behind the main line of resistance. One Tiger covers the northern part of Feuguerolles-sur-Orne. Eight Tigers operational; Tiger 214 of (SS-Unterscharführer Kuhlemann suffers track damage after being hit by artillery.

24 July 1944: Assault of eight Churchills from Maltot towards St. Martin; all are knocked out by the 1./schwere SS-Panzer-Abteilung 102.

The 2nd Platoon of the 2./schwere SS-Panzer-Abteilung 102 supports offensive operations east of the Orne from positions northeast of Feuguerolles-sur-Orne. Due to the low visibility and the extreme ranges, the operation meets with no success. Seven Tigers operational.

25 July 1944: The 2./schwere SS-Panzer-Abteilung 102 is still in covering positions; it suppresses enemy movements on Hill 67 and on the northern outskirts of St. Andre-sur-Orne. Three tanks and four antitank guns are destroyed. Seven Tigers in action. Tiger 222 of SS-Unterscharführer Oberhuber is hit; the radio operator is killed. The 1./schwere SS-Panzer-Abteilung 102 is relieved on Hill 112 by the 3./schwere SS-Panzer-Abteilung 102. The company is then employed at Cropton.

26 July 1944: The 1./schwere SS-Panzer-Abteilung 102 is employed containing enemy advances on Hill 67 and on the north outskirts of St. Andre-sur-Orne (from positions west of Feuguerolles-sur-Orne). Three tanks and four antitank guns are destroyed. Tiger 222 of SS-Unterscharführer Oberhuber is knocked out by antitank-gun fire from the flank. *Total tanks: 38.*

The situation for the 2./schwere SS-Panzer-Abteilung 102 remains unchanged. Before noon, this company directs gunfire on enemy forces east of the Orne River. Operational tanks: 7.

27 July 1944: Mission unchanged: Covering the area west of Feuguerolles-sur-Orne. Operational tanks: 7.

28 July 1944: No operations. Operational tanks: 9.

29 July 1944: Operational tanks: 10.

30 July 1944: Operational tanks: 30.

31 July 1944: Operational tanks: 11. The 2./schwere SS-Panzer-Abteilung 102 has knocked out or destroyed eighteen tanks and fifteen antitank guns in July.

1 August 1944: Disengagement and march via La Caine, Hamars and Campandre to Roucamp. The 1./schwere SS-Panzer-Abteilung 102 occupies covering positions in Vire.

2 August 1944: The battalion is attached to the 9. SS-Panzer-Division "Hohenstaufen" and forms Kampfgruppe Weiss. It is assembled near Roucamps and then relocates to the area southwest of St. Jean.

Together with SS-Panzer-Aufklärungs-Abteilung 9, the 1./schwere SS-Panzer-Abteilung 102 is ordered to attack in the direction of the 2./schwere SS-Panzer-Abteilung 102 (from Estry to the northern outskirts of La Bistiere). Twenty-two enemy tanks are knocked out.

At 0440 hours, the 2./schwere SS-Panzer-Abteilung 102 reaches Roucamps. It assembles 300 meters to the northwest. At 0555 hours, the company receives a new mission: Attack via St. Jean; once there, advance west to the road bend three kilometers to the northwest; occupy covering positions (the 1./schwere SS-Panzer-Abteilung 102 would be south of the company once this was done).

At 1300 hours, the order is received to attack behind the 1./schwere SS-Panzer-Abteilung 102 via Estry, Pierres, Chenedolle, Viessoix and Vaudry to the north to La Bistiere. The company was then to occupy covering positions at the northern outskirts of La Bistiere. The 1./schwere SS-Panzer-Abteilung 102 is three kilometers west of this location (near La Graverie).

The 2./schwere SS-Panzer-Abteilung 102 starts movement at 1500 hours and reaches the road crossing 500 meters west of Chenedolle. The 1./schwere SS-Panzer-Abteilung 102 engages armor of the Guards Division in Chenedolle. A pincer movement is initiated to the south; it follows the road south from Vassy to Vire. Near Le Hauts, the leading platoon is engaged by antitank guns positioned in Vire; one Tiger knocked out. The 2./schwere SS-Panzer-Abteilung 102 outflanks further north via Pierres and reaches the road Tinchebray-Vire, where it occupies covering positions and resupplies during the night.

Total tanks: 37.

3 August 1944: The 2./schwere SS-Panzer-Abteilung 102 is ordered to attack north in conjunction with the 3./Panzer-Aufklärungs-Abteilung 9 along the road Vire-Caen in order to block the road north of La Bistiere. At the crossroads three kilometers north of Vire, the leading platoon (SS-Untersturmführer Loritz) encounters enemy forces; three Cromwells knocked out. Afterwards, several enemy attacks are pushed back; six more tanks and one scout car are knocked out. Hill 119 is seized. Several enemy counterattacks are repelled; seven tanks are knocked out. Tiger 233 of SS-Hauptscharführer Rowsovski) starts burning after seven hits from enemy tanks.

During the night, withdrawal to the northern outskirts of Vire, followed by an advance on Pierres. The 1./schwere SS-Panzer-Abteilung 102 reaches La Papillonniere, attacks further north towards La Graviere and makes contact with the 3. Fallschirmjäger-Division. Two more Tigers of the 1./schwere SS-Panzer-Abteilung 102 are knocked out.

Total tanks: 34.

4 August 1944: The 2./schwere SS-Panzer-Abteilung 102 remains in an overwatch position with seven tanks north of La Bistiere. During the day, six enemy tanks are knocked out. Due to enemy pressure, withdrawal during the night to the northern outskirts of Vire. One Tiger (Rodinger) breaks down after the engine catches fire. The other Tigers of the Kampfgruppe are in fighting positions between La Graviere and Hill 145 east of it.

Total tanks: 33.

5 August 1944: Redeployment of the 2./schwere SS-Panzer-Abteilung 102 (seven Tigers) via Pierres to Chenedolle. Three tanks—Tigers 212, 213 and 214—reinforce the 1./schwere SS-Panzer-Abteilung 102 and remain in the northern part of Chenedolle. The rest of the company concentrates near the road Tinchebray-Vire for maintenance, rearming and refueling. In the afternoon, the Tiger 212 is immobilized by an artillery hit. Operational tanks: 20. The battalion is relieved from attachment to the 9. SS-Panzer-Division "Frundsberg."

Total tanks: 32.

6 August 1944: The situation for the 2./schwere SS-Panzer-Abteilung 102 remains unchanged. The two tanks in Chenedolle are immobilized after several artillery and anti-tank-gun hits and are replaced by Tiger 224 and 242. Parts of the 1./schwere SS-Panzer-Abteilung 102 are employed west of Chenedolle. A counterattack is conducted with elements of the 10. SS-Panzer-Division "Hohenstaufen" on Le Bas Perrier; four tanks are knocked out. The British infantry (1st Norfolks) is erroneously attacked by US Thunderbolts, leaves its fighting positions in panic and suffers heavy casualties. German infantry fails to take advantage of this situation in a timely manner and is subsequently stopped by artillery.

7 August 1944: The operational tanks of the 1./schwere SS-Panzer-Abteilung 102 march to Vassy. Dismounted tank crews blow-up a US 9-centimeter antitank gun. Both tanks of the 2./schwere SS-Panzer-Abteilung 102 covering Chenedolle are hit by artillery and have to be replaced. Enemy positions of the 2nd Fife and Forfar on the hills around Bas Perrier are shelled by the tanks; the shelling continues the following day.

8 August 1944: Operational tanks: 21. Despite an order to withdraw by the battalion commander, one tank—Tiger 134 of the 1./schwere SS-Panzer-Abteilung 102—repels the attack of a company of Shermans of the 23rd Hussars west of Chenedolle; 15 tanks are knocked out. During the night, the immobilized tank is recovered by three Tigers of Schwab's platoon.

9 August 1944: After the enemy breakthrough north of Falaise, the 2./schwere SS-Panzer-Abteilung 102 (minus the tanks attached to the 1./schwere SS-Panzer-Abteilung 102) is ordered to move to Falaise via Condé-sur-Noireau.

After being resupplied, the march is continued to the northern entrance of Bons Tassily. Orders are received to move via Ussy to Martainville. An assembly area is occupied in the woods northwest of Tournebu; the company is directed to support the 271. Infanterie-Division. The company becomes the division reserve and assembles near the Bois Halbout.

The remaining thirteen operational tanks are moved early in the morning from the Vire area to the sector of the 12. SS-Panzer-Division Hitlerjugend" in order to defend the line Bretteville-sur-Laize-St. Sylvain. Together with SS-Panzer-Regiment 12, they decimate a tank attack of the Canadian II Corps near Hill 140, knocking out 47 out of 55 tanks.

10 August 1944: Two tanks of the 2./schwere SS-Panzer-Abteilung 102 are employed on the left flank of the 271. Infanterie-Division; four enemy tanks are knocked out.

11 August 1944: Six tanks of the 2./schwere SS-Panzer-Abteilung 102 are employed near the Bois Halbout; two tanks conduct an immediate counterattack on an armor concentration southwest of Le Moncel and four enemy tanks are knocked out. During the night, the company withdraws to the Bois Halbout.

12 August 1944: Getting the report that twenty-six enemy tanks were advancing south from east of Barbery, the 2./schwere SS-Panzer-Abteilung 102 covers the road to Espins and Fresney with two tanks. It then advances with its remaining six tanks along the road to Barberie (via Cingal). Seven enemy tanks and one reconnaissance vehicle are knocked out. Five Tigers are moved back to the Bois Halbout. This area is now occupied by the enemy and has to be recaptured; three enemy tanks are knocked out). Two Tigers stay in covering position southeast of Tournebu; the rest are resupplied 200 meters southeast of

Clair-Tison. The company receives a new mission: It moves to Chateaux la Motte and occupies covering positions to the north.

13 August 1944: In the morning, the 2./schwere SS-Panzer-Abteilung 102 (3 Tigers) assembles in the woods 500 meters southeast of Tournebu and screens to the north; two enemy tanks and one Tiger knocked out. The company's next mission—to clear the terrain along a small river from Clair-Tison to the north—is cancelled because the requested infantry does not arrive in time. A local attack along the road from Clair-Tison to the north; following this, the company withdraws to a spot 100 meters south of Clair-Tison. In the evening, one Tiger in a covering position on Hill 184 northeast of Soulangy knocks out three Shermans.

Total tanks: 31.

14 August 1944: A tank attack out of Soulangy is repelled by three tanks—Tigers 212, 231 and 241—in front of St. Pierre-Canivet; ten enemy tanks are knocked out. Orders are received to withdraw to the northeast outskirts of Falaise. Having arrived there, the 2./schwere SS-Panzer-Abteilung 102 is involved in the engagements around the cathedral and pulls back after dawn to the outskirts of the city. Tiger 231 of SS-Untersturmführer Loritz is a total loss. One Tiger (Münster) is destroyed by infantry during close combat.

Total tanks: 29.

15 August 1944: Tiger 134 repels an enemy assault on Versainville and then withdraws to Eraines. The rest of the 1./schwere SS-Panzer-Abteilung 102 and two operational tanks of the 2./schwere SS-Panzer-Abteilung 102 are in fighting positions on the northern outskirts of Potigny; one enemy tank is knocked out.

16 August 1944: Movement to Vignats. Blocking positions are occupied on the road crossing 500 meters north of Falaise. The sole operational tank of the 2./schwere SS-Panzer-Abteilung 102—Tiger 241—mows down an infantry assault; late in late afternoon, it relocates to the northeast outskirts of Falaise. Two Tigers stay in Falaise supporting elements of the 12. SS-Panzer-Division "Hitlerjugend."

Total tanks: 27.

17 August 1944: The 1. and 2./schwere SS-Panzer-Abteilung 102 (only Tiger 241 from the latter unit) withdraw to Villy and get resupplied. The 2./schwere SS-Panzer-Abteilung 102 is ordered to cover the northern exit road out of Villy, together with some assault guns. A reconnaissance patrol and an armor attack from the area north of Damblainville are pushed back. One Tiger (Liebeskind) is destroyed.

Total tanks: 26.

18 August 1944: Tiger 241 is ordered to withdraw to the château two kilometers south of Fresne-la-Mere and screen to the north; friendly forces to the right is the 1./schwere SS-Panzer-Abteilung 102. When the enemy infiltrates La Hogouettes at noon, a quick attack towards the railway crossing west of Abbaye is ordered. On the way to the northwest exit road out of Abbaye, Tiger 124 is given a tow. At 1700 hours, an enemy attack is repelled. After dawn, the order is given to blow up Tiger 124 and to close in to the battalion command post 500 meters east of Vignats.

Total tanks: 25.

The badly wounded battalion commander, SS-Obersturmbannführer Weiss, is captured near Trun.

19 August 1944: Orders are issued to break through via Vignats to Necy to the 1./schwere SS-Panzer-Abteilung 102; two barrels of fuel are carried on board. After refueling, the company withdraws to the northeast (still three Tigers). Enemy forces are encountered west of Brieux. After two antitank-gun hits, Tiger 241 (SS-Untersturmführer Schroif) starts burning. The Tiger following Schroif runs into his tank and is also lost. The lead tank—that of the company commander of the 1./schwere SS-Panzer-Abteilung 102, SS-Hauptsturmführer Kalls—is able to get through.

Tigers 214 and 222 are employed on the road Trun-Vimoutiers; one enemy tank is destroyed. Several enemy air raids are sustained without damage. During the defense of the command post of the 12. SS-Panzer-Division "Hitlerjugend" in Necy, three Tigers are lost. A single Tiger is destroyed in close combat by the infantry of the South Alberta Regiment advancing on Saint-Lambert-sur-Dive.

Total tanks: 19.

20 August 1944: Several Tigers conducts a counterattack from Vimoutiers to Trun. In addition, there are engagements near Champosoult, with several enemy tanks being knocked out. One Tiger (Reisske), which suffers mechanical problems suspiciously often, has its pistons seized by a lack of motor oil and is abandoned near Vimoutiers. (It remains there today as a national monument.)

Total tanks: 18.

21 August 1944: Employment near Coudehard and Champosoult. After a skirmish with US tanks, one Tiger (Lenz) is hit in the engine and is towed away by Kalls' tank. Both vehicles seeks cover west of Aubry-le-Panthou, but they have to be blown up after running out of fuel. Two tanks of the 3./schwere SS-Panzer-Abteilung 102—Rosowsky's Tiger with a "Swiss Cheese" turret, which is towing Streng's Tiger—get as far as Le Sap. They manage to get fuel from a column of vehicles belonging to the 9. SS-Panzer-Division "Hohenstaufen"; they then continue to move in the direction of Broglie.

Total tanks: 14.

22 August 1944: The tank column reaches Broglie in the early afternoon. In the meantime, the Maintenance Company has changed position and is no longer there. Other tanks only make it as far as Rouen. One immobilized tank of the 3./schwere SS-Panzer-Abteilung 102 is abandoned on the outskirts of Mandeville after having knocked out three Canadian tanks. Three tanks are abandoned at the previous location of the Maintenance Company in Aubry-le-Panthou.

Total tanks: 9.

23 August 1944: Two Tigers transit Brionne after passing a burning column of ambulances that had been strafed by ground-attack fighters.

24 August 1944: The two tanks make contact with their company, the 2./schwere SS-Panzer-Abteilung 102.

25 August 1944: One Tiger (Streng) gets to Elbeuf and has to be blown up there. The company commander's tank of the 1./schwere SS-Panzer-Abteilung 102 is lost during an attempt to cross the Seine River by means of the deep-wading equipment. Some tanks gather in Fleury and succeed in reaching the assembly area of the battalion west of Amiens. Tiger 223 is abandoned in Tostes.

Total tanks: 6.

28 August 1944: When crossing the Seine River, Tiger 001 comes off the ferry and sinks into the crossing point at Rouen. It cannot be recovered. In the rally point near Amiens, the battalion is reorganized and assembled for a further march to the east.

Total tanks: 5.

29 August 1944: Road march with the wheeled vehicles from the area north of Albert to Arras; elements resupplied in deserted army depots. At night, this battalion element passes Vimy and later reaches Lens.

30 August 1944: At the Seine River, most of the remaining tanks have to be blown up.

Total tanks: 1.

1 September 1944: March from Roubaix through Ath and Enghien into the area of Leeuw. Passing the outskirts of Brussels, the march route passes through Mechelen and continues to Diest. A single Tiger makes it as far as Genval, where it has to be abandoned by its crew, which disables the main gun by means of an explosive charge.

Total tanks: 0.

3 September 1944: Redeployment to Limburg (near Maastricht). Arrival of the new battalion commander, SS-Sturmbannführer Hartrampf.

7 September 1944: March via Aachen into the area east of Düren.

9 September 1944: Transiting Arnsberg and Soest, the new bivouac area is reached. The battalion is reconstituted at the Senne Training Area. It is redesignated as schwere SS-Panzer-Abteilung 502. The battalion is temporarily headquartered at Anröchte; the 2./schwere SS-Panzer-Abteilung 102 at Neuengeseke; and the 3./schwere SS-Panzer-Abteilung 502 at Horn. It later relocates to Paderborn.

According to the Wehrmacht Daily Report of 8 October 1944, the battalion destroyed 227 tanks and 28 antitank guns on the invasion front from 10 July to 20 August 1944.

27 December 1944: Six Tiger II tanks are delivered, which are later transferred to schwere SS-Panzer-Abteilung 503.

14 February–6 March 1945: Delivery of thirty-one Tiger IIs.

In early March 1945, the order is received to move to Stettin (Senne Training Area-Bielefeld-Hanover-Stendal). Shortly before the battalion can move out, the commander of the 2./schwere SS-Panzer-Abteilung 502, SS-Obersturmführer Soretz, is killed in a traffic accident. SS-Untersturmführer Schroif is given acting command until the new commander, SS-Hauptsturmführer Neu, can arrive.

11 March 1945: Arrival in Stettin (Torney Station) and detrainment.

17–18 March 1945: Railway transport again via Eberswalde, Rüdersdorf and Erkner to Fürstenwalde and Berkenbrück. This is followed by a road march via the Autobahn into the area around Briesen.

19 March 1945: During the night, march via Wilmersdorf and Falkenhagen to Dolgelin; positions occupied in a near-by forest. Preparations for the relief attack on Küstrin.

22 March 1945: In the afternoon, order received for a night attack on Sachsendorf. The line of departure is to be crossed shortly before midnight; due to poor communications with the attached infantry, the attack slows down.

23 March 1945: After midnight, the first enemy position is penetrated by the 2./schwere SS-Panzer-Abteilung 502. At sunrise, the tanks are shelled by numerous artillery and antitank guns. The 1./schwere SS-Panzer-Abteilung 102 under SS-Hauptsturmführer Kalls tries to close in south of the road and destroys parts of the antitank-gun belt and knocks out three tanks. The combat-inexperienced infantry that accompanies the tanks and the incessant fire from antitank guns finally cause the advance to stall. Altogether, more than twenty enemy tanks are knocked out. Three Tiger commanders are killed by head wounds.

During the night, the disabled tanks are recovered. The operational tanks of the battalion seek cover among the buildings of Hackenow and Tucheband. Three Tigers are detailed to screen. SS-Obersturmführer Schienhofen argues with the battalion commander, urging him not to have the tanks concentrated, since they have already come under constant massed artillery and Stalin-organ fire. Out of control, he draws his pistol and aims at Hartrampf, who has already issued a number of odd orders. At this moment, there is a mortar barrage, which wounds Schienhofen in the head. The wounding of Schienhofen "cools down" this unfortunate situation. Four Tigers of the 3./schwere SS-Panzer-Abteilung 502 and two Bergepanthers are damaged due to the ill-advised positioning of the vehicles.

24 March 1945: Covering positions occupied at Golzow.

26 March 1945: The covering force knocks out two tanks. At 2100 hours, the tanks at in their jump-off positions for another assault on Küstrin. The battalion commander, who suffered a broken arm the previous day, is leading from inside his Sd.Kfz. 251/1 (normally only a used as command post).

27 March 1945: Shortly after crossing the line of departure, the 1./schwere SS-Panzer-Abteilung 502 is stopped by a minefield; three Tigers are immobilized. The same thing occurs in the attack sector of the 3./schwere SS-Panzer-Abteilung 502 (SS-Obersturm-führer Schienhofen), which is advancing on the right side of the main road Manchnow-Kietz. One tank—Tiger 321—is immobilized after running over a mine; it then knocks out two Soviet tanks before it is knocked out by a captured Panzerfaust.

Before sunrise, a passage through the minefield is cleared in the sector of the 1./schwere SS-Panzer-Abteilung 502; the 2./schwere SS-Panzer-Abteilung 502 is then ordered to break through. After the destruction of four enemy tanks, the attack again stops due to the fact that the infantry loses contact

The new commander of the 2./schwere SS-Panzer-Abteilung 502 is unfit for the stress of combat and gets on the nerves of tank commanders by constantly issuing nonsensical orders. His tank gets stuck in a large bomb crater during a withdrawal movement. One after another, five Tigers are hit and immobilized. After darkness falls, the battalion moves back to Seelow. The operational tanks of the battalion assemble in Neu Tucheband. Operational tanks: 13.

28–29 March 1945: During the night, the immobilized tanks can be recovered.

31 March 1945: Relief-in-place and withdrawal behind Seelow.

March 1944: Four tanks of the battalion are repaired by Panzer-Instandsetzungs-Abteilung 559 (559th Ordnance Battalion) and another three by the Krupp-Drucken-Müller factory in Berlin (Tempelhof).

3 April 1945: The battalion redeploys to the area of Diedersdorf-Lietzen.

6 April 1945: Operational tanks: 27.

8 April 1945: In expectation of the Soviet main offensive, the tanks occupy positions behind berms.

10 April 1945: Operational tanks: 28.

15 April 1945: Operational tanks: 29. The battalion is now in the area Petershagen-Sieversdorf (the 2./schwere SS-Panzer-Abteilung 502 is in Dolgelin).

16 April 1945: Operational tanks: 29. Start of the Soviet main offensive. The 1./schwere SS-Panzer-Abteilung 502 is in fighting positions with six tanks on the eastern outskirts of Dolgelin, where it covers the open terrain towards the Oder River. Many enemy tanks cannot be fired upon, because they are already beneath the depression angle of the main guns. Despite this, several enemy columns are hit and eleven tanks are knocked out.

The 2./schwere SS-Panzer-Abteilung 502, attached to Panzer-Grenadier-Division "Kurmark," is ordered to Alt Zeschdorf at 0900 hours. It starts a counterattack towards Schönfließ at 1430 hours that lasts until the evening. Having broken through the small town, the attack stalls in front of two field positions. The reluctant company commander is unable to coordinate the operation with the German infantry. (The situation is additionally complicated by the fact that whole units of the Soviets operate in German uniforms! Many traitors of the Nationalkommitee Freies Deutschland—the "National Committee for a Free Germany," an organization formed by defectors in Russian captivity—also cause confusion among the defending forces. At night, the company withdraws to its assembly area and recovers its immobilized tanks.

17 April 1945: Employment in the Libbenichen Sector. The 1./schwere SS-Panzer-Abteilung 502 repels several attacks with the assistance of the Flak platoon.

18 April 1945: The commander of the 2./schwere SS-Panzer-Abteilung 502, pulling back from Schönfließ, is erroneously engaged by SS-Untersturmführer Kuhnke. Kuhnke is relieved of all duties at once, but he must be reinstalled later due to a lack of officers.

19 April 1945: The 1. and the 3./schwere SS-Panzer-Abteilung 502 engage in heavy fighting in the area of Lietzen-Marxdorf. The 2./schwere SS-Panzer-Abteilung 502 is withdrawn to Berkenbrück.

20 April 1945: Orders to withdraw during the afternoon into the area east of Fürstenwalde.

21 April 1945: The 2./schwere SS-Panzer-Abteilung 502 relocates in the darkness via Demnitz to the Steinhöfel Castle. The battalion command tank and the 3./schwere SS-Panzer-Abteilung 502 are in fighting positions 1 kilometer southwest of Heinersdorf; the headquarters Tiger and several other tanks are abandoned after having used up all their ammunition and suffering suspension damage.

22 April 1945: The 2./schwere SS-Panzer-Abteilung 502 takes up battle positions on the northern outskirts of Steinhöfel, 500 meters east of the woodline of the Tempelberg Forest. Later on, it changes position to 300 meters left of the road Tempelberg-Heinersdorf and covers Müncheberg. At approximately 1000 hours, the company changes positions again and moves to the hillside near the Heinersdorf Mill. The Tiger of SS-Untersturmführer Schroif was knocked out there on the previous day after having destroyed several Soviet tanks.

After destroying several antitank guns and a mortar battery at a distance of 2,400 meters, the company transits Hasenfelde and withdraws via Hasenwinkel to the western outskirts of Steinhöfel. It occupies a covering position that is oriented towards Neuendorf and Buchholz.

At 1600 hours, the 2./schwere SS-Panzer-Abteilung 502 moves to Hasenfelde; 4 tanks that have been repaired by the Maintenance Company join the group. The 3./schwere SS-Panzer-Abteilung 502 is in position 300 meters north of the 2./schwere SS-Panzer-Abteilung 502 on the road in front Heinersdorf.

Enemy infantry on the march from Dolgelin to Heinersdorf are shelled at a distance of approximately 3,500 meters. Shortly before dawn, the tanks are ordered to Arensdorf. Eleven enemy tanks that are approaching this town are knocked out there; the rest escape. All tanks are very short of fuel. Several tanks have to be blown up the next few days after they run out of fuel. The enemy continues his offensive during the night and pushes back the German infantry. One Tiger (Kuhlemann) is hit by an antitank gun and has to be left behind in the western part of Arensdorf. All tanks are nearly out of fuel. Due to the fact that hostile infantry has infiltrated into the village, it has to be abandoned.

23 April 1945: After midnight, withdrawal through partially occupied terrain towards Wilmersdorf. Breakout near Arensdorf. March is continued via Wilmersdorf to the southwest. The 1. and the 3./schwere SS-Panzer-Abteilung 502 push back several armor assaults near Demnitz-Steinhöfel; approximately fifteen tanks are knocked out. New defensive fighting near Berkenbrück.

24 April 1945: The rest of the battalion gets to the area of Bad Saarow.

25 April 1945: The operational tanks assemble near Kersdorf (north of the Autobahn) and throw back the Russian forces that had crossed the Spree River.

Withdrawal via Storkow to the north shore of Lake Wolzing; engagement with the enemy. Further withdrawal to the Prieros Isthmus; covering positions are occupied to the west. One Tiger (SS-Hauptscharführer Schmidt) is blown up outside of Storkow after being hit several times.

Five operational tanks coming from the maintenance facility are assembled in the wooded area around Wolzig.

The order is issued that any wheeled vehicle not essential for combat has to be blown up or disabled.

One Tiger (Streng) positioned on the Prieros Bridge engages enemy forces crossing the river in boats. Withdrawal to the wooded area south of Prieros and Märkisch-Buchholz. One tank of the 3./schwere SS-Panzer-Abteilung 502 is ordered back to Prieros in order to contain an enemy penetration there.

26 April 1945: During the movement to the assembly area for the breakout east of Halbe, Tiger 331 burns out when the fire suppression system fails.

27 April 1945: The last Tigers of the battalion assemble near the forestry building at Hammer for the breakout attempt of the remnants of the 9. Armee to the west. The attack starts in the evening with seven Tigers of the 2./schwere SS-Panzer-Abteilung 502 in the lead and seven Tigers of the 1./schwere SS-Panzer-Abteilung 502 functioning as the rearguard.

Several assault groups tried to clear the obstacles fiercely defended by the Soviets in Halbe. While moving back, the leading tank (Kuhnke) is set aflame with a tank round in the engine compartment. The second tank (Münster) then collides with a wheeled vehicle as it backs up. The hot exhaust pipes ignite the leaking fuel and Münster's tank also burns out. The column takes a detour to the south and then turns west again later.

28 April 1945: Early in the morning, a Tiger (Harlander) is knocked out by a tank hunter/killer team. Early the same morning, an enemy artillery position is shot to pieces.

The tanks wait for the rest of the breakout forces to close up in front of the Autobahn (Berlin-Cottbus). They then attack via the Autobahn bridge southwest of Halbe into the Baruth Forest; the infantry closes up again.

The breakout forces then parallel the Autobahn to the south, where they reach the forestry building at Massow. When the Autobahn is crossed, Tiger 123 collides with the lead tank; both tanks become immobilized.

Massive resistance has to be broken again south of the Motzen Hills on the road Zossen-Baruth. Near the forestry building at Wunder, the wheeled vehicles are defueled to allow the tanks to continue their movement. At night, the German Army's Kummersdorf test and firing ranges are captured.

One Tiger (Hellwig) has to be blown up south of Neuhof. Tiger 111 (Stehmann) is blown up between Sperenberg and Fernneuendorf.

In the late afternoon, an antitank-gun belt on the road Trebbin-Luckenwalde is eliminated. The road north of Luckenwalde is crossed.

In the forest outside of Luckenwalde, all of the equipment of the Maintenance Company is blown up.

29 April 1945: Near midnight, the area between Berkenbrück and the forestry building at Mürten's Mill is reached. In front of the mill, the commander's tank of the 2./schwere SS-Panzer-Abteilung 502 has to be abandoned, because it has water in its fuel. On Kalls's tank, the final drive is ripped off; it finally has to be blown up.

30 April 1945: Attack on Hennickendorf. Further advance west in the area of Wittbrietzen-Rieben-Zauchwitz. In the morning, the western edge of the training area north of Schönefeld is reached.

1 May 1945: Only two Tigers—both of which are loaded with wounded—are still operational. No crewmember is without wounds! Shortly before reaching the forward elements of the 12. Armee, the next-to-last Tiger (SS-Hauptscharführer Streng) is knocked out near Markendorfer Hufen by a Panzerfaust, where it explodes. A short time later, the last tank—that of SS-Untersturmführer Klust of the 1./schwere SS-Panzer-Abteilung 502—has to be abandoned near Elsholz due to a lack of fuel.

During the last few days, the battalion destroyed more than seventy enemy tanks.

Together with the other forces of the 12. Armee, many members of the battalion cross the Elbe River and are captured by the US forces.

During its time of existence, the battalion destroyed about 600 tanks.

BATTALION COMMANDERS

SS-Sturmbannführer Laackmann	January 1944–March 1944
SS-Sturmbannführer Weiss	March 1944–18 August 1944
SS-Sturmbannführer Hartrampf	August 1944–May 1945

KNIGHT'S CROSS RECIPIENTS

SS-Sturmbannführer Kurt Hartrampf	28 April 1945
SS-Oberscharführer Paul Egger	28 April 1945

TOP SCORER

SS-Oberscharführer Paul Egger	113 kills

Two views of the rail movement from Argentan to the Netherlands at the end of march 1944. The Sd.Kfz. 250's are equipped with a rear-mounted MG 42.

The battalion finished its activation/reconstitution at Argentan, where it initially had no tanks. This photograph shows Sd.Kfz. 250's of the battalion's reconnaissance platoon preparing to depart for a training exercise. The vehicles bear the insignia of the headquarters Company and the Blitzrune ("lightning rune") formation insignia. WINKELMANN

The first tanks were delivered in late April 1944, and the crew training started almost immediately. TURK

SS-Hauptscharführer Haak sitting on Tiger 142 at the Wezep Training Area in Holland. KLÖCKNER

Personnel train on the quad 2-centimeter Flak under poison-gas conditions.

After arriving at Versailles, the tanks attempt to make their way to the front. In this picture, SS-Oberscharführer Bauman's Tiger is heavily camouflaged with natural foliage but displays evidence of fighter-bomber attacks on the turret sides. FINK

An idyllic picture in May 1944 at the Zwolle Training Area in the Netherlands. The relaxed crew waits for the next phase of training to start. TURK

Flak was a highly prized commodity on the Western front in 1944, but it also had to be camouflaged.

During the day, the tanks sought concealment to avoid being spotted by enemy aircraft.
WINKELMANN

SS-Oberscharführer Schroif in his Tiger. The battalion insignia of schwere SS-Panzer-Abteilung 102—the Blitzrune (lightning rune)—is clearly visible on the left front of the hull.

Tiger 211 in a camouflage scheme typical in Normandy: natural foliage. This was fine when stationary, but a moving "tree" is quite easy to spot from the air.

There was always time to take a snapshot with friends. Tank commanders of the battalion keep smiling despite the difficult situation. FINK

Three high scorers of the battalion (left to right): SS-Oberscharführer Fey, SS-Oberscharführer Egger and SS-Oberscharführer Glagow.

Tiger 214 is refueled and rearmed prior to its next encounter.

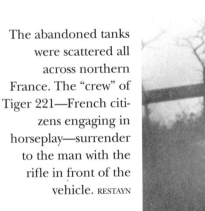

The abandoned tanks were scattered all across northern France. The "crew" of Tiger 221—French citizens engaging in horseplay—surrender to the man with the rifle in front of the vehicle. RESTAYN

Tiger 231 of SS-Untersturmführer Loritz, also had to be abandoned and was left behind at Ussy on 14 August 1944. VARIN

The few tanks that escaped the Falaise Pocket tried to reached the Seine River, such as this Tiger passing through a battered French town.

Tiger 223 was stopped by track damage near Tostes, just a few miles from the Seine. It was examined by this Canadian soldier on 30 August 1944.

NATIONAL ARCHIVES OF CANADA

The Tiger of SS-Unterscharführer Reisske broke down on 20 August 1944 near Vimoutiers and was later pushed into the roadside ditch to clear the road. Years later, it started a new life as a battlefield monument.

This is the battalion's Tiger that made it farthest to the east. It is shown here passing through the Belgian city of Enghien in early September 1944. DE MEYER

The tank ran out of fuel a short distance down the road at Genval and had to be destroyed by its own crew.
DE MEYER

SS-Obersturmführer Schienhofen in front of his Tiger II at the Camp Senne Training Area in early 1945. By this time, the battalion had been redesignated as schwere SS-Panzer-Abteilung 502.

After being reconstituted at Camp Senne, the battalion was moved by rail to Stettin. WESTERMANN

In Mid-March 1945, the tanks were employed near the Oder River near the encircled strongpoint of Küstrin.

This photograph of SS-Untersturmführer Winkelmann's Tiger II taken during these operations indicates that many tanks did not even have vehicle identification markings. WINKELMANN

One of the very rare photographs of German armor in 1945 show this Tiger of schwere SS-Panzer-Abteilung 502 in a German town.

The battalion commander's tank—Tiger 555—is being prepared for recovery after having run over a mine near Golzow on 27 March 1945. RECKZIEGEL

Tiger 321 also ran over a mine during the counterattack on Kietz. It was then destroyed by a captured Panzerfaust early in the morning of 28 March 1945. Only the gunner, SS-Rottenführer Filor, was able to escape with his life.

A poor photograph, but one that is reproduced here because of its rarity. It shows a Bergepanther recovering a Tiger II, while being assisted by two 18-ton prime movers.

The battalion command halftrack was busy during the fierce fighting in the Seelow Sector. RECKZIEGEL

Tiger 213 had to be destroyed by it own crew after it collided with another tank on 28 April 1945.

The fighting has taken its toll on an exhausted SS-Sturmmann Reckziegel, who is resting on the gun tube of his tank. RECKZIEGEL

The Soviets used this schwere SS-Panzer-Abteilung 502 Tiger for antitank gunnery training for many years at the former Wehrmacht training area at Kummersdorf.

SCHWERE SS-PANZER-ABTEILUNG 102 (502)

Vehicles on Hand/Deliveries

Date	Tiger I	Tiger II	On hand	Remarks
21 April 1944	6		6	
20-22 May 1944	24		30	
26-29 May 1944	15		45	
22 August 1944	6			Not arrived
27 December 1944		6		To schwere SS-Panzer-Abteilung 503
14 February 1945		10	10	
20 February 1945		9	19	
27 February 1945		3	22	
2 March 1945		7	29	
6 March 1945		2	31	
Grand Total	45	31		

Losses

Date	Losses	On hand	Remarks
10 July 1944	5	40	2 destroyed in an air raid, 2 knocked out and 1 missing
11 July 1944	1	39	Knocked out
26 July 1944	1	38	Knocked out by an antitank gun
2 August 1944	1	37	Knocked out by an antitank gun
3 August 1944	3	34	Knocked out
4 August 1944	1	33	Self-ignition
5 August 1944	1	32	Destroyed by artillery
13 August 1944	1	31	Knocked out
14 August 1944	2	29	1 knocked out and 1 destroyed by infantry
17 August 1944	1	28	Knocked out
18 August 1944	1	27	Knocked out by a Sherman
19 August 1944	3	24	2 knocked out and 1 destroyed by infantry
20 August 1944	1	23	Abandoned
21 August 1944	4	19	Destroyed by own crew
22 August 1944	4	15	Destroyed by own crew
25 August 1944	3	12	2 destroyed by own crew and 1 lost during a river-crossing attempt

Losses

Date	Losses	On hand	Remarks
28 August 1944	1	11	1 lost during a river-crossing attempt
30 August 1944	10	1	?
1 September 1944	1	0	Destroyed by own crew
27 March 1945	1	30	Knocked out by a Panzerfaust
21–25 April 1944	15	15	2 knocked out and remainder destroyed by own crew
26 April 1945	1	14	Self-ignition
27 April 1945	2	12	Burnt out
28 April 1945	5	7	4 knocked out and 1 knocked out by infantry
29 April 1944	2	5	1 knocked out by a T-34 and 1 abandoned
1 May 1945	2	0	1 abandoned and 1 destroyed by an antitank round
Late April 1945	3		?
Grand total:	76		

Of the losses suffered by the battalion, 38% were due to self-destruction (to prevent capture), 50% were lost in combat operations and 12% were lost due to other causes.

Schwere SS-Panzerabteilung 102 – 1 June 1944

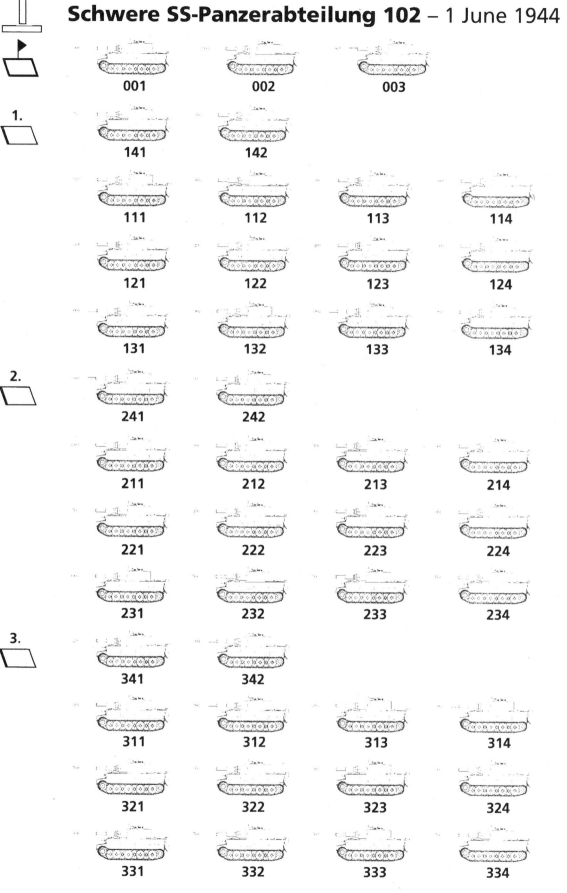

001   002   003

1.

141   142

111   112   113   114

121   122   123   124

131   132   133   134

2.

241   242

211   212   213   214

221   222   223   224

231   232   233   234

3.

341   342

311   312   313   314

321   322   323   324

331   332   333   334

Schwere SS-Panzerabteilung 502 – 6 March 1945

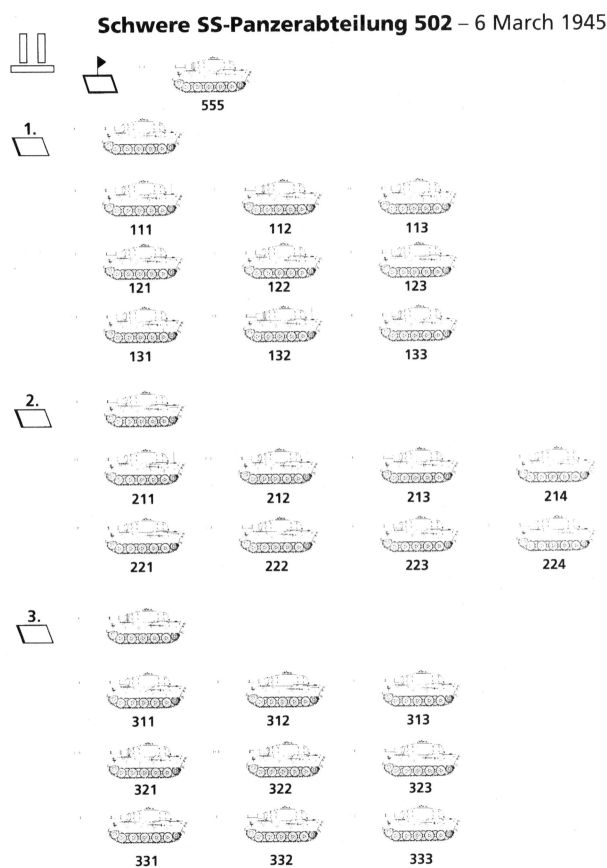

Schwere SS-Panzer-Abteilung 103 (Schwere SS-Panzer-Abteilung 503)

The battalion is established as corps troops for the III. (germanisches) SS-Panzer-Korps in the spring of 1944 in Paderborn. Personnel are provided from SS-Panzer-Regiment 11 and other SS divisions. Initial battalion commander is SS-Sturmbannführer Paetsch; SS-Sturmbannführer Hartrampf assumes acting command following him.

✛

1 July 1943: Established as the II./SS-Panzer-Regiment 11 at the Grafenwöhr Training Area.

End of July 1943: Deployment to Croatia.

8 August 1943: Disarmament of an Italian tank regiment in Presco (near Agram).

Early September 1943: Relocation to Jastrebarsko. Tank training with assault guns and former Italian tanks.

Until mid-December 1944: Employment as infantry against partisans in the area of Agram-Jastrebarsko-Karlovac.

1 November 1943: Reorganization as schwere Panzer-Abteilung 103. The Tiger-Ausbildungs-Kompanie (Tiger Training Company) of SS-Hauptsturmführer Flügel is consolidated with the battalion. SS-Hauptsturmführer Flügel becomes the new commander of the 1./schwere Panzer-Abteilung 103. His predecessor, SS-Obersturmführer Schubert, is sent to a course for general-staff officer training.

January 1944: Redeployment to Kampen (near Zwolle).

4 February 1944: Six Tiger Is are issued for training purposes.

February–March 1944: Tank training courses in Paderborn.

Spring 1944: The six Tigers are issued to the 9./SS-Panzer-Regiment 3. Relocation of the battalion to the Oldebroek Training Area. SS-Obersturmführer Ther becomes the new commander of the 2./schwere Panzer-Abteilung 103.

Summer 1944: Relocation to Epe (Netherlands). SS-Obersturmbannführer Leiner becomes the new battalion commander. Improvised training is conducted by using three Panzer Is (Model C).

15 May 1944: Right before the invasion in Normandy, trained crews are transferred from the battalion to schwere SS-Panzer-Abteilung 101 and schwere SS-Panzer-Abteilung 102.

26 May 1944: Delivery of six Tiger Is. Each tank company receives two tanks for training.

1 June 1944: Operational tanks: 6.

1 July 1944: Operational tanks: 6.

22 August 1944: Delivery of four Tiger Is. These and another six are handed over to schwere Panzer-Abteilung (Funklenk) 301. Training commences on Tiger II tanks.

Early September 1944: Transport to the Senne Training Area (North). Afterwards, the companies establish their headquarters as follows: 1./schwere SS-Panzer-Abteilung 103 in Pivitsheide; the 2./schwere SS-Panzer-Abteilung 103 in the Augustdorf guesthouse; the 3./schwere SS-Panzer-Abteilung 103 in Billinghausen; Headquarters Company in Höste; and the battalion headquarters in the Heidekrug guesthouse in Pivitsheide.

19 October 1944: Reception of the first four Tiger II tanks. Trained crews are sent back to the 11. SS-Freiwilligen-Panzer-Grenadier-Division Nordland."

14 November 1944: The battalion is redesignated as schwere Panzer-Abteilung 503.

1 December 1944: Operational tanks: 3.

27 December 1944: Six new Tiger II tanks are issued that were originally intended for delivery to schwere SS-Panzer-Abteilung 502.

11 January 1945: The battalion receives six tanks.

12 January 1945: The battalion receives three tanks.

16 January 1945: The battalion receives three tanks.

18 January 1945: The battalion receives four tanks.

25 January 1945: The battalion receives thirteen Tiger II tanks.

26 January 1945: Entrainment of thirty-nine Tiger IIs in Lage for transport to the Eastern Front. The battalion is to report directly to Heeresgruppe Weichsel (Army Group Vistula). One week prior, SS-Sturmbannführer Herzig relieves the unpopular SS-Obersturmbannführer Leiner, the son-in-law of the deceased SS-Brigadeführer Eicke. SS-Hauptsturmführer Birnschein and SS-Obersturmführer Ther, who sent reports against Leiner to the SS Main Office, are transferred for law, order and discipline reasons to schwere SS-Panzer-Abteilung 501.

28 January 1945: Detrainment of parts of the battalion in Kalies in the Wedell area of Pomerania.

The 3rd Platoon of the 2./ (four tanks) and the Flak platoon are directed to Küstrin. Some how, this is the homeland of SS-Untersturmführer Haake, the platoon leader!

Employment of some elements at the Driesen Bridgehead (the 1./schwere SS-Panzer-Abteilung 503 of SS-Obersturmführer Lippert).

One train (690739) with six Tigers stops near Mückenberg; the transport leader is ordered by the local commander, Generalmajor Hauschulz, to detrain as quickly as possible and move to Friedeberg.

29 January 1945: Instead, the tanks move to Stolzenberg and are taken by surprise by Russian tanks at 0400 hours; all are lost.

The battalion is attached to the II. Armee-Korps.

31 January 1945: The 1./schwere SS-Panzer-Abteilung 503 attacks with seven to eight tanks towards Regentin with a Fallschirmjäger-Bataillon; eight antitank guns are destroyed. During the movement to contact, SS-Oberscharführer Dienersberger uses his submachine gun against Russian infantry in a wooded area that is being passed. He is mortally wounded in the head.

One Tiger (SS-Untersturmführer Bromann)becomes immobilized after several hits from antitank guns. The remaining elements hit an antitank position right outside of Regentin. The leading tank (SS-Unterscharführer Lindl of the 1./schwere SS-Panzer-Abteilung 503) receives twenty-two hits, but it is able to get through. One Tiger (SS-Untersturmführer Meinl) , which is covering the left flank, is hit by a Russian tank and starts burning. The crew suffers severe burns.

Total tanks: 38.

The other elements of the battalion are attached to the XX. -Armee-Korps.

1 February 1945: The attack is resumed and covers more than ten kilometers.

2 February 1945: An advance of five kilometers towards Deutsch Krone and Schneidemühl. The acting commander of the 2./schwere SS-Panzer-Abteilung 503, SS-Untersturmführer Schäfer, is wounded. The tanks later withdraw. One immobilized tank (SS-Unterscharführer Bender) is recovered during the night hours.

3 February 1945: Four Tigers make their way to Arnswalde.

4 February 1945: The 1./schwere SS-Panzer-Abteilung 503 (with four tanks) relieves a surrounded infantry element five kilometers from Arnswalde. Four Tiger IIs are immobilized; two enemy tanks are destroyed.

In a second engagement, four other tanks stop several enemy attacks near Hohenwalde and north of Samenthin. Several enemy tanks are knocked out. One tank—the Tiger II of SS-Untersturmführer Bromann—becomes immobilized after being hit in the drive sprocket by an antitank gun; it is pulled back during the night by the other three tanks to the Marienkriche churchyard in Arnswalde.

Seven Tiger IIs remain in the encircled Arnswalde in order to stabilize the local defense.

5 February 1945: Several enemy attacks on Arnswalde are repelled.

The local commander, Generalmajor Vogt, considers capitulation; after a threat by those elements of the battalion there to break out alone, this intention is not realized.

7 February 1945: SS-Untersturmführer Kauerauf picks up three tanks in Zachan that were repaired in Stargard. He is ordered to break through to Arnswalde via Reetz. Just outside the enemy-occupied town of Reetz, these tanks are diverted to support SS-Panzer-Regiment 11 "Hermann von Salza" in Jacobshagen. The tanks attached to the 11. Armee are further attached to Kampfgruppe Munzel.

Several enemy tanks are knocked out in Arnswalde.

8 February 1945: One Tiger II of the 1./schwere SS-Panzer-Abteilung 503 (SS-Untersturmführer Kauerauf) and two tanks of the 2./schwere SS-Panzer-Abteilung 503 (SS-Obersturmführer Kaes) attack towards Ziegenhagen. They are joined in this effort by twelve assault guns from SS-Panzer-Abteilung "Hermann von Salza" and, later on, by additional assault guns from SS-Sturmgeschütz-Abteilung 11 "Nordland" and one Fallschirmjäger-Kompanie. Three JS IIs and several antitank guns are destroyed. After sundown, all-round defensive positions are established at the southern outskirts of Klein Silber (in the direction of Reetz).

The Arnswalde Tigers repel several enemy assaults near Schönwerder and Sandow.

9 February 1945: Two Tiger IIs are knocked out by tank hunter/killer teams in Klein Silber. The third Tiger II is immobilized by a malfunction of its electrical system and is destroyed by the crew.

Total tanks: 35.

Several enemy attacks are repelled at the southern outskirts of Arnswalde.

10 February 1945: The tanks not trapped in Arnswalde are sent from Preussisch Stargard to Zachan and directed to support the 11. SS-Freiwilligen-Panzer-Grenadier-Division "Nordland," which represents the center assault group for Operation "Sonnenwende" (Operation "Solstice").

Several Tiger IIs crush an enemy force assembled near Kühnsfelde in conjunction with Bataillon "Groß" and knock out several T-34s.

11 February 1945: Defensive fighting in Arnswalde.

12 February 1945: Ammunition gets scarce in Arnswalde. Instead of 8.8-centimeter main-gun rounds, ammunition for the 8.8-centimeter Flak is airdropped. Operational tanks: 16.

14 February 1945: Defensive operations against repeated enemy assaults on Arnswalde.

15 February 1945: This successful defense forms the prerequisite for the relief attack on Arnswalde. Operational tanks: 17.

17 February 1945: The next attack—into the area of Landsberg—has to be suspended due to enemy numerical superiority.

All Tiger IIs that fought in Arnswalde—four operational tanks with the Tiger II of SS-Oberscharführer Körner in tow—withdraw via Marienberg to Zachan for urgent repair and maintenance.

17–18 February 1945: All the tanks around Zachan are entrained for movement to Danzig (Gdansk) together with one maintenance platoon and the supply trains. The other tanks are put under command of Hauptmann Natterer, the commander of the Headquarters Company; the battalion commander moves with the elements dispatched to Danzig.

25 February 1945: The battalion reports fourteen operational tanks and twenty-five tanks in repair status.

26 February 1945: Twelve tanks being repaired are towed to Massow and put onto rail cars.

3 March 1945: An enemy attack on the 5. Jäger-Division (5th Light Infantry Division) east of Reetz is pushed back.

The train with the damaged tanks derails due to its excessive weight and high speed. More than eighty refugees also using this train are killed. The tanks that are still conditionally operational are detrained and move to Neuendorf, which is already under enemy pressure. One Tiger II (SS-Oberjunker ?) that is lacking ammunition is quickly set on fire by the crew and forms a roadblock. The following tank—the Tiger of SS-Oberscharführer Körner)—knocks down a large lime tree and is able to proceed towards Gollnow. On the way out of Neuendorf, a second crew-disabled Tiger II is passed.

Total tanks: 30.

4 March 1945: One after the other, the tanks to be repaired are towed to Gollnow and entrained there again so they can be moved to Pasewalk.

7 March 1945: The tanks are loaded on the flatcars with their combat tracks. This causes some collisions with passing trains on the opposite track. Due to destroyed railway sections, the train gets stuck in Christinenberg.

9 March 1945: After reconnoitering the situation, the movement commander (SS-Oberscharführer Körner) requires the rail movement be continued to Altdamm using the undamaged opposite track. This succeeds and the tanks are later transported to Pasewalk.

During the next few days, the Tigers have to stay on the flatcars and are used as security for the salon train of the Commander-in-Chief of Heeresgruppe Weichsel, Reichsführer SS Heinrich Himmler! Later detrainment in Zarenthin.

12 March 1945: Counterattack together with the I./Grenadier-Regiment 7 two kilometers northeast of Groß Mischau. Withdrawal to Pempau.

8 March 1945: Three Tigers of the 1./schwere SS-Panzer-Abteilung 503 are employed around Küstrin. SS-Unterscharführer Hoffmann's tank runs out of fuel in Kuhbrücke and SS-Oberscharführer Reitert's tank breaks its track tensioning device beside the road bridge across the Oder River. They are left behind by the crews, who are captured a short while later. The fate of the third tank is unclear. It hit a tree along the highway on its march from the detrainment station at Landsberg/Warthe on its way to Küstrin and wrecked its final drive. The fourth tank was refueled by mistake with coolant instead of gasoline, and it suffered engine failure. It was evacuated to a depot-level maintenance facility in Berlin.

Total tanks: 29.

The platoon leader (SS-Untersturmführer Haake) deserts and finds time to marry. In the weeks that follow, he is transported by his wife to Northern Germany, hidden in a horse cart.

Employment of the elements around Danzig.

20 February 1945: Departure to Wangerin.

21 February 1945: Arrival in Gotenhafen.

22 February 1945: Detrainment in Dirschau and road march into the area south of Preussisch Stargard; this brings the total of Tiger II's in the Danzig Pocket to 17. The battalion elements are initially attached to the XXIII. Armee-Korps and then to the XXVII. Armee-Korps.

First employment south of Preussisch Stargard with five to six Tigers.

27 February 1945: After knocking out two enemy tanks, SS-Obersturmführer Kaes is killed near Grabau by a hit from an antitank rifle through the vision block.

Mopping-up actions in a nearby unidentified town.

28 February 1945: Blocking positions are occupied. A single tank—the Tiger of SS-Oberscharführer Heinrich of the 1./schwere SS-Panzer-Abteilung 503—positioned on the front slope of a piece of high ground receives a fatal hit through the ventilator on the turret roof, and the turret crew is killed by fragments.

3 March 1945: Two Tigers are employed in Vossberg with SS-Panzer-Aufklärungs-Abteilung 11. An enemy tank company is eliminated. Some time later, another four tanks moving in the direction of Freienwalde are also knocked out.

7 March 1945: Further defensive fighting north of Preussisch Stargard.

The battalion elements are designated as a reserve of the XXIII. Armee-Korps for several days.

Two Tigers—the rest are at the maintenance facility—are in covering positions together with one Panzer IV, one Sturmgeschütz, and one 8.8-centimeter Flak when a massive enemy tank attack starts from the southwest. Out of eighty tanks, fifty-seven are destroyed. Nevertheless, the Russians continue their advance on the Preussisch Stargard fort. One tank—the Tiger of SS-Untersturmführer Bromann—relieves an encircled corps command post at the Hermannshof estate. The other tank—the Tiger of SS-Hauptscharführer Becker—receives a hit to the engine and starts burning. The dismounted crew is murdered by the Russians.

10 March 1945: Skirmishes near Groß Mischau.

16 March 1945: Employment near Ramkau.

20 March 1945: Two of six tanks operational.

21 March 1945: Operations around Bastenhagen.

21–22 March 1945: Blocking positions occupied at Groß Katz.

Tank maintenance takes place on the Danzig wharf. Employment around Danzig, occasionally accompanied by a forward observer from the heavy cruiser Prinz Eugen.

25 March 1945: First air raid on Danzig. Two Tigers (Bromann and the radio officer, SS-Obersturmführer König) reconnoiter towards Zoppot. Later on, they occupy a blocking position on the edge of Oliva-Zoppot.

26 March 1945: Several attacks are repelled, and six Josef Stalin tanks are knocked out. One Josef Stalin, which was captured by Sturmgeschütz-Brigade 190, is put under German command; when it becomes non-operational, it is finally sunk in the harbor.

The rest of the battalion is attached to the 11. SS-Freiwilligen-Panzer-Grenadier-Division "Nordland" (six operational and seven damaged Tigers).

After sunset, the tanks pull back to the battalion command post in the Oliva Castle, which is also the site of the corps command post. During the night, the last four Tigers change position to the Weißhof Estate southeast of Oliva.

Total tanks: 12.

30 March 1945: The crews under command of SS-Untersturmführer Städler in the Danzig area are partially employed as infantry until 1 May 1945 in the woods near Bohnsack.

2–3 May 1945: The majority of the personnel of the battalion elements in the Danzig area are transported by sea from Schnackenburg to Swinemünde and then on to the other battalion elements in the Berlin area.

6 April 1945: Operational tanks: 9.

1–15 April 1945: Assembly of the ten Pasewalk Tigers at Frauenhagen.

10 April 1945: The Wehrmacht Daily Report mentions SS-Untersturmführer Bromann, who is employed in the Gotenhafen area. He is credited with sixty-six enemy tanks and forty-four antitank guns from 2-18 March 1945. Operational tanks: 9.

13 April 1945: Inventory: 12.

16 April 1945: The battalion elements are ordered into the area north of Straußberg (via Angermünde and Eberswalde). Operational tanks: 10.

18 April 1945: Blocking positions occupied on the road from Protzel to Bollersdorf (at Ernsthof). An enemy armor assault originating from Grunow is repelled; sixty-four enemy tanks and one Tiger II are knocked out.

Total tanks: 11.

19 April 1945: A Soviet breakthrough hits the Maintenance Company; most of it falls into enemy hands.

Breakthrough to Berlin; four enemy tanks knocked out.

Tiger 314 of SS-Unterscharführer Diers is in a blocking position on the hills northeast of Klosterdorf (three kilometers east of Straußberg); thirteen enemy tanks approaching between Prötzel and Grunow are knocked out. Due to a hit on the turret roof, the crew has to use the emergency firing circuit. The tank pulls back with another Tiger (SS-Oberscharführer Bootsmann) in tow!

After several miles, the tanks are stopped by SS-Gruppenführer Harmel. He orders Diers' tank to turn east and knock out several enemy tanks. After heading in this direction, the crew learns that the reported Soviet tanks have already been destroyed. On its way back to its original location, the tank gets stuck in the deep snow and has to be recovered by two Panzer IVs of the 10. SS-Panzer-Division "Frundsberg" that just happen to be moving through the area. Due to the enemy breakthrough, Bootsmann's tank, which was left behind, cannot be recovered.

Total tanks: 10.

Five Tigers under SS-Obersturmführer Müller are occupy firing positions on the high ground near Grunow. The engagement against the attacking enemy tanks is opened too early. When ammunition runs scarce, the three Tigers of SS-Oberscharführer Körner, which have been kept in reserve, have to join the fight. Together, the Tigers destroy more than seventy tanks. SS-Obersturmführer Müller is killed outside of his tank during a barrage by "Stalin organ" rockets.

In support of a counterattack on the high ground near Bollersdorf, SS-Oberscharführer Körner spots an entire Soviet armor brigade, which has assembled carelessly and is being resupplied. On the road to Straußberg, a Josef Stalin company is lined up; at the edge of Bollersdorf more than 100 T-34/85s are crowded together.

He opens the engagement by knocking out the lead and trail Josef Stalin tanks. The remaining Josef Stalins are not able to traverse their turrets due to the density of the trees.

Within a few minutes, the three Tigers wipe out the T-34/85s. They then dispatch the remaining Josef Stalins.

SS-Oberscharführer Körner is credited with knocking out thirty-nine; SS-Hauptscharführer Harrer is credited with another twenty-five. The tanks then rearm behind the defensive area. The other tanks are relocated in the direction of Werneuchen.

In the late afternoon, the 3 Tigers are attacked by around thirty T-34s. With the assistance of a fourth Tiger (SS-Untersturmführer Schäfer), all the enemy tanks are put out of action. After that, the accompanying Soviet infantry assault is wiped out by using delayed-fuse rounds.

After sunset, more Josef Stalins restart their advance and are knocked out by using night flares. The Tigers then pull back to Straußberg. During this day, his 25th birthday, SS-Oberscharführer Körner knocks out his 76th enemy tank.

20 April 1945: Several tanks are knocked out at the edge of Sraußberg; following this, there is a delaying action towards Altlandsberg. SS-Oberscharführer Körner has to change tanks and gets the one from SS-Untersturmführer Schäfer. Schäfer's tank is being repaired in Berlin-Tempelhof at the Krupp & Druckemüller plant until late in the afternoon. When it returns, it is ordered to move to Nieder Schönhausen along with a second Tiger (SS-Untersturmführer Feige) to push back the enemy from the R 158.

SS-Unterscharführer Diers's tank is repaired in Hönow (near Altlandsberg). The welding inside the turret of the tank, however, catches it on fire. The gunner SS-Rottenführer Kothe neutralizes the fire using the fire extinguisher. Due to the acid, the gun sight and the turret machine gun are ruined.

21 April 1945: The road march to Berlin is started (via Marzahn, Lichtenberg and Biesdorf).

SS-Oberscharführer Körner and SS-Untersturmführer Feige crush an enemy armor assault, knocking out fifteen tanks, some of them from virtually pointblank range. Retreat to the Hermannstraße in Neukölln. Due to a hit from a rifle grenade into the commander's cupola, SS-Untersturmführer Feige's head is sheared off.

Tiger 314 starts its march to the Krupp & Druckemüller plant in Britz (via Marzahn and Lichterfelde).

22 April 1945: Movement through sections of Berlin (Biesdorf, Köpenick, Oberschöneweide and Neukölln across the Teltow Canal Bridge); one ISU-122 is knocked out. Screening positions occupied on the Sonnenallee in the direction of the bridge. Later on, employment in the direction of the Bergstraße and on the Richardstraße in front of the Hertie department-store warehouse. The Tigers are ordered to retake the Köpenick Railway Station by advancing from the Berliner Straße. Six Tiger IIs are employed with the 33. Waffen-SS-Grenadier-Division "Charlemagne."

23 April 1945: Early in the morning, SS-Oberscharführer Körner knocks out a Josef Stalin. Due to limited observation, a second Josef Stalin is spotted too late a little while later. In a freak hit inside the gun tube of the Tiger, the loader is torn to pieces. The tank is ordered to the last-known location of the Maintenance Company.

Total tanks: 9.

Tiger 314 is repaired and ordered to be employed in Britz (the Siemens facilities); the crew heads in this direction without a tank commander. During the movement, the crew "picks up" SS-Untersturmführer Gast from the 3. SS-Panzer-Division "Totenkopf" as an interim commander. There are no engagements, and the tank returns back in the afternoon. It subsequently occupies a covering position in Marienfelde.

24 April 1945: The remaining tanks are scattered around Berlin. One tank (SS-Unterscharführer Bender) is employed on the Mecklenburgische Straße, where it knocks out four tanks. The tank of SS-Unterscharführer Turk is employed in the area of the Schloßbrücke, the Gertraudenbrücke, the Reichsbank, Wallstraße and the Spitalmarkt.

SS-Untersturmführer Gast, still in command of the orphaned tank, knocks out an ISU-122 on the Teltow Canal Bridge in Neukölln. After the intercom system malfunctions, the commander directs the driver by means of a string. Afterwards, the tank occupies a covering position on the left-hand antitank barrier in the Sonnenallee (oriented towards the bridge). It sees its last ration run from the first sergeant of the 3./schwere SS-Panzer-Abteilung 503. At noon, it moves to the main command post at the Neukölln Court House. Order are given for it to move via the Bergstraße, the Richardstraße and the Hertie warehouse in the Berliner Straße to a position opposite to the main post office.

25 April 1945: SS-Unterscharführer Bender is employed with his Tiger II near the railway station at the Heerstraße. The Tiger II near the Neukölln main post office is knocked out. One tank conducts a counterattack together with elements from the 33. Waffen-SS-Grenadier-Division "Charlemagne" from the Hasenheide district; several enemy tanks are knocked out. It then breaks through enemy blocking forces using the Richardstraße, where it knocks out three enemy tanks in the vicinity of Jahnstraße 3. Following this, it relocates to the Hertieplatz.

Total tanks: 8.

26 April 1945: The Tiger of SS-Oberscharführer Diers supports a counterattack south of SS- Panzer-Regiment 11 of the 11. SS-Freiwilligen-Panzer-Grenadier-Division "Nordland" and two companies of the 33. Waffen-SS-Grenadier-Division "Charlemagne" from the Neukölln Town Hall towards the Berliner Straße. Diers' tank is later joined by another Tiger II. After expending all the main gun rounds, the tanks are ordered to move back to the Hermannsplatz. When SS-Untersturmführer Gast dismounts, he is badly wounded. During the night, the tanks move to the Potsdamer Platz. Maintenance is also conducted in the Uhlandstraße during the night. The gunner reports to the battalion command post on the Potsdamer Straße and SS-Oberscharführer Diers joins his crew again.

27 April 1945: The tank of SS-Oberscharführer Diers is in a covering position at the central subway station and orients in the direction of the Belle-Alliance-Platz. After replacing the tank of SS-Untersturmführer Feige, SS-Oberscharführer Körner is employed together with SS-Untersturmführer Schröder in Wilmersdorf (on the Kurfürstenstraße) and at the Halensee Railway Station. Two enemy tanks are knocked out.

28 April 1945: An enemy attack supported by flamethrowers on the right side of the Luisenstadt Church is pushed back. One Tiger supports a counterattack of the 33. Waffen-SS-Grenadier-Division "Charlemagne."

The battalion commander, SS-Untersturmführer Schäfer and SS-Hauptscharführer Körner are ordered to report to the Reich Chancellery.

29 April 1945: All of the above are decorated with the Knight's Cross by SS-Brigadeführer Mohnke; SS-Untersturmführer Bromann is presented this award in absentia.

Two tanks block the city freeway and the Kurfürstendamm; the other tanks are assembled at the city zoo.

The tank of SS-Unterscharführer Diers moves to the Potsdamer Platz in the direction of the Saarlandstraße and the Anhalter Railway Station. The tank of SS-Unterscharführer Turk is on the other side of the road. One ISU-122 and several T-34s are knocked out.

Two Tigers are in action at the Halensee Railway Station (SS-Oberscharführer Stolze and SS-Unterscharführer Bender, who is replaced by Semik after he is wounded).

30 April 1945: SS-Oberscharführer Stolze knocks out one tank at the Halensee Railway Station. SS-Unterscharführer Diers is ordered by radio to the Reichstag and knocks out around thirty T-34s there. SS-Unterscharführer Turk remains at the Potsdamer Platz and repels another enemy assault, before his tank receives a hit that damages the right track. It is recovered by a Bergepanther to the area of the Reich Chancellery. About three hours later, the tank moves to the Saarlandstraße. It is employed later at the entrance to the Potsdamer Platz subway station, where it was ultimately abandoned.

Total tanks: 7.

1 May 1945: Five more enemy tanks knocked out at the Halensee Railway Station.

Counterattack by SS-Unterscharführer Diers' tank towards the Kroll Opera House. Orders are received from Goebbels: Assemble at the Friedrichstraße Railway Station and break through via the Weidendammer Brücke in the direction of Oranienburg. Link up with Kampfgruppe Steiner and then move to Schleswig Holstein. Link up with Canadian forces and attack towards the east!

At 2100 hours, four enemy tanks are knocked out in the Friedrichstraße in front of the Weidendammer Brücke. SS-Oberscharführer Körner "takes possession" of an abandoned Panther tank.

2 May 1945: About midnight, the breakthrough attempt is started. One of the passengers on the rear engine deck is a high-ranking person. At the next intersection, heavy shelling is received from the right flank and all outside passengers are shredded to pieces. An SS-Untersturmführer, who was Goebbels' driver and adjutant, subsequently identifies the high-ranking person: Martin Bormann. The movement continues to the Züricher Straße and then to the Schönhauser Allee. The tank runs over a German mine after crashing through a tank barrier. The tank has to be blown up. SS-Unterscharführer Turk's tank receives an order to break out via the Weidendammer Brücke. The tank is eventually abandoned when it has only a few rounds left and one of the tracks will no longer steer.

Total tanks: 5.

Two Tiger II tanks attempt to break through to the west at the Schulenburger Brücke. One of them belongs to the 1./schwere SS-Panzer-Abteilung 503 of SS-Obersturmführer Lippert; the other one is from the 3./schwere SS-Panzer-Abteilung 503 of SS-Untersturmführer Schäfer. Desperate fighting ensues.

The Tiger from the 3./schwere SS-Panzer-Abteilung 503 is knocked out at close range shortly before it reaches the Heerstraße by an 8.8-centimeter Flak manned by Russians (two men are killed and Schäfer suffers severe burns). The other tank is destroyed by its crew.

Two other tanks under SS-Oberscharführer Stolze try in vain to break through at the Spandauer Brücke. During the night, the tanks are abandoned.

Total tanks: 1.

SS-Oberscharführer Körner and his Panther moves via Staaken towards Döberitz. There, he knocks out a Josef Stalin that is blocking the Reichsstraße 5. He then proceeds to knock out two assault guns. During the night, the Panther is set on fire after it suffers alternator damage.

A single Tiger in action south of Perleberg bogs down in a meadow and is abandoned.

Total tanks: 0.

3 May 1945: SS-Obersturmführer Lippert is killed in action.

The majority of the battalion, including SS-Sturmbannführer Herzig, makes its way into the area of Ketzin (on the Havel River), where it is trapped by the Soviets. Most of it is captured.

9 May 1945: The rest of the battalion around Danzig is taken prisoner near Schievenhorst.

✝

Total score of the battalion is more than 500 tanks.

BATTALION COMMANDERS

SS-Sturmbannführer Paetsch	1 July 1943–4 February 1944
SS-Obersturmbannführer Leiner	4 February 1944–18 January 1945
SS-Sturmbannführer Herzig	18 January 1945–8 May 1945

KNIGHT'S CROSS RECIPIENTS

29 April 1945:	SS-Sturmbannführer Herzig
29 April 1945:	SS-Untersturmführer Schäfer
29 April 1945:	SS-Untersturmführer Bromann
29 April 1945:	SS-Oberscharführer Körner

TOP SCORERS

SS-Oberscharführer Körner	100+
SS-Untersturmführer Bromann	66

The training for many SS tank crews started with SS-Panzer-Ersatz-Abteilung 1 at the Grafenwöhr Training Area. Obsolete tanks such as these panzer III's were used. KOTHE

Old versions of the Panzer IV were also used. The limited and resource-intensive Panthers and Tigers could only be used sparingly for training purposes. KLÖCKNER

Radio training was also conducted in a similarly cost-conscious way. KOTHE

Other elements of the battalion also continued their training as well. Here we see a soldier of the supply section cleaning his Büssing truck after drivers' instruction. In this relatively peaceful environment, everything had to be according to regulation, to include the placing of a Fahrschule ("Drivers' School") sign on the front of the vehicle above the license plate.

At the end of July, the battalion—initially formed as the II./SS-Panzer-Regiment 11—was sent to Croatia. In August of that year, the battalion took part in the disarmament of an Italian tank regiment. The operational Italian tanks—such as this M13/40—were then used for the continued training of the German crews.

The battalion trained on its new Tigers at the Zwolle Training Area in the Netherlands. The tanks were parked under these shelters to help avoid detection by Allied aircraft. KOTHE

In late January 1944, a detail was sent to Königsborn to pick up tanks. As seen in the above photograph, factory reconditioned tanks were also issued to the battalion in addition to brand-new ones. TURK

STAHL.

More views from the Zwolle Training Area. In the lower photograph, crews practice rail loading a tank by driving over an improvised loading ramp (bundles of hay over which two sections of track have been laid).

More instances of having to train without the actual formation vehicles. Here we see use being made of the rare C version of the Panzer I (VK 601). KOTHE

Gunnery training at Zwolle. The tanks sported a highly unusual three-color camouflage scheme. No turret numerals have been applied, since the battalion was still short its final complement of tanks.

Some new tanks move out for field training. The battalion still did not have its complete issue of tanks. KOTHE

Crew training at Zwolle. The fact that that tanks do not have any natural camouflage or have their air-defense machine guns mounted indicates that the Allied air threat had not yet made an impact in the spring of 1944. KLÖCKNER

In order to enable its sister battalion, schwere SS-Panzer-Abteilung 102, to deploy for combat operations, the battalion had to transfer some of its trained crews. This photograph shows some of them after being welcomed by their new superiors. HAAK

For a short time, SS-Sturmbannführer Hartrampf was the battalion commander. He then left the battalion to assume command of schwere SS-Panzer-Abteilung 102 in August 1944. He is seen here inspecting training; a "gas attack" may be on the training schedule based on the two soldiers seen to his right.

SS-Sturmbannführer Hartrampf issues orders to his commanders prior to the start of a field-training exercise.

The battalion tried to make the best of its understrength status. It used a number of former Italian Army vehicles that it brought back with it from Croatia. Getting spare parts was difficult, however.

Some standard vehicles were available, however, such as this Kübelwagen staff car.

In early May, the battalion lost another six Tigers, this time to the 9. SS-Panzer-Regiment 3. This Tiger had been loaded on the train; its outer road-wheels have been removed and the transport tracks mounted.

On 22 August 1944, a pick-up detail was dispatched to Magdeburg to be issued another four Tigers. The tanks have been loaded and the detail gets ready to depart, apparently having found enough time in Magdeburg to make new friends!

After being issued with Tiger IIs, the battalion was sent to the front in the Oder Sector. Here we see SS-Unterscharführer Reichel observing the rearming of his Tiger.

The first major encounter of the battalion with Soviet forces was in and around Arnswalde, which was finally relieved by the Tigers. On 4 February 1945, the Tiger of SS-Untersturmführer Bromann was hit by an antitank gun. The tanks was towed to Arnswalde during the night and was positioned in front of the battered Arnswalde church.

These tanks were subsequently turned in to schwere Panzer-Abteilung (Funklenk) 302, marking the end of the Tiger I phase of schwere SS-Panzer-Abteilung 103. TURK

Damaged roadwheels are being replaced in this photograph. The spare track links that were normally mounted on the turret sides seems to already have been used. Many tanks did not have either Balkenkreuze or identification markings on them. BROMANN

After the first few engagements, there was not much time to perform maintenance or effect repairs on the tanks. Here, however, we see the remounting of a drive sprocket after a final drive has been repaired.

After the fighting at Arnswalde, an awards ceremony is conducted. SS-Sturmbannführer Herzig decorates tankers with both classes of the Iron Cross. All of the tanks seem to have a number of "kill" rings painted on the gun tubes. STAHL

This photograph of the slightly wounded SS-Untersturmführer Bromann also clearly shows an interesting aspect of methods applied in the field. The double-ended hooks were left permanently attached to the tow shackles. This helped speed up the attachment of tow cables. The noncommissioned officer on the ground is SS-Oberscharführer Böde, the company's maintenance sergeant.

STAHL

Camouflage was also essential on the Eastern Front. It is difficult to identify this Tiger II, but the alert reader will be able to make out one of the identifying features of this tank—the rain guard that was added over the gunner's sights. OTT

Two small groups were separated from the battalion and went on to fight in the Danzig (Gdansk) Pocket. One of the tanks can be seen after the fighting, where it had got stuck in a bomb or shell crater.

A Tiger II that was involved in the final fighting in Berlin! The last 10 tanks of the battalion were used up in the defense of the capital. This was the tank of SS-Unterscharführer Turk and was abandoned on 30 April 1945 in front of the subway station at Potsdamer Platz.

Having lost their tanks, most of the crews were shipped to Swinemünde in late April. The First Sergeant of the 2./schwere SS-Panzer-Abteilung 503, SS-Stabsscharführer Feiler, can be seen second from the right. For uniform enthusiasts, it would appear that many members of this company had rose-pink or red piping applied around their collar tabs and, in some cases, even around their collars in a manner that was similar to Army armor formations. BROMANN

SCHWERE SS-PANZER-ABTEILUNG 103 (503)

Vehicles on Hand/Deliveries

Date	Tiger I	Tiger II	On hand	Remarks
4 February 1944	6		6	Handed over to the 9./SS-Panzer-Regiment 3
24 May 1944	6		6	Handed over to schwere Panzer-Abteilung 301 (Funklenk)
22 August 1944	(4)		10	Sent off for depot-level maintenance and handed over to schwere Panzer-Abteilung 301 (Funklenk)
19 October 1944		4	4	
27 December 1944		6	10	Received from schwere SS-Panzer-Abteilung 502
11 January 1945		6	16	
12 January 1945		3	19	
16 January 1945		3	22	
18 January 1945		4	26	
25 January 1945		13	39	
Grand Total	0	39		

Losses

Date	Losses	On hand	Remarks
31 January 1945	1	39	Knocked out by a tank
9 February 1945	3	36	1 destroyed by own crew and 2 destroyed by infantry
23 February 1945	1	35	Knocked out
3 March 1945	2	33	Destroyed by own crew
7 March 1945	1	32	Knocked out
28 March 1945	4	28	Abandoned
April–May 1945	15	13	?
18 April 1945	1	12	Knocked out
19 April 1945	1	11	Knocked out
23 April 1945	1	10	Knocked out by an JS 2
25 April 1945	1	9	Knocked out
2 May 1945	7	2	6 destroyed by own crew and 1 knocked out by a captured 8.8-centimeter Flak
May 1945	2	0	?
Grand total:	39		

Of the losses suffered by the battalion, 56% were due to self-destruction (to prevent capture) and 44% were lost in combat operations.

Schwere SS-Panzerabteilung 503 – 25 January 1945

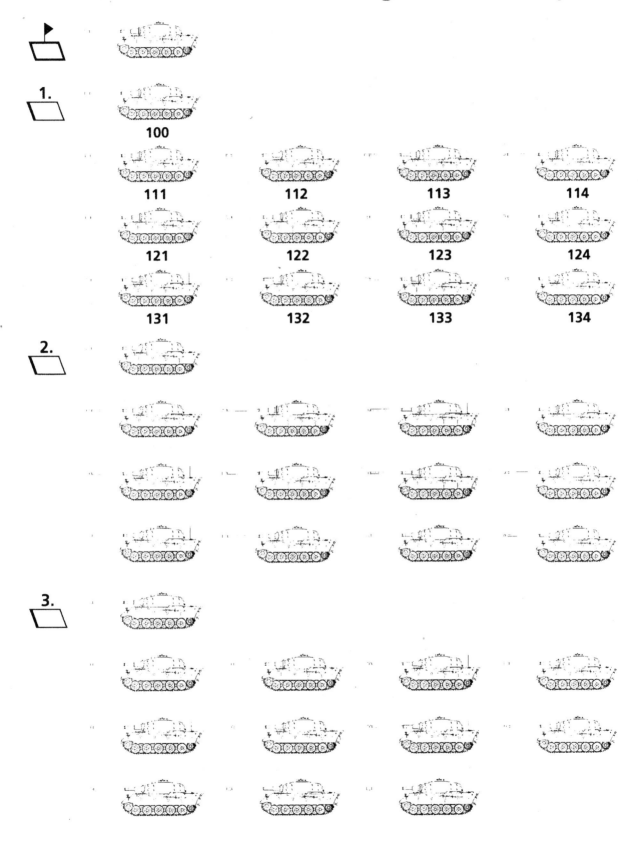

1.

100

111   112   113   114

121   122   123   124

131   132   133   134

2.

3.

Schwere SS-Panzer-Abteilung 104

22 October 1943: An order is issued to activate the battalion, which will establish a habitual command and control relationship with the IV. SS-Panzer-Korps.

May 1944: The activation order is rescinded and the formation is stricken from the rolls (field-post identity number deleted).

Formations with Individually Attached Tigers

TIGERS OF THE ARMOR SCHOOL AT BERGEN

Several tanks of different types that were part of the training inventory for the Panzer-Lehr-Abteilung were moved to the hastily established armor school at Bergen. These were then employed in the vicinity of the school during the final weeks of the war.

Among the armored vehicles: six Tiger Is, eleven Panthers, twenty-nine Panzer IVs, and twelve assault guns and tank destroyers. It was originally intended for them to join Panzerausbildungsverband "Thüringen" (Armor Training Formation "Thuringia"), which was established when the training establishment was mobilized and put on a war footing on 24 March 1945. This order was later suspended by the General der Panzertruppen West (the senior armor officer responsible for armor-related activities in the western theater).

One of the formations that was actually formed was Tiger-Gruppe Fehrmann, which later fought with Kampfgruppe Schulze (see the separate section).

April 1945: Two Tigers are issued to Kampfgruppe (Oberst) Grosan of the 2. Marine-Infanterie-Division (2nd Naval Infantry Division). The mixed tank and anti-gun company of this Kampfgruppe consists of one Panther, two assault guns, the aforementioned two Tiger I tanks, and approximately six 7.5-centimeter Pak. The Kampfgruppe attack enemy forces near Engehausen on 11 April 1945; several antitank guns are knocked out. Enemy attempts to break through the German lines from Hademstorf in the direction of Ostenholz are spoiled for two days.

14 April 1945: Kampfgruppe Grosan is relocated to Soltau for the local defensive effort (movement via Ostenholz-Bergen-Achterberg-Tetendorf). One of the two Tigers is left behind at a tank barrier in Bassel due to lack of fuel. The Panthers and the assault guns are used as flank cover in the direction of Ahlften; the Tiger and the antitank guns orient towards the western outskirts of Wolterdingen.

16 April 1945: Skirmishes around Soltau, which is then bypassed by the British.

17 April 1945: The British 8th Armoured Reconnaissance Regiment attempts to out-flank Soltau to the east; its forward elements are pushed back to Bassel by a single Tiger. In the meantime, the other Tiger repels the British assaults on Wolterdingen.

18 April 1945: The second Tiger is positioned at the outskirts of Bispingen and puts to flight the lead elements of the British 7th Armoured Division after knocking out several scout cars. The Tiger has to be abandoned later on due to mechanical failure.

PANZER-DIVISION "CLAUSEWITZ"

This division is established in early April 1945 in the area of Lüneburg-Lauenburg and forms a so-called mixed tank regiment (Panzer-Regiment 106 "Clausewitz"), using elements from the armor-school instructional detachment from the gunnery school at Putlos (Kampfgruppe (Major) von Benningsen).

13 April 1945: On the southern outskirts of Uelzen-Verssen, the British 15th Scottish Division is encountered. Several enemy tanks are knocked out. The attack is continued and the division's Panzergrenadier battalion outflanks the Scots, inflicting heavy casualties.

14 April 1945: Mission: Attack to the south via Helmstedt to the Harz Mountains! (The ultimate intent was for the division to take part with Wenck's forces in relieving Berlin.)

15 April 1945: A Tiger batters British formations at Nettelkamp.

16 April 1945: Kampfgruppe Benningsen joins the division.

18 April 1945: At midnight, Kampfgruppe Benningsen captures the wooden area 12 kilometers northeast of Wittingen.

19 April 1945: In the darkness, Kampfgruppe Benningsen loses contact south of Hasselhorst with the other Panzer-Division "Clausewitz" elements advancing on Lindhof. As a result of this, a US blocking force is unwittingly outflanked and subsequently decimated. The Kampfgruppe of the XXXIX. Panzer-Korps (General der Panzertruppe Decker) concentrates its armored vehicles and advances on Süderwittingen in order to escape from US envelopment. In the evening, the woods near Ehra-Lessien are reached.

20 April 1945: Attack on the only intact bridge across the Weser-Elbe Canal near Fallersleben is prepared.

21 April 1945: Early in the morning, the road Gifhorn-Brome is seized, and a column of US supply trucks is eliminated. The German column continues its road march with its lights on and threads into a US column without problems. Many soldiers at traffic control points wave to the column.

Just in front of the canal bridge, the leading armor elements hit an antitank-gun position. The lead tank is knocked out. Two Panthers equipped with infrared searchlights destroy it and capture the bridge. In Fallersleben, a Tiger runs over a mine and is immobilized. Assault with the last tanks towards Ehmen, passing a refueling US tank company. The column then advances via Destedt to the Elm Mountains. The Kampfgruppe is disbanded when its vehicles run out of fuel.

19 April 1945: A single Tiger stops the advance of the 3rd Royal Tank Regiment towards Sassendorf (south of Lauenburg).

1 May 1945: The same Tiger again stops elements of the 3rd Royal Tank Regiment on the northeast outskirts of Schwarzenbek and knocks out two enemy tanks before it is also hit and knocked out.

TIGER-GRUPPE FEHRMANN

After the Panzer-Lehr-Division was formed at the Fallingbostel Training Area, an activation staff remained in Camp Oerbke under command of Major Schulze. Using several tanks from the Armor School at Bergen, he formed Kampfgruppe Schulze in early April 1945 and received the mission to make contact with the division (by then trapped in the Ruhr Pocket).

The Kampfgruppe consisted of five Panthers and six Tiger I tanks. The latter ones are put under command of Oberleutnant Fehrmann. The tanks were marked with a large letter F and numbered 1, 2, 3, 4, 5, and 13.

✙

6 April 1945: After marching in the direction of the Weser River, the Kampfgruppe reaches the Aller River near Rethem. Due to transmission failure, 1 Tiger breaks down.

7 April 1945: Nienburg is transited. Near Stolzenau, a light-infantry company joins the Kampfgruppe.

8 April 1945: Relocation to the forestry building at Landwehr (northeastern outskirts of the Schaumburger Forest near Wiedensahl).

9 April 1945: Assault of the Panthers on Wietersheim. Only one returns with the Kampfgruppe commander. The Kampfgruppe does not realize that it is approximately thirty kilometers behind the enemy's lines. Tiger-Gruppe Fehrmann then attacks. Tiger F02 is hit in the turret by a PIAT—a British handheld antitank rocket similar to a bazooka in its capabilities—at the western outskirts of Frille. It then sustains another hit on the mantlet, which jams the elevating and depressing mechanism of the main gun. The two Tigers that are following continue the advance and take approximately thirty British air-borne soldiers prisoner.

The Tiger with the blocked gun elevating and depressing mechanism is driven back to Fallingbostel by Unteroffizier Franzen. It receives a new mantlet over the course of the next few days.

11 April 1945: The five remaining tanks fight their way through enemy-controlled territory as far as Bückeburg. The Kampfgruppe moves only on trails in the woods. In the course of this, two Tigers bog down. The attempt by a Panther to recover them results in the Panther also getting bogged down. All three tanks are blown up. The crews—including Oberleutnant Fehrmann—are taken prisoner by US forces after moving several kilometers on foot.

The other two Tigers face several US tanks near Achum. Tiger F13 of Feldwebel Bellof is knocked out; there are no survivors. Tiger F05 with Major Schulze on board knocks out three Shermans and one armored car advancing on the road; it then manages to evade the superior enemy, despite three hits. The tank refuels from an US fuel truck near Wendthagen. Major Schulze plans his route using a captured US map. During the night, the Autobahn bridge near Lauenau is crossed.

12 April 1945: The enemy held town of Nienstedt is transited early in the morning. A gregarious US military policeman waves to the German vehicles traveling with their head-lights on as they move towards the Nienstedt Pass. In front of the high ground, they encounter a US column. An accompanying Sherman and one armored car are knocked out. The US surrender and about 200 German soldiers held in a barn are freed. With two captured US trucks, the march continues.

13 April 1945: At dawn, Major Schulze notices in Egestorf that a large US command post is located in Barsinghausen. Major Schulze decides to try to wipe it out. After continued movement to the northeast edge of the dominant high ground, the Tiger runs out of fuel in front of the forestry building at Hohenbostel and has to be blown up. Major Schulze dissolves the Kampfgruppe.

The Way of Tiger F02

10 April 1945: After his tank is repaired, the commander gets the order to report to the command post of Kampfgruppe Grosan in Ostenholz.

12 April 1945: The tank is ordered to participate in a counterattack south in the direction of the British Aller Bridgeheads near Essel. After knocking out two Comets, one half-track, and one scout car, the Kampfgruppe withdraws to the northern edge of the forest.

13 April 1945: Advance from Ostenholz to the south. The tank is knocked out by a Comet of A Squadron of the 3rd Royal Tank Regiment as it moves along Drebber Creek without infantry accompanying infantry. The flank shot from the Comet comes from a distance of only sixty meters; the crew evades to Ostenholz.

Tiger F02 got separated from the rest and was knocked out by a British Comet on 13 April 1945 near Ostenholz.
BOVINGTON TANK MUSEUM

Feldwebel Bellof's Tiger F13 was knocked out on 11 April 1945 near Achum. BOVINGTON TANK MUSEUM

The Comet's hit is being examined by this British officer. Two fragments caused by the solid-shot projectile are visible on both sides of the penetration. The round hit the engine and brought the vehicle to a sudden stop.

Several days later, the tank was towed to the road and recovered. The vehicle reveals a strange mixture of components, e.g., an old turret with the drum-shaped commander's cupola and the late-version steel-rimmed road-wheel suspension. BOVINGTON TANK MUSEUM

FALLSCHIRM-PANZER-KORPS "HERMANN GÖRING"

15 March 1945: One Tiger available; it is not operational.

10 April 1945: Two Tigers on hand; one operational.

15 April 1945: Three Tigers on hand.

17 April 1945: In the morning, three Tigers attack Neu Krauscha; one Tiger is knocked out by antitank guns. In the evening, the town is attacked again and finally captured; two antitank guns and five enemy tanks destroyed.

18 April 1945: Screening mission at Neu Krauscha.

19 April 1945: The last operational tanks of the regiment—approximately seventeen Panthers, two Tigers and four armored Flak vehicles—are pooled under the command of Oberleutnant Wallhäußer. They start an attack out of an assembly area at Ebersbach and pass Kodersdorf to the west. They then pass Heide Hill and head in the direction of the road to the forestry building at Freischütz. Just outside of the meadows of Kodersdorf, a meeting engagement starts with the armored corps of the 2nd Polish Army. Within a short time, forty-three enemy tanks are knocked out and twelve more are captured undamaged.

20 April 1945: Twelve Tigers on hand.

25 April 1945: Assault as far as the hill along the Ratibor-Holscha railway line.

29 April 1945: Disengagement and entrainment in Bautzen; transport to Dresden.

PANZER-KOMPANIE KUMMERSDORF

31 March 1945: Formed out of the logistics battalion at the Kummersdorf Training Area. There are three very mixed platoons. They include one Tiger II, one Jagdtiger, four Panthers, two Panzer IVs, one Panzer III, one Nashorn tank destroyer, one Hummel self-propelled gun, two Shermans, and one Porsche Tiger 8.8-centimeter L/70 main gun (immobile).

19 April 1945: Company on the march to Luchau.

21 April 1945: Battalion staff and the company are attached to Kampfgruppe Möws.

PANZER-GRENADIER-DIVISION "KURMARK"

26 January 1945: Kampfgruppe (Oberst) Langkeit is formed, which later establishes the basis for Panzer-Grenadier-Division "Kurmark." Worn-out training tanks, including two Tiger Is, of Panzer-Ersatz- und Ausbildungs-Abteilung "Großdeutschland" in Cottbus are integrated.

30 January 1945: Defensive operations southwest of Neu Bischofsee (Nowo Biskupice).

3 February 1945: The first attempt to break out of the Neu Bischofsee Pocket in the direction of Kunersdorf (Kunowice) fails. In the afternoon, the attack gains ground after integration of a antitank company equipped with the Hetzer tank destroyer.

5 February 1945: Covering positions occupied west of Reitwein.

6 February 1945: Covering positions are occupied in the area Rathstock-Herzershof. Enemy movements in the area Neu Manchnow are engaged.

7 February 1945: Enemy penetrations along the road Podelzig-Reitwein are cleared.

10 February 1945: The tanks are relocated to Podelzig (via Dolgelin and Carzig), where they support an attack of the Potsdam Military Academy against the Reitwein Heights at 1700 hours (only short notice given). After sunset, any further attack on Reitwein has to be suspended. An enemy counterattack on Podelzig is pushed back with the assistance of the tanks. The II./Panzer-Regiment "Kurmark" remains in the Sachsendorf area during the next few days.

15–17 February 1945: The gap between Lebus and Klessin is held by two Panzergrenadier squads and one Tiger. The Tiger has only around ten rounds of main-gun ammunition but plenty of machine-gun ammunition. From positions on the embankment, it hold the enemy at bay.

18 February 1945: Support of the counterattack of Kampfgruppe Wetzlar on the Lebus Bridgehead on both sides of the road Podelzig-Lebus; the tanks are employed east of the road. After hitting a strong antitank-gun belt, the assault is called off. The tanks are moved to Altzeschdorf as divisional reserve.

22 February 1945: The division's armored group is assembled in the western part of Schüfergrund for another attack on Lebus (via Haaker Grund and Point 55). Later in the night, the southern portions of Sichelgrund are seized.

23 February 1945: Continuation of the attack from the northern part of Hakengrund towards Hill 55; withdrawal of the tanks.

1 March 1945: One Tiger operational.

2 March 1945: Counterattack out of the assembly area at Sachsendorf towards enemy elements that have penetrated near Rathstock. The German assault is contained by the Soviets west of Rathstock; the tanks move back to the assembly area at Sachsendorf.

15 March 1945: One Tiger operational. Relief attack on Klessin fails; five enemy tanks are knocked out.

20 March 1945: Klessin is relieved, but Podelzig remains in enemy hands.

30 March 1945: Attack on Sachsendorf; fifty-five tanks are knocked out. The division is relieved-in-place and is designated a reserve in the Falkenhagen Forest.

27 March 1945: Operational Tigers: 1.

6 April 1945: Operational Tigers: 1.

8 April 1945: No Tigers operational.

16 April 1945: Several tanks in position in Dolgelin are constantly shelled by artillery.

18 April 1945: Blocking positions occupied between Diedersdorf and Neuentempel.

19 April 1945: Withdrawal into the area southeast of Fürstenwalde.

20–25 April 1945: Employment in a blocking position near Bad Saarow.

25 April 1945: Assault across the Autobahn in the direction of Ketschendorf. Ultimate destruction of the division in the fighting for and within the Halbe Pocket.

PANZER-ABTEILUNG KUMMERSDORF/MÜNCHEBERG

Early February 1945: Formed from the Armor Experimentation and Instructional Group at Kummersdorf. Initially earmarked for assignment to Kampfgruppe Panzer-Division "Jüterbog" (two tank companies).

25 February 1945: On hand: four Tiger IIs, one Tiger I, and one Jagdtiger. Five Tiger Is due in from depot-level maintenance.

5 March 1945: Panzer-Brigade "Müncheberg," which had been formed in February 1945, is directed to expand to Panzer-Division "Müncheberg" (order: OKH/GenSt d.H./Org.Abt. I/1270/45 g.Kdos). The tank elements include Panzer-Abteilung "Müncheberg," the I./Panzer-Regiment 29 and Panzer-Abteilung Kummersdorf. The regimental staff is to be formed from Panzer-Regiment Stab z.b.V. Coburg (Coburg Special-duty Tank Regiment Staff).

14 March 1945: Panzer-Abteilung Kummersdorf is consolidated with Panzer-Abteilung "Müncheberg:" The 1./Panzer-Abteilung "Müncheberg" has eleven Panzer IVs (different models), the 2./Panzer-Abteilung "Müncheberg" has ten Panthers and the 3./Panzer-Abteilung "Müncheberg" has eleven Tigers).

15 March 1945: Eight Tigers are operational. One Tiger is in short-term maintenance, two Tigers are in long-term maintenance and one Tiger is due in.

17 March 1945: Assembly for the relief attack on Küstrin.

22 March 1945: The Russians attack after a ninety-minute artillery preparation. South of Reichsstraße 1, they hit the at Tucheband. They assault the 2./Panzer-Abteilung

"Müncheberg" north of Reichsstraße 1 at Gorgast. The Tiger company, in reserve in Golzow, cannot start engaging in time due to the artillery shelling of the rear combat zone, but it is able to knock out several enemy tanks.

27 March 1945: Two Tigers operational; five in short-term maintenance; and two in long-term maintenance.

5 April 1945: Nine out of thirteen Tigers operational.

6 April 1945: Operational tanks: 7.

10 April 1945: Operational tanks: 9.

15 April 1945: Operational tanks: 10. One Tiger due in.

14–17 April 1945: Defensive operations in the Seelow area followed by the occupation of blocking positions around Müncheberg. Following this, defensive operations in the "Hardenberg" Position. Finally, withdrawal to Berlin.

1 May 1945: The last five tanks are spotted in the vicinity of the Flak bunker near the city zoo. The last cohesive elements are eliminated there as well. Most of the tank crews continue the fight as infantry. The last Tiger I is abandoned several hundred meters away from the Brandenburg Gate.

This sensational image shows a Tiger I of Panzer-Division "Müncheberg" in front of the Brandenburg Gate just a few days after the Battle for Berlin had ended. ANDERSON

PANZERKAMPFGRUPPE NORD

Using the vehicle inventory of the training facilities at Bergen—the evacuated Armor School—and Putlos—the armor gunnery school—the establishment of a Panzerkampfgruppe Nord (Armored Task Force North) was ordered on 13 February 1945 by the Inspector General of the Armored Forces. This took place as part of Aktion Gneisenau, which was the code name for calling up elements of the training base for reinforcing the field army.

It was directed for the headquarters to come from Bergen, along with a signals platoon (with two command Panzer IIIs), an engineer platoon, a scout platoon (with motorized bicycles), a reconnaissance platoon (seven Sd.Kfz. 250/1's), a reconnaissance platoon with six armored cars and an air-defense platoon (with 4 3.7-centimeter and 3 quad 2-centimeter Flak all mounted on Panzer IV chassis).

The tank battalion of Panzerkampfgruppe Nord was to be composed of a headquarters, a mixed tank company with ten Panthers and six Tigers, a light tank company with twenty-two Panzer IVs and an assault-gun company with nine Sturmgeschütz IIIs and five Jagdpanzer IVs. These elements were to be provided from the assets at Bergen. For the rest of the battalion, the gunnery school at Putlos was to provide a mixed tank company with a total of thirteen Panthers and Tigers and a light tank company with a total of fifteen Panzer IVs and/or Jagdpanzer IVs.

The Panzergrenadier battalion of Panzerkampfgruppe Nord was to consist of a headquarters with two SPWs, two grenadier companies (without vehicles) and a heavy company (with trucks). The heavy company was to consist of one 15-centimeter infantry gun, two 10.5-centimeter infantry guns, two heavy mortars, and three heavy machine-guns. The aforementioned assets were also to come from Bergen. The gunnery school at Putlos was to provide the mechanized infantry battalion with a mixed company consisting of two SPWs, three SPWs with 7.5-centimeter guns, two SPWs with 8-centimeter mortars, and three SPWs with heavy machine guns.

This planning was suspended by a Führer order after intervention by Generaloberst Guderian. It was revived later during the Aktion Leuthen, another stage of all-out mobilization of the home army (see the section on Panzergruppe Paderborn as well).

These forces were later allocated for local fighting or to the formation of Panzer-Division "Clausewitz."

PANZER-KOMPANIE PADERBORN

On 21 October 1944, Panzer-Ersatz- und Ausbildungs-Abteilung 500 was ordered to create a quick-reaction Kampfgruppe for employment in the Aachen sector.

There is contradictory information concerning the strength and the make-up of this unit. The originally ordered strength of fifteen Tigers was not achieved.

Two sources confirm a strength of three Tiger Is and two Panzer IVs, which probably represented the combat power of the unit. The tactical markings on the tanks were quite odd; it was an alphanumeric starting with R followed by a single digit. The Tigers were apparently numbered R3, R4 and R7, while the two Panzer IVs were R5 and R6.

This unit, perhaps even only portions of it, was employed in November 1944, but no further details are known.

PANZERGRUPPE PADERBORN

When the Allies approached Paderborn at the end of March 1945, a provisional task force was formed out of the operational tanks of the Panzer-Lehr- und Ausbildungs-Abteilung Tiger (the new unit designation for the former Panzer-Ersatz- und Ausbildungs-Abteilung 500). It was intended to assign these forces to Panzerausbildungsverband "Westfalen"

(Armor Training Formation "Westphalia"),which was formed as part of the Aktion Leuthen on 24 March 1945. The Panzergruppe was initially ordered to move to the area of Recklinghausen and report to Heeresgruppe H (Army Group H).

A total of eighteen Tiger Is and nine Tiger IIs were available. (In a report dated 28 March 1945, the following armored assets were available at Paderborn: four Panzer IIIs, five Panzer Vs, eleven Panzer VIs (Model E), six Panzer VIbs and three prime movers.) Two Tiger Is were manned by crews from the 3./schwere Panzer-Abteilung 424 and three Tiger IIs were manned by crews from schwere Panzer-Abteilung 508. (One of the Tiger IIs had a Porsche turret.)

In the end, Panzergruppe Paderborn had fifteen Tiger Is and three Tiger IIs and also four Panthers and four Panzer IIIs. The commander of the Kampfgruppe was Hauptmann Uckert.

✠

30 March 1945: Fourteen Tigers are sent to Kirchborchen. 160 soldiers of the Panzer-Lehr- und Ausbildungs-Abteilung Tiger are in position as infantry in Wewer, where they repel the initial attacks of the US 3-33 Armor.

31 March 1945: The tanks are positioned at the airport south of Paderborn. The Maintenance Company of the Panzer-Lehr- und Ausbildungs-Abteilung Tiger operates out of Paderborn, where it conducts operations with six repaired Panthers.

1 April 1945: Eight Tigers march through Marienloh to Schlangen, where the command post is established. Attack on Nordborchen. A single Tiger employed west of the road to Borchen and south of the railway line destroys two lead tanks of Task Force Boles. It then pulls back to the north and is immobilized after being attacked by fighter-bombers. Three Tigers are trapped in the limestone quarry south of Paderborn.

2 April 1945: Fifteen to sixteen Tigers road march between Bad Lippspringe and Horn, with approximately half then moving on to Detmold and the other half heading south. One after the other, the tanks run out of fuel.

Hauptmann Uckert is taken prisoner and is replaced by Hauptmann Scharfe.

Increasing employment as infantry in the area around Paderborn.

4 April 1945: Parts of Kampfgruppe Dettmar from Paderborn—including one Tiger—reach German forces at Veldrom.

12 April 1945: All tanks are either lost or inoperable.

PANZER-KOMPANIE "PANTHER"

This unit was formed on 30 January 1945 by Military District III (Silesia) as a Gneisenau unit (units formed out of the training base to supplement the field army). The company had different types of tanks, and its 1st Platoon had three Tigers. No details are known concerning the possible combat employment of this unit.

TIGERS IN THE PANZER-LEHR-DIVISION

It was originally planned to field this division with a heavy tank company of fourteen Tigers. The fielding would start with a mixed company within the II./ Panzer-Lehr-Regiment with nine Panzer IVs and three Tiger Is.

✠

15 January 1944: The Chief-of-Staff of the Inspector General of the Armored Forces, Generalmajor Thomale, assure the division that it will receive a company with Tiger II tanks.

29 January 1944: The division asks whether the fielding of a Tiger II company is still on schedule.

1 February 1944: Three Tiger I tanks are operational. According to a request to alter the table of organization and equipment, the division prefers to equip the radio-control tank company with Tigers instead of assault guns.

3 February 1944: The Chief-of-Staff of the Inspector General of the Armored Forces approves the exchange of personnel from Panzer-Kompanie Versailles, who have been trained on Tigers, with soldiers from the Panzer-Lehr-Regiment.

17 February 1944: The reorganization of the radio-control tank company into a Tiger II unit is ordered. The 3./Panzerjäger-Lehr-Abteilung is ordered to Paderborn to start training on Tigers, because it is earmarked for being equipped with Jagdtigers.

14 March 1944: Panzer-Kompanie (Funklenk) 316 receives the first five Tiger II tanks produced (with Porsche turrets). (See the section devoted to this unit in *Tigers in Combat I*.)

1 April 1944: Five Tiger IIs operational.

1 June 1944: Six Tigers operational; two of them in the maintenance facility (five of them Tiger IIs).

1 July 1944: Three Tigers on hand, none operational.

1 August 1944: All divisional Tigers turned in.

PANZER-LEHR-ABTEILUNG PUTLOS

In April 1945 the instruction personnel of the tank gunnery school at Putlos and the personnel of Panzer-Lehr-Abteilung Putlos (including the Supply Company) form a small Kampfgruppe under command of Major von Benninggsen. The armor inventory consists of a heavy tank company (ten Panthers and two Tiger Is), a mixed tank company (seven Panzer IVs [unknown variants], four Panzer IVs [long-barreled variants], one Panzerjäger IV and one Sturmgeschütz) and a light motorized infantry company (sixteen SPWs). On 16 April 1945, Kampfgruppe von Benninggsen was absorbed into Panzer-Division "Clause-witz" in the Lüneburg area. The combat engagements are described in that section.

TIGERS IN THE FORTRESS OF POSEN

Several tanks and tank destroyers were to be found fighting in the city of Posen, which had been declared a fortress on 20 January 1945: two Panthers, one Panzer IV, one Tiger I, and one Jagdpanzer Hetzer. In addition, the remnants of Sturmgeschütz-Ersatz-Abteilung 500 (with seventeen assault guns) were also incorporated into the city's defenses. Before the struggle was over, an additional eight new assault guns that had been earmarked for Panzer-Grenadier-Division "Großdeutschland" were diverted and integrated into the fighting there.

✠

22 January 1945: During the night, the first enemy elements approach the outskirts of the city.

23 January 1945: The Tiger and one of the Panthers, positioned in the eastern part of the city, receive the mission to reconnoiter the terrain. On request of the local defense forces, the Tiger of Fahnenjunker-Oberfeldwebel Sanders (an officer candidate with the temporary rank of Oberfeldwebel) destroys the spire of a water tower where a forward artillery observer has been spotted. The Panther is hit on the track; the crew is covered by the Tiger as it repairs the track. As it starts to pull back, the accelerator linkage breaks. The loader jumps outside, opens the heavy engine deck (by himself!), and actuates the throttle control rod manually, enabling the tank to withdraw.

26 January 1945: In the southern part of the city, the Tiger guards a crossing with its engine shut off. A T-34 closes in from behind. It is identified relatively late, and the turret can only be traversed manually, because the engine would not fire up immediately. Just in time, the engines starts, and the enemy tank is knocked out, even though it opens fire first.

29 January 1945: During the night, the Tiger is ordered to recover a Panther near the Rochus Bridge. The Panther had received sixteen hits from an antitank gun. During the recovery operation, the Soviets try to knock out the Tiger with a captured Panzerfaust. The Soviet gunner only hits the turret hatch.

Some time later, the Tiger destroys two enemy tanks advancing from the Schillerpark towards a government building. It also destroys two antitank guns.

30 January 1945: A raid on the Handwerkerhaus (craftsmen's building) is supported by firing ricochets. A 9.2-centimeter antitank gun is destroyed.

1 February 1945: Four T-34s at the Schloßbrücke are knocked out by the Tiger.

2 February 1945: With the support of the Tiger, Kampfgruppe Köhler relieves the soldiers trapped in the Gestapo grounds.

15 February 1945: Defensive positions occupied in Süd Weinern.

16 February 1945: During an artillery barrage on the citadel, the Tiger's gearbox is damaged as it pulls back. With the help of a assault gun, it is recovered to the edge of Zeppelin Field. Two Josef Stalins are knocked out there

17 February 1945: The immobilized Tiger destroys 4 tanks and a 9.2-centimeter antitank gun.

23 February 1945: The few survivors surrender.

TIGERS IN SLOVAKIA

The 1. Panzer-Armee employed twenty-eight Panzer IVs, sixteen assault guns, and two Tigers to suppress the uprising in Slovakia that started on 29 August 1944. The exact type of Tigers used is not clear, with some sources saying they were the Porsche version (VK 4501 [P]).

After conclusion of this operation on 31 October 1944, these two tanks remained in the country. In the vicinity of Lucky (near Ruzomberok) in the Velky Choc Mountains, they disappeared in a marshy area.

Vehicles Issued to Units

PANZERKAMPFWAGEN VI "TIGER"

Year	Month	Number	Entity	Arrival	Identified Chassis Numbers (250... or 251...)
1942	April	1	Waffenamt[1]	April	V1
	May	1	Waffenamt	May	001
	August	9	502[2]	19 August to 25 September	035–705
	September	2	501	30 August	035–775
	October	8	501	October	013–020
	November	10	501	November	021, 023, 024, 028 and 031–033
		4	503	November	
	December	16	503	December	045,046,050 and 065
		9	2./502	21–28 December	
		1	Waffenamt	December	V3
		1	SS LAH	December	053
		2	SS DR	December	049
		5	SS LAH	December	048 and 066–068
		1	501	9 December	059
1943	January	3	502	5 February	
		4	SS LAH	January	071–073 and 075
		8	SS DR	January	076–078, 083–086, 088 and 092

[1] German Army Weapons Procurement Agency.
[2] Formation designations are abbreviated for reasons of space.

PANZERKAMPFWAGEN VI "TIGER"

Year	Month	Number	Entity	Arrival	Identified Chassis Numbers (250... or 251...)
		9	SS T	January	079, 080, 089, 094–096 and 101–103
		7	GD	February	082, 087, 090, 098–100 and 104
	February	1	Waffenamt	February	V2
		2	GD	February	106 and 108
		2	501	5 March	
		4	502	20 February	
		20	504	February	109, 111, 112, 117 and 122–126
		2	505	February	
	March	18	505	March	137,139,143,154 and 157
		10	503	31 March	164
		6	Putlos	March	
	April	14	503	30 April to 10 May	188
		6	504	June	200, 204 and 206–208
		13	SS PzAbt	May	
		5	SS LAH	13 May	194, 210, 214, 223 and 226
		5	SS DR	13 May	201, 213, 217, 219, 220 and 225
		5	SS T	20 May	152, 211, 212, 216, 224 and 230
	May	1	SS DR	13 May	
		1	SS T	20 May	
		6	GD	13 May	215, 218, 228, 229, 231 and 236
		31	502	18-26 May	196, 222, 232, 234, 242 and 246
		1	500	27 May	
		7	502	31 May–1 June	259, 263 and 268
		7	500	06 June	
		2	504	20 May	

PANZERKAMPFWAGEN VI "TIGER"

Year	Month	Number	Entity	Arrival	Identified Chassis Numbers (250... or 251...)
	June	11	505	20 June	272 and 304
		14	3./505	10 June	
		14	3./501	27 June	
		14	3./504	02 June	279 and 339
		3	GD	29 June	195, 199 and 247
1943	July	1	Waffenamt	July	
		5	SS LAH	16 July	
		27	SS 101	August	255, 323, 344, 345, 348, 350 351, 354, 355, 357, 359, 362, 372 and 377
	August	8	Meyer	28 July	
		3	506	16 August	
		12	503	23 August	386
		6	GD	August	295, 368, 379, 379, 381 and 383
		42	506	28 August	
		6	500	25–30 August	
		6	509	30 August	
	September	9	500	September	
		20	509	07 September	456
		5	SST	03 October	
		5	SS DR	?	
		5	505	27 September	491, 494 and 496
		3	PzLehr (GD)	lost	
		19	509	30 September	456–544
		7	PzLehr (GD)	lost	502, 506 and 515
	October	1	500	October	
		2	Waffenamt	October	
		2	509	12 October	569 and 575
		1	Japan (SS 101)	January	455
		27	501	19–28 October	
		10	SS 101	29 October	
		5	501	4 November	
	November	13	501	8-12 November	
		1	500	November	
		1	Waffenamt	November	

PANZERKAMPFWAGEN VI "TIGER"

Year	Month	Number	Entity	Arrival	Identified Chassis Numbers (250... or 251...)
	December	17	508	10–19 December	
		16	507	23–26 December	603 and 682
		45	503	3–7 January 1944	
		18	502	?	608, 610, 615, 618, 632, 636, 665, 686–688, 693, and 700–702
		6	SS 101	January	
		4	502	?	704–706 and 708
		2	SS 101	January	
		2	508	14 January	
		5	SS DR	10 February	617, 626, 678, 722 and 729
		3	507	20 January	732–734
1944	January	6	Waffenamt	January	
		20	508	14–19 January	
		10	502	20 January	712–715, 719, 753, 755–757 and 759
		6	508	24 January	
		12	506	29-30 January	
		6	509	2 February	762, 779, 794
		6	SS 103	4 February	
		2	509	5 February	803
		14	502	21 January	
		5	506	10 February	
		5	SS LAH	10 February	
		6	502	?	
	February	1	508	February	
		6	503	10 February	
		10	GD	?	
		6	SS LAH	February	
		26	507	24–25 February	822 and 871
		3	503	26 February	
		11	504	29 February to 1 March	
		6	GD	6 March	

PANZERKAMPFWAGEN VI "TIGER"

Year	Month	Number	Entity	Arrival	Identified Chassis Numbers (250... or 251...)
		6	503	9 March	870, 872, 878, 879, 883 and 886
		12	503	31 March	881, 882, 885 and 888–896
	March	6	504	14 March	
		6	503	21 March	901, 903, 914, 915, 917, 925 and 933
		6	507	16 March	922, 923, 926, 931, 934 and 938
		28	504	17–21 March	
		5	508	10 April	
		45	506	29 March to 8 April	
	April	6	GD	6 April	
		12	507	7–14 April	973, 974, 979, 984, 986–988, 994, 995, 999, 003 and 026
		12	505	13–25 April	980, 997, 998, 005, 008, 009, 012 and 019
		26	SS 101	April	
		6	SS 102	21 April	
		6	508	25 April	
		9	SS T	2 May to 7 June	
		1	505	1 June	
		12	505	26 April	041, 057, 066, 068, 072, 079, 083, 086, 092, 098 and 101
		8	GD	6 May	
	May	6	GD	18 May	
		6	509	20 May	
		24	SS 102	20–22 May	
		12	509	23 May	
		6	SS T	June	
		15	SS 102	26–29 May	114
		12	509	30 May to 2 June	
		6	GD	1 June	

PANZERKAMPFWAGEN VI "TIGER"

Year	Month	Number	Entity	Arrival	Identified Chassis Numbers (250... or 251...)
	June	27	508	14–18 June	
		33	503	11–15 June	214
		11	510	20–22 June	
		6	501	25 June	
		16	510	25–30 June	
		2	507	30 June	
		6	510	1 July	
	July	12	510	3–7 July	
		6	507	27 June	
		12	504	21–22 July	
		3	Hungary	29 July	
		6	506	23 July	
		5	SS T	26 June	
		6	509	30 July	
		12	GD	17 August	
		6	509	4 August	
		6	510	10 August	
	August	6	507	8 August	
		6	SS 102	?	
		4	301	1–20 September	

Grand Total   1353

PANZERKAMPFWAGEN TIGER II

Year	Month	Number	Entity	Arrival	Identified Chassis Numbers (280...)
1944	February	5	316	14 March	001–005
	March	1	500	1 April	
	April	1	500	1 April	
		3	Waffenamt	April	
	May	4	500	30 June	
		6	Waffenamt	May	
	June	12	503	12 June	023, 030, 031 and 035

PANZERKAMPFWAGEN TIGER II

Year	Month	Number	Entity	Arrival	Identified Chassis Numbers (280...)
		6	501	25 June	
		4	500	30 June	
		2	Waffenamt	June	
	July	1	500	3 July	
		3	Waffenamt	July	
		25	501	7–14 July	
		6	505	26 July to 7 August	
		14	503	31 July to 2 August	
		14	SS 101	28 July to 1 August	092, 093, 101, 103, 105 and 112
	August	14	501	4–7 August	
		2	500	10 August	100
		39	505	10–29 August	
		17	506	20 August to 1 September	
	September	1	Waffenamt	September	
		28	506	3–12 September	215
		45	503	19–22 September	
		11	509	28 September to 3 October	243 and 260
	October	14	SS 501	17–18 October	273 and 278
		4	SS 503	19 October	
	November	20	SS 501	12–26 November	288 and 302
		9	509	5–7 December	
		6	506	8 December	317–319
	December	36	509	9 December to 1 January	
		6	506	13 December	
		6	SS 502	27 December	
1945	January	29	SS 503	11–25 January	
		6	SS 501	26 January	
		3	1./511	21 May	
		3	1./510	21 May	

PANZERKAMPFWAGEN TIGER II

Year	Month	Number	Entity	Arrival	Identified Chassis Numbers (280...)
	February	13	SS 501	12 March	
		27	SS 502	14 February to 2 March	
	March	4	SS 502	2–6 March	
		4	507	9 March	
		5	FHH	16 March	
		13	506	?	
		11	507	22 March	
		6	510	16 March	
		7	511	31 March	

Grand Total   496

BIBLIOGRAPHY (SUPPLEMENT TO VOLUME I)

SECONDARY SOURCES: BOOKS

Adair, Paul	*Hitler's Greatest Defeat*
Agte, Patrick	*Michael Wittmann*
Alman, Karl	*Panzer vor*
Armstrong, Richard	*Red Army Tank Commanders*
Astor, Gerald	*A Blood-dimmed Tide*
Balck, Hermann	*Ordnung im Chaos*
Baumann, Günther	*Posen '45*
Beale, Peter	*Tank Tracks*
Becker, Waldemar	*Das Kriegsende 1945 im ehemaligen Hochstift Paderborn*
Bernage/Benaumou	*Goodwood*
Bismark, Günter	*Uelzen 1918–45*
Brisset/Bates	*The Charge of the Bull*
Colby, John	*War From the Ground Up*
Delaforce, Patrick	*Churchill's Desert Rats*
————	*The Black Bull*
MacDonald, Charles	*A Time for Trumpets*
Dropsy, Paul	*Mon village dans la tourmente*
Duffy, Christopher	*Der Sturm auf das Reich*
Dupuy, Trevor	*Hitler's Last Gamble*
Ford, Ken	*Assault Crossing*
————	*Assault on Germany*
Gaujac, Paul	*L'armée de la victoire*
Gaul, Roland	*The Battle of the Bulge in Luxembourg*
Gosztony, Peter	*Der Kampf um Berlin 1945*
Hastings, Max	*Overlord*
Hinze, Rolf	*Letztes Aufgebot*
How, J.J.	*Normandy—The British Breakout*
Jensen, Marvin	*Strike Swiftly!*
Jentz, Tomas	*Panzertruppen*
John, Antonius	*Kursk '43*
Jordan, Franz	*Einsatz der deutschen Verbände im nordöstlichen Niederösterreich* (manuscript)

Kern, Erich	*Kampf in der Ukraine*
Kershaw, Robert	*It Never Snows in September*
Lakowski, Richard	*Seelow 1945*
Lakowski/Stich	*Der Kessel von Halbe*
Leuthen, Hanns	*Am Rande der Straßen*
Ludewig, Joachim	*Der deutsche Rückzug aus Frankreich 1944*
Maier, Georg	*Drama zwischen Budapest und Wien*
Marie, Henri	*Villers-Bocage*
Mennel, Rainer	*Der nordafrikanisch-italienische Kampfraum 1943–45*
Mörke, Fritz	*Der Kampf um den Kreis Arnswalde 1945*
Newton, Steven	*Retreat from Leningrad*
Osten, G.	*Kämpfe um Uelzen und Stadensen 1945*
Poralla, Peter	*Unvergänglicher Schmerz*
Puntigam, Josef Paul	*Vom Plattensee bis zur Mur*
Rahier, Josef	*Die Front an Rur und Inde*
Rahne etc.	*Kriegsschauplatz Sachsen 1945*
Ramm, Gerald	*Gott mit uns*
Rauchensteiner, Manfried	*Der Krieg in Österreich '45*
Read/Fisher	*Der Fall von Berlin*
Reynolds, Michael	*The Devil's Adjutant*
Russell, John	*No Triumphant Procession*
Saft, Ulrich	*Krieg in der Heimat (2)*
Siegert, Richard	*Der Tiger von Posen*
Trees, Wolfgang	*Schlachtfeld zwischen Maas und Rhein*
Tieke, Wilhelm	*Bis zur Stunde Null*
Thompson, R.W.	*Die Schlacht um das Rheinland*
Thrams, Hermann	*Küstrin 1945*
Veeh, Helmut	*Die Kriegsfurie über Franken 1945*
Westemeier, Jens	*Joachim Peiper*
Wilhelmsmeyer, Helmut	*Der Krieg in Italien 1943–1945*
Zaloga, Steven	*Bagration 1944*

SECONDARY SOURCES: PERIODICALS

AFV News
Armor
Der Freiwillige
Fahrzeug
G2
Militaria
Military History
Military Miniatures
Military Modeling
Modeler's World
Modell-Fan
Panzer
Steelmaster
Tankette
Tank Magazine
39–45

SECONDARY SOURCES: UNIT HISTORIES
Infantry Divisions

5. Infanterie-Division:	Sievert, Gert	Sandmaier/Buchau (1982)
6. Infanterie-Division:	Großmann, H.	Podzun (1958)
10. Infanterie-Division:	Schmidt, August	Podzun (1963)
21. Infanterie-Division:	Allmayer-Beck	Schild (1990)
25. Infanterie-Division:	Boehm, Erwin	Self-published (1985)
29. Infanterie-Division:	Lemelsen, Joachim	Podzun (1960)
31. Infanterie-Division:	Hinze, Rolf	Self-published (1997)
32. Infanterie-Division:	Schröder, J.	Self-published (1956)
35. Infanterie-Division:	Baumann, Hans	Braun (1964
56. Infanterie-Division:	Diverse	Self-published
58. Infanterie-Division:	von Zydowitz, Kurt	Podzun (1952)
61. Infanterie-Division:	Hubatsch, Walther	Podzun (1983)
65. Infanterie-Division:	Velten, Wilhelm	Vowinkel (1974)
71. Infanterie-Division:	AG Kleeblatt	Self-published (1973)
76. Infanterie-Division:	Löser, J.	Biblio (1988)
81. Infanterie-Division:	Haupt, Werner	Podzun (1985)
83. Infanterie-Division:	Tiemann, Reinhard	Podzun (1986)
98. Infanterie-Division:	Gareis, Martin	Podzun (1956)
125. Infanterie-Division:	Breymaer, Helmut	Self-published (1983)
131. Infanterie-Division:	Blankenhagen, Wilhelm	Giebel (1982)
134. Infanterie-Division:	Haupt, Werner	Self-published (1971)
161. Infanterie-Division:	Kippar, Gerhard	Self-published (1994)
198. Infanterie-Division:	Graser, Gerhard	Self-published (1961)
205. Infanterie-Division:	Kammerer, Fritz	Self-published (1969)
207. Infanterie-Division:	Diverse	Self-published (1961)
225. Infanterie-Division:	Miehe, Walter	Patzwall (1980)
281. Infanterie-Division:	Diverse	Self-published (1961)
290. Infanterie-Division:	Behrens, Heinrich	Self-published (1970)
292. Infanterie-Division:	Nitz, Günther	Bernard & Graefe (1957)
305. Infanterie-Division:	Hauck, Friedrich-Wilhelm	Podzun (1975)
363. Infanterie-Division:	Gohlke, Helmut	Self-published (1977)

ABOUT THE AUTHOR

Wolfgang Schneider is the author of numerous articles and books concerning the development and combat history of armored vehicles. He is the editor of the reference book *Tanks of the World.*

Oberst (Colonel) Schneider is an active officer in the armor branch of the Bundeswehr. He has served as a tank platoon leader with the Leopard 1 Main Battle Tank, a mechanized-infantry platoon leader with the Marder mechanized infantry combat vehicle, a tank company commander with the Leopard 1 Main battle, an antitank company commander with the Jaguar Tank Destroyer and as a battalion commander with the Leopard 2 main battle Tank within the prestigious Panzer-Lehr-Brigade. Oberst Schneider presently works in the German Ministry of Defense as the chief development officer for the next generation of German main battle tanks.

He is married, with three daughters, and lives in northern Germany.

A Panzer III (Model J) of the light platoon of the 8./SS-Panzer-Regiment 2 during the Kharkov offensive in February 1943. *Insert:* The Wolfsangel was painted in different colors on both the front and rear of the vehicles. This was the standard vehicular insignia of SS-Panzer-Grenadier-Division "Das Reich" prior to Operation "Citadel."

Tiger I of the 4./SS-Panzer-Regiment 1 during the retaking of Kharkov in February 1943. *Insert:* Vehicular insignia of SS-Panzer-Grenadier-Division "Leibstandarte SS Adolf Hitler."

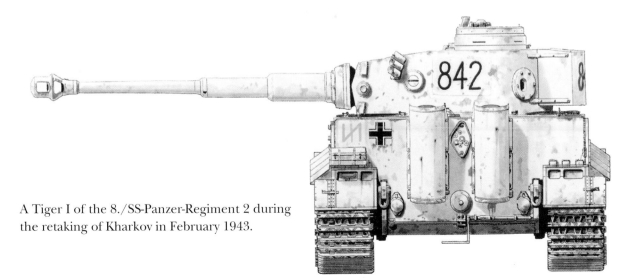

A Tiger I of the 8./SS-Panzer-Regiment 2 during the retaking of Kharkov in February 1943.

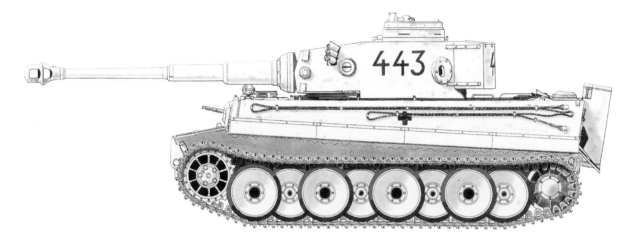

A Tiger I of the 4./SS-Panzer-Regiment 3 during the retaking of Kharkov in February 1943.

A Tiger I of the 4./SS-Panzer-Regiment 3 in the company base camp northwest of Kharkov in April 1943.

A Tiger I of the 13./SS-Panzer-Regiment 1 during Operation "Citadel" in July 1943.

A Tiger I pf the 9./SS-Panzer-Regiment 3 during Operation "Citadel" in July 1943. The Dreizackrune (three vertical bars) was the divisional vehicular insignia of SS-Panzer-Grenadier-Division "Totenkopf" during the operation and for several months afterwards.

A Tiger I of the 13./Panzer-Regiment "Großdeutschland" while engaged in operations in the Brjansk Sector (Heeresgruppe Mitte) in July 1943.

A Tiger I of the 10./Panzer-Regiment "Großdeutschland" during operations in the Achtyrka area (Heeresgruppe Süd) in August 1943.

A Tiger I of the 13./SS-Panzer-Regiment 1 near Lisovka (central Russia) in November 1943.

A Tiger I of the 8./SS-Panzer-Regiment 2 during Operation "Citadel" in July 1943. *Insert (left):* The "dancing hobgoblin" was the vehicular insignia of the 8./SS-Panzer-Regiment 2 during Operation "Citadel." It retained this insignia until the end of 1943. *Insert (right):* The Doppelrune was the divisional vehicular insignia of SS-Panzer-Grenadier-Division "Das Reich" during Operation "Citadel."

A Tiger I of schwere Panzer-Kompanie Meyer during operations south of Rome in December 1943.

A Tiger I of the 3./schwere SS-Panzer-Abteilung 101 during the battalion's activation period at Mons (Belgium) in January 1944.

A Tiger I of schwere SS-Panzer-Abteilung 103 at the Oldebroek Training Area (Holland) in May 1944.

A Tiger I of the headquarters section of schwere SS-Panzer-Abteilung 101 during operations in Normandy in July 1944.

A Tiger I of the 1./schwere SS-Panzer-Abteilung 101 during operations in Normandy during July 1944.

A Tiger I of the 2./schwere SS-Panzer-Abteilung 101 during operations in Normandy in July 1944.

A Tiger I of the 3./schwere SS-Panzer-Abteilung 101 during operations in Normandy in July 1944.

A Tiger I of the 2./schwere SS-Panzer-Abteilung 102 during operations in Normandy in July 1944. ***Insert:*** The Blitzrune was the vehicular insignia of schwere SS-Panzer-Abteilung 102 during the Normandy Campaign. It was painted on the front and rear of the vehicles in pink.

A Tiger II of the 1./schwere SS-Panzer-Abteilung 501 in the Beauvais sector in August 1944.

A Tiger I of the 9./Panzer-Regiment "Großdeutschland" during Operation "Cäsar" (Heeresgruppe Nord) in September 1944.

A Tiger I of the 4./schwere Panzer-Abteilung 506 during operations around Geilenkirchen (western Germany) in October 1944.

A Tiger I of the Panzer-Kompanie Paderborn in the Aachen area in October 1944.

A Tiger II of the 3./schwere SS-Panzer-Abteilung 501 during the Ardennes Offensive in December 1944.

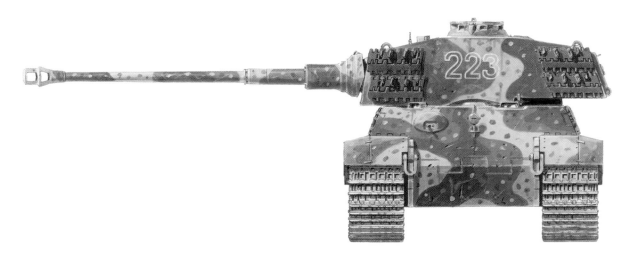

A Tiger II of the 2./schwere SS-Panzer-Abteilung 502 during the breakout attempt at Halbe in April 1945.

A Tiger II of the 1./schwere SS-Panzer-Abteilung 503 during the fighting east of Berlin in April 1945.

A hybrid Tiger I of Tiger-Gruppe Fehrmann during operations in the Bückeburg area of central Germany in April 1945.

A Tiger I of schwere Panzer-Kompanie Hummel in an area north of Siegen (Germany) in April 1945.

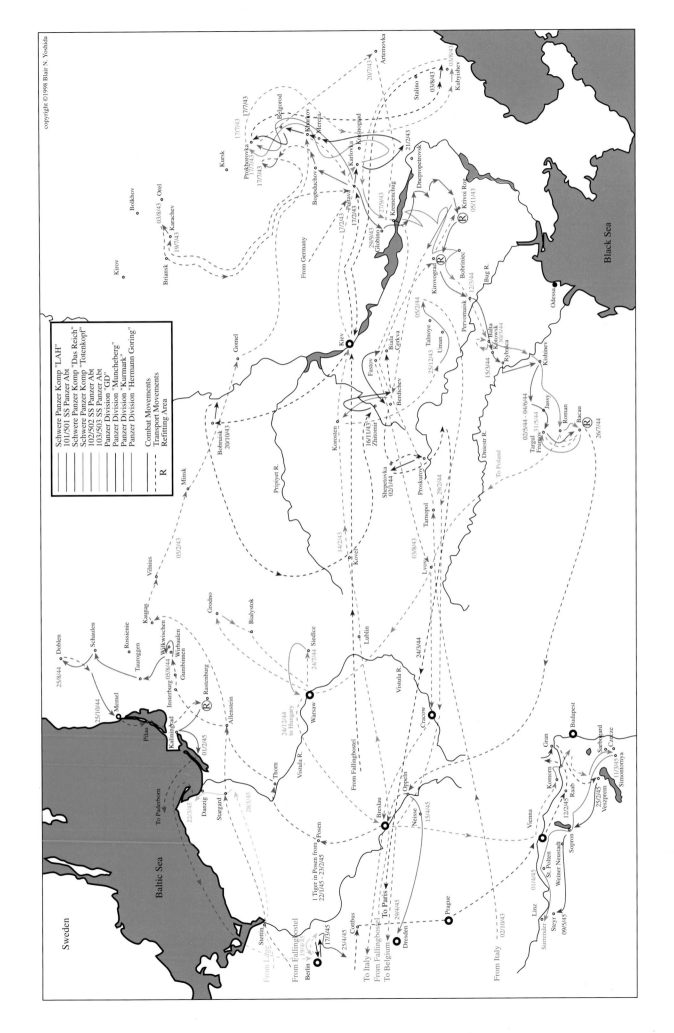

copyright ©1998 Blair N. Yoshida

Sweden

Baltic Sea

Black Sea

Legend:
- Schwere Panzer Komp "LAH"
- 101/501 SS Panzer Abt
- Schwere Panzer Komp "Das Reich"
- Schwere Panzer Komp "Totenkopf"
- 102/502 SS Panzer Abt
- 103/503 SS Panzer Abt
- Panzer Division "GD"
- Panzer Division "Muncheberg"
- Panzer Division "Kurmark"
- Panzer Division "Hermann Goring"

Combat Movements
Transport Movements
R   Refitting Area

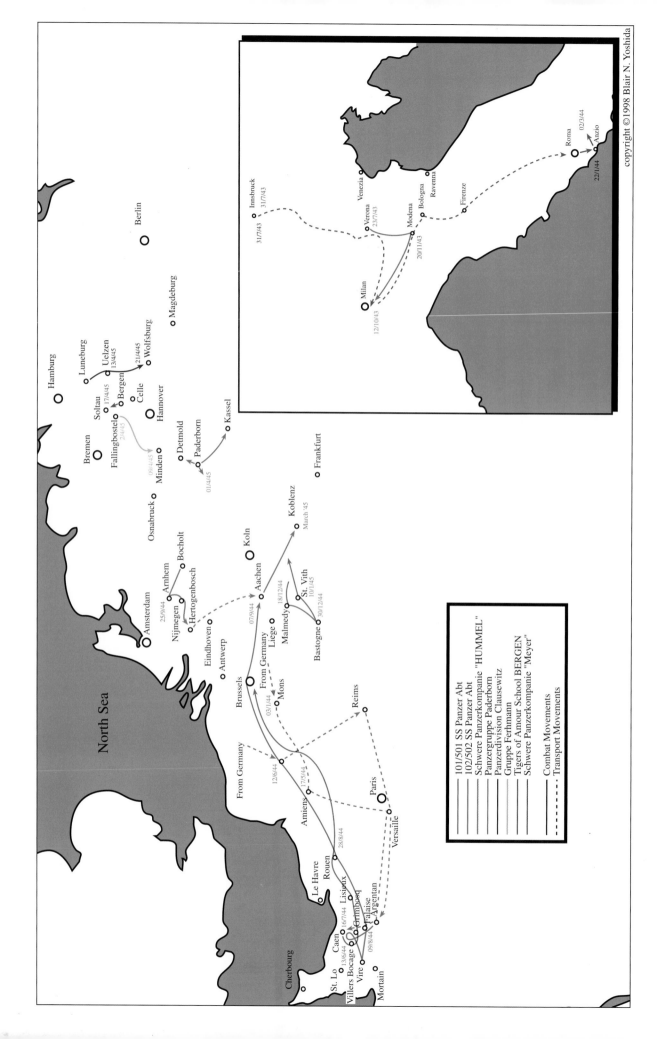

North Sea

Berlin

Hamburg
Luneburg
Uelzen
13/4/45
Soltau 17/4/45 Bergen 21/4/45 Wolfsburg
Bremen Fallingbostel Celle Magdeburg
2/4/45
09/4/45 Hannover
Detmold
Minden Paderborn Kassel
01/4/45

Osnabruck Frankfurt

Amsterdam Bocholt
Arnhem
25/9/44 Hertogenbosch Koln Koblenz
Nijmegen Aachen March '45
Eindhoven 07/9/44
Antwerp From Germany St. Vith
Liege 18/12/44 10/1/45
Malmedy
Brussels Bastogne 30/12/44
From Germany 03/1/44 Mons

Reims

12/6/44
17/5/44
Amiens Paris

Le Havre Versaille
Rouen 28/8/44
Lisieux
Cherbourg Caen Grimbosq
13/6/44 16/7/44 Falaise Argentan
St. Lo Villers Bocage 09/8/44
Vire
Mortain

101/501 SS Panzer Abt
102/502 SS Panzer Abt
Schwere Panzerkompanie "HUMMEL"
Panzergruppe Paderborn
Panzerdivision Clausewitz
Gruppe Ferhmann
Tigers of Amour School BERGEN
Schwere Panzerkompanie "Meyer"
Combat Movements
Transport Movements

Innsbruck
31/7/43
31/7/43 Venezia
Verona
23/7/43 Ravenna
Modena
20/11/43 Bologna
Firenze
Milan
12/10/43
Roma 02/3/44
Anzio
22/1/44

copyright ©1998 Blair N. Yoshida